Global Sport Marketing

Contemporary issues and practice

**Edited by Michel Desbordes and
André Richelieu**

Routledge
Taylor & Francis Group

LONDON AND NEW YORK

First published 2012 by Routledge
2 Park Square, Milton Park, Abingdon, Oxfordshire OX14 4RN

Simultaneously published in the USA and Canada
by Routledge
711 Third Avenue, New York, NY 10017

First issued in paperback 2014

Routledge is an imprint of the Taylor & Francis Group, an informa business

British Library Cataloguing in Publication Data
A catalogue record for this book is available from the British Library

Library of Congress Cataloging in Publication Data
Global sport marketing : contemporary issues and practice / edited by Michel Desbordes and André Richelieu.
    p. cm.
    1. Sports–Marketing–Cross-cultural studies. 2. Sports and globalization–Cross-cultural studies. 3. Sports–Economic aspects–Cross-cultural studies. I. Desbordes, Michel. II. Richelieu, André.
    GV716.G56 2012
    796.068′8–dc23   2011046309

ISBN: 978-0-415-50720-2 (hbk)
ISBN: 978-1-138-79582-2 (pbk)

Typeset in Times New Roman
by HWA Text and Data Management, London

Global Sport Marketing

Globalization has had a profound impact on the sports industry, creating an international market in which sports teams, leagues and players have become internationally recognized brands. This important new study of contemporary sports marketing examines the opportunities and threats posed by a global sports market, outlining the tools and strategies that marketers and managers can use to take advantage of those opportunities.

The book surveys current trends, issues and best practice in international sport marketing, providing a useful blend of contemporary theory and case studies from the Americas, Europe and Asia. It assesses the impact of globalization on teams, leagues, players, sponsors and equipment manufacturers, and highlights the central significance of culture on the development of effective marketing strategy. *Global Sport Marketing* is key reading for any advanced student, researcher or practitioner working in sport marketing or sport business.

Michel Desbordes is Professor at the University of Paris Sud 11, France, and Associate Professor at the ISC School of Management (Paris, France). He is a specialist in sports marketing, and his research focuses on the management of sport events, sports sponsorship and marketing applied to football.

André Richelieu is Professor in the Marketing Department at Laval University, Canada. He specializes in brand management and sports marketing. His research relates to how sports teams can leverage their brand equity by capitalizing on the emotional connection they share with their fans, and on how sports teams can internationalize their brand.

Routledge Research in Sport Business and Management

Available in this series:

Global Sport Marketing
Contemporary issues and practice
Michel Desbordes and André Richelieu

Contents

Figures

Tables

Boxes

Contributors

Wladimir Andreff is Professor Emeritus at the University of Paris 1 Panthéon Sorbonne, and Honorary President of the International Association of Sport Economists.

His statistical summary consists of 373 scientific publications in Economics and 98 published scientific book reviews, including 10 books as an author, 12 books as an editor, 56 articles in peer-reviewed economic journals (*EconLit* listed). He has participated in 317 scientific conferences since 1973 (of which 138 were abroad, across 38 countries) and 21 keynote speeches.

Contact: andreff@club-internet.fr

Christoph Breuer is an expert on sport demand, sporting organizations and sponsoring. His research mainly addresses (i) forecasts of sporting demand; (ii) the identification of key variables for the viability of sporting organizations; and (iii) measurement of the economic value of sports sponsorships. Christoph is a prolific author: an overview of his publications is available at www.dshs-koeln.de/wps/portal/oekonom_en/.

Michel Desbordes is Professor of Sports Marketing at Université Paris Sud 11 and an associate professor at ISC Paris. He is a holder of a University tenure degree in Economics and Marketing, and a graduate of the Ecole Normale Supérieure at Cachan. He holds a DEA (*Diplôme d'études approfondies*) from Université Paris IX-Dauphine, and a doctorate in Management Science from Université Strasbourg I (management of innovation in sporting products). He created and from 1999 to 2005 directed the 'Events and Recreational Sports Management' diploma programme at Université Paris Sud 11. He has been the director of the MBA programme in Sports Marketing and Management at ISC Paris since 2006.

His research work covers sports events, the marketing of football, sporting venues and experiential marketing as applied to sporting events. Since 1999 Professor Desbordes has published 18 books, in French, English, Spanish and Russian. He has also published 28 articles in academic journals (*European Sport Management Quarterly, International Journal of Sport Marketing & Sponsorship, International Journal of Sport Management and Marketing, International Journal of Sport Communication and the Journal of Sponsorship*) and 18 chapters in collective works. Since 2008 he has been the scientific editor for the *International Journal of Sport Marketing & Sponsorship* (www. imrpublications.com/journal-landing.aspx?volno=L&no=L).

He has been an invited professor in Canada, China, the United States, The Netherlands, Spain, Finland, England and South Korea.

In addition, he acts as a consultant for a variety of institutions: the Union of European Football Associations (UEFA), Adidas, New Balance, the Tour de France, Dakar, the Paris Marathon, the French Federations of Football, Judo, Swimming, Triathlon and Rowing, Rip Curl, Columbia, Amaury Sport Organisation (ASO, organizer of the Tour de France), the French "Sports for All" Federation, TNS Sport, Reebok, Sport 2000, the Stade de France, GDF Suez, Audi, the French Cycling Federation and Renault Sport.

Contact: mdesbordes@iscparis.com

Frank Go has held the Bewetour chair at the Rotterdam School of Management, Erasmus University, The Netherlands since 1996. He received his PhD from the Faculty of Economics and Econometrics, University of Amsterdam. He has been visiting professor at the Catholic University Leuven, the University of Antwerp and is currently a visiting professor at the Open University Business School, Rikkyo University, Tokyo, Japan. Prior to his present post he was affiliated with the University of Calgary, Alberta, Canada, and the Hong Kong Polytechnic University. He is an editorial board member of seven international journals. His research interests are in travel and hospitality marketing relationship issues, information technologies and social interaction, brand identity and image formation and scenario planning. He is co-editor of the *International Place Branding Yearbook* series (2010, 2011 and 2012) and co-authored *Place Branding*, all issued by Palgrave Macmillan, London.

Boris Helleu is Senior Lecturer in Sports Management at Université de Caen Basse-Normandie. His thesis was devoted to the geographic aspects of the regulation of professional sport; he holds a doctorate in Sports Sciences from Université de Rouen.

His work examines sport as event by combining contributions from economics (models of sports regulation), geography (the globalization and metropolization of professional sport) and marketing (fans and stadiums).

He was the scientific advisor on the ministerial reports devoted to the competitiveness of French professional football (2008) and big arenas (2010).

Christian Kolmer is a media scientist and historian working with the Media Tenor Institute in Zurich, where he is the head of non-governmental organization (NGO) analysis. Born 1965 in Essen, he studied history, communication science and economics in Bochum and Mainz. After his MA thesis on the ascent of Christianity as a process of public opinion, he specialized on research on news selection and did extensive research on the media image of the German

Treuhandanstalt, the body in charge of the privatization of the East German state enterprises. After his graduation from Johannes Gutenberg University in Mainz with an input–output analysis on news selection he joined Media Tenor, where he is responsible for political and societal research, science contacts and corporate clients as well. His fields of interest centre on agenda-setting research and cross-country comparisons, especially in the field of country images.

Tim Pawlowski specializes in the management of marketing by football teams. His research covers the economic aspects of sports leagues and the micro-economics of sporting demand. Tim has published articles in a number of books and journals, and his thesis was awarded the Toyota prize for excellence in research. A summary of his work is available at www.dshs-koeln.de/wps/portal/oekonom_en/

André Richelieu is a full professor in the Faculty of Business Administration at Laval University, Quebec City, Canada. He specializes in sports marketing. His research relates to how sports teams can leverage their brand equity by capitalizing on the emotional connection they share with their fans, and on how sports teams can internationalize their brand. His research covers both North America and Europe, and has led to comparative studies whose results are summarized in this book.

André is a sports fan who also loves travelling. He spent eight years in Africa, in the country formerly known as Zaire. There he encountered the legendary 'Leopards' football team, of which General Mobutu was so proud. He discovered that the world of sport did not revolve exclusively around ice hockey and baseball, as he and other North Americans believed, but rather around soccer – sorry: football!

André recovered well enough from Canada's loss to France at the 1986 World Cup in Mexico, but found it harder to forget the departure of the Montreal Expos baseball team for Washington.

He eventually channelled his energies into becoming a prolific author of scientific articles, with nearly 30 papers and 50 academic lectures to his credit. André is also a showman, always ready to apply the humour of a Roberto Benigni and the energy of a Tom Jones if it helps his audiences learn! His prizes and awards bear this out, for example the 2007 'Prize for Excellence in Teaching' from Laval University and the prize for 'Best Marketing Professor' awarded by his students in 2011.

André has been an invited professor in North America and Europe, lecturing on his recent work, always radiating the same enthusiasm. In this era of 'sportainment' even academics must now leave their ivory towers and engage with the media: in this regard André has given over 500 interviews on the marketing of sport, brand management, and marketing in general.

An overview of his work can be found at http://www.andrerichelieu-sportsmarketing.com/

Contact: andre.richelieu@fsa.ulaval.ca

Christopher Rumpf is a research assistant in the Institute of Sports Economics and Management at the German Sports University in Cologne. Christopher is currently studying for his doctorate under Professor Breuer's direction.

Guojun Zeng has been an associate professor, vice-director of hospitality in the Management Department in the School of Tourism Management, Sun Yat-sen University since 2005 and is currently a visiting scholar at the Rotterdam School of Management, Erasmus University, The Netherlands. He received his PhD from the School of Business Management, Sun Yat-sen University (Zhongshan University). He has published independently and in co-authorship in several journals. His research interests are in strategic management for the travel and tourism industry, standardization of tourism, as well as tourism marketing.

Introduction

Michel Desbordes and André Richelieu

During the last decade the sports business has expanded rapidly, which has led to a growing interest in the marketing of sport.

This interest in sports marketing has been driven by the practical issues of the sports business. For example, in 1998, France became champion of the world in football (soccer) and a number of questions were immediately raised:

- How do I create and manage a partnership?
- Why would I sponsor an event or a team?
- What type of stadium is the best for creating the right atmosphere at a sporting match?
- How do I acquire the television rights? What is a 'fair' price for them?
- How should I determine my sponsorship policy? What methods are available? What time horizon should I consider? When should I terminate a sponsorship arrangement? How do advertising and sponsorship complement each other? Should one replace the other?
- Is it more efficient to manage your partnerships yourself or to employ an agency?
- Is it a good idea to be a sponsor in more than one sport?
- What is the value of my brand if I am a sports team? How is that value estimated?

The initial answers to these questions will come from marketing agencies and companies that promote sports events, aided by an improved theoretical understanding of the subject. 1998 may thus be viewed as the end of the 'prehistoric' period of this discipline in France. Like others in the Internet and new-technology fields, firms in this business (particularly sponsors and equipment manufacturers) are discovering that sport offers a means to make profits, improve your competitive position, publicize your brand, and change your image. Not long afterwards the same team won the Euro 2000 championship, confirming its position as the world's best. Meanwhile the French rugby team beat the All Blacks in 1999 (in an unforgettable match where every bounce went the French way) and took second place in the World Cup. The women's handball team also finished second in the world that year, and the men won the world title in Paris in 2001.

Lastly, the French basketball team won silver in the 2000 Olympics behind the Americans, which almost amounted to a victory in the eyes of the public.

Why are we revisiting all this sporting news, when the topic is 'sports marketing'? Simply because the 'sports marketing' discipline is also practiced in sports-marketing agencies (Havas Sports, Carat Sport, IMG, Octagon...), by broadcasters (ESPN, TNT, TBS, BBC, Sky, TF1, Canal +, France Télévision, Eurosport, M6...), equipment manufacturers (Adidas, Nike, Reebok, Salomon, Rossignol...), the leagues (National Basketball Association (NBA), National Football League (NFL), Major League Basketball (MLB), Professional Football League, National Rugby League...), international federations (Union of European Football Associations (UEFA), Fédération Internationale de Football Association (FIFA), International Olympic Committee (IOC)) and with some difficulty by the national federations (Fédération Française de Football (FFF), Fédération Française de Rugby (FFR), and the Fédération Française de Tennis (FFT) for the tennis championship at Roland-Garros). A researcher must therefore look for inspiration among their everyday management practices, while also contributing the insights provided by theory. If the concepts of CRM (customer relationship management), of yield management (a management technique consisting of optimizing the occupancies of aircraft, trains, hotels and sports arenas) and of ambush marketing are now so popular in the agencies, it is because academics introduced these ideas some years ago. It is very unsettling, however, to find that these 'professionals' still believe that they started it all, and are unaware of the primary sources.

Ambush marketing, which was introduced by Tony Meenhagan in 1994 in a still-famous article and then reworked in another article in 1998, is now an increasingly popular technique.

Ambush marketing first appeared following the dramatic climb in the price of rights to broadcast major events. The strategy involves obtaining an impact comparable to that of the official sponsor, but without being contractually associated with the event – and of course at a lower cost. David Stotlar (2001a, 2001b) quotes the words of Lisa Ukman,[1] who defined ambush marketing in 1995 as 'A promotional strategy whereby a non-sponsor attempts to capitalize on the popularity/prestige of a property [holder] by giving the false impression that it is a sponsor. [This tactic is] often employed by the competitors of a property's official sponsors.'

'Anti-ambush' strategies are now available and are being developed in the agencies. The organizers of major events are especially affected by this type of problem, and have to face situations that might be described as 'guerilla marketing'. To deal with these practices, international authorities are now seeking legal solutions, finding themselves in situations comparable to that of counterfeiting.

For example, the International Olympic Committee (IOC) is currently very concerned about ambush marketing.[2] Since 2000, because of this concern, the IOC has used the term 'parasitic marketing' to indicate that it is an underhand and reprehensible practice, which injures the real investors.

Box 0.1 The Olympic Games: all rights reserved (13 February 2010)

'It's a fierce competition, but it's not a sporting competition, it's in the commercial arena' explains Benoît Séguin, a University of Ottawa professor who specializes in sports marketing. At the heart of this confrontation the International Olympic Committee (IOC) and the Vancouver Organizing Committee for the Olympic Games (VANOC), along with the Canadian government, are acting as referees so that the contest remains civilized – and profitable.

A number of firms are nevertheless seeking to profit from the universal fame of the Games, without paying as much as the official sponsors. Professor Séguin mentions 'ambush marketing' [in French: '*marketing insidieux*']. At the national level, for example, Petro-Canada will spend between $60 and $70 million, quite legally, to produce glasses with the Olympic Games symbol. He notes that its competitor Esso is more closely associated with Hockey Canada. Although it costs a lot less, unwary consumers could assume that this oil company was also part of the Olympics, since it is funding the hockey players.

In Turin, four years ago, an 'ambush' firm had rented all the giant billboards located near the official sites. Vast numbers of spectators then made a connection between the Games and the company, without its paying anything to the IOC.

'The danger for the official sponsor is that if the ambush marketing works properly, it will reduce the value of its investment.'

Source: www.cyberpresse.ca/le-soleil/dossiers/vancouver-2010/201002/13/01-949322-les-jeux-olympiques-tous-droits-reserves.php (last accessed 15 June 2010).

In France, 2002 marked the passing of the sports-marketing euphoria. The French team, favourites for the 2002 Football World Cup, failed miserably in the first round. Accused, no doubt wrongly, of having interfered with the team, the French squad's principal sponsors at the time (SFR, Adidas, Canal +, and Carrefour) found themselves in a jam and obliged to rethink their advertising strategy, which had relied on a victorious outcome.[3] Events, then, force sports-marketing practices to change. Today, a major section of the literature addresses 'risk-management applied to sponsorship' (Amis and Cornwell, 2005; Arthur and Chadwick, 2007; Beech and Chadwick, 2007).

By way of counterpart in the academic world, the 1990–2010 period saw the emergence of a genuine literature in the field of sports marketing. Although the seminal work of Mullin *et al.* (1993) may be taken as the start of a new field of research in the Anglo-Saxon world, the French literature barely mentioned the subject before 1999. It was often necessary to settle for managerial studies inspired by the sociology of sporting practices, sports history, sporting law, sports economics, and so on. The publication of *Marketing du sport* (Desbordes *et al.*, 1999) then became one of the cornerstones of the discipline in the francophone world. Today, however, when we look at the approach taken in that work, it seems very traditional, even old-fashioned. Indeed, adopting the marketing of sports-services providers and sellers of goods to meet the concerns of the sports consumer is a very 'marketing-mix' approach. Nevertheless, at the time it was the only one available. Today, this work has given birth to many offspring, which afford a much more comprehensive view of distribution, events and strategic marketing as applied to sport. The discipline has matured, become more complex, and has incorporated the elements of neo-marketing; it now represents a fertile breeding ground of ideas for marketing in general.

For example, from the standpoint of events, the BNP Paribas Masters tennis tournament has involved its spectators since 2007, making them on-court participants, adopting the idea of experiential marketing tested over many years by the promoters of NBA basketball games. In the same way, in the distribution of sporting products brands such as Nike (through its Nike Towns) and Adidas (in its concept stores) are employing this notion of the experience (Hetzel, 2002). From the standpoint of the relationship with its users, all of the brands are attempting to forge links with them on their home turf. New Balance has created an Internet platform (www.runningclub.fr/), in line with the precepts of relational marketing and CRM.

The development of this discipline can also be studied with respect to the topics addressed by researchers and their areas of investigation. In recent years, researchers have tended to abandon the marketing of sporting products for that of sporting services (Desbordes, 2001). On the epistemological level, a product, unlike a service, possesses no specificity.

Although it may be fair to say that being interested in 'automobile marketing' is simplistic from a scientific point of view because there is no reason why the conclusions in that field should be any different from those in other industrial sectors, the special organization of sport creates specific features that justify the existence of a marketing of sport.[4]

- As regards products, specific features are certainly harder to distinguish. A sports product, especially those intended for instrumentalized activities in the great outdoors, ultimately requires the same properties as a 'traditional' product, but of superior quality. The product must be a little better-made than the average (because practical requirements cause athletes to look for lightness, rigidity or resistance to the elements), a little more attractive than average (because sporting activities require us to display our bodies in a contest where social interactions will occur), a little more 'trendy' than the average (because sport is often synonymous with progress and innovation in our society), and have stores that are ahead of their time[5] (because consuming a sports product is above all a pleasure more than a utilitarian act of consumption). Ultimately, the marketing of sports products remains a rather traditional matter, with a few characteristics that are more strongly pronounced than for other products, but it is certainly the most limited area of sports marketing, and for this reason most researchers have moved away from it after making it the central topic of their theses (Hillairet, 1992; Desbordes, 1998a, 1998b).

- The marketing of services, however, is much more complex. Unlike the sports-products sector, which is exclusively the domain of market companies that are all essentially seeking to maximize their profit, according to the neo-classical definition of the firm, sports services operate in a kind of 'hodgepodge' environment, where commercial firms rub shoulders with non-profit associations, federations authorized by ministries to develop their sport, schools and local governments. The situation then becomes much more complicated to manage and leads its participants to ask themselves a number of questions. Who are their competitors? What resources do they possess? Who regulates this system? Who has the power to sell what is being produced?[6] All these questions are complex and force the marketing function to become involved in organizational theory, and in the legal and strategic aspects.

Similarly, a sports service differs from a traditional service:

- A sports service has an emotional dimension. The intangible nature of a sports service is combined with a highly emotional character, which gives it density.[7] A sports event may lose much of its drama in the absence of an impassioned commentary from a journalist, or if unaccompanied by the emotional displays of a crowd.
- A sports service has an environmental dimension. The environment of the event has a great influence on the experience of pleasure and the sports consumer's level of satisfaction. We might even say that the environment is an integral part of the service (Minquet, 1992).
- A sports service assumes the active participation of the consumer. The particular character of a sports service is also a function of the way in which a sports consumer cooperates in the production of the service (Pigeassou and Garrabos, 1997, 56–57). Players consume the service by involving their own bodies in it, sweating and dusty, even sometimes in pain. It is their own energy (not that of the service provider), their efforts and their resources that give substance to the service. In a sense, the body is the primary instrument of this production (Pigeassou and Garrabos, 1997, 180).
- A sports service has a symbolic dimension. The final characteristic feature of sports services is their particularly pronounced symbolic dimension. Of course, all forms of consumption, sporting and non-sporting alike, have a symbolic aspect connected to social portrayal, but sports consumption perhaps more than others (Ohl, 1995). Sport enables an individual to play a role in front of other people and convey a social position to them.

The concept of a sports service is thus both complex and fertile, and fully deserves to become a priority subject for research. Among the various existing sports services, the concept of the sports event is a topic that marketers have often neglected.

However, sporting events, too, have specific features that are inherent to their sector of activity. Consider the example of a sporting competition such as the Formula 1 season. In a traditional industrial sector, maximum profits and efficiencies are associated with peak performance and power. It is quite different in sports, because the events rely on uncertainty. In 2002, Formula 1 racing lost 30 per cent of its audience because the domination of Schumacher and Ferrari spoiled the show (Duchemin, 2002). This is the paradox of sport: one must dominate while at the same time maintaining a sufficient number and quality of adversaries; otherwise the overall value of the spectacle will fall.[8] The Microsoft model would be disastrous in the field of sporting events. These conclusions apply to all types of competition (football, tennis, rugby, etc.). These aspects of regulation are very interesting to a researcher because they introduce ethical concepts into the method of management – but this is not the only attraction of events. When we look inside the 'black box', the one that produces, that in neo-classical theory transforms capital and labour into output, we become aware of the complexity of the production system. From a functional viewpoint, this makes project management a challenging task. Desbordes and Falgoux (2007) illustrate the necessity of coordinating all these functions: logistics, security, marketing, production, and the sporting, legal and human-resources functions. Although such organization is not unique to sport, since in general all businesses have to coordinate these functions, sporting events introduce special features that greatly complicate the organizer's task:

- An event is usually a 'one-shot' thing, with no room for error.
- A sports event is by definition uncertain (the result, sometimes the duration, the weather, environment, etc.).
- These random factors may alter the course of the event and create unforeseen circumstances (security in particular).
- Ultimately, the organizer's mission is to guarantee the quality of a service that is uncertain by its very nature!

This special feature of sports services leads to very specific marketing studies and behaviours.

As a consequence of all these considerations, the management and marketing of sport have become scientific fields in their own right. Since the 1990s, these publications have been followed by a stream of other productions, leading to a field that is increasingly specialized by subject. It is now possible to find manuals on the distribution of sports products, sponsorship, sporting brands, sporting venues, the relationships between sport and the media, patronage, and marketing applied to football, among others.

This specialization of the field did not occur in isolation from the real world, as we have already mentioned.

Table 0.1 Increase in the cost of television rights to the Olympic Games (in US$ millions)

Year	Host city	TV rights (USA)	TV rights (Europe)	TV rights (World)
1960	Rome	0.5	0.7	1.2
1964	Tokyo	1.0	0.4	1.5
1968	Mexico	4.5	1.0	9.8
1972	Munich	7.5	1.70	11.8
1976	Montreal	25.0	4.5	34.8
1980	Moscow	85.0	6.0	101.0
1984	Los Angeles	225.0	19.8	287.0
1988	Seoul	300.0	28.0	407.0
1992	Barcelona	401.0	90.0	636.0
1996	Atlanta	456.0	250.0	907.0
2000	Sydney	715.0	350.0	1350.0
2004	Athens	793.0	400.0	1700.0
2008	Beijing	894.0	460.0	2000.0

Source: Bourg and Gouguet, 1998.

The link between the realities of management and the world of research is particularly conspicuous during the organization of great sporting events: the 1998 Football World Cup in France, the Sydney Olympics in 2000, the 2007 Rugby World Cup in France, the Beijing Olympics in 2008, the Vancouver Olympics in 2010 – all world-class events that gave rise to numerous research programmes and the development of young research workers in their respective countries.

We are currently witnessing an expansion of the publishers of scientific books and reviews. Human Kinetics, Fitness Information Technology (FIT), Elsevier, Edward Elgar and others distribute English-language books, while Economica, De Boeck, les éditions d'Organisation, Vuibert, and Armand Colin distribute French-language ones.

In the area of reviews, the *Journal of Sport Management, Sport Marketing Quarterly, Sport Management Review, International Journal of Sport Marketing and Sponsorship, European Sport Management Quarterly, International Journal of Sport Management and Marketing, Journal of Sponsorship, International Journal of Sport Communication*, as well as general reviews in marketing and management science, present the work of English-language researchers.

This abundance of publications is explained by the place that sport occupies in our society, with the frenetic merchandizing of major sporting events, well illustrated by the dizzying increase in the cost of television rights (see Table 0.1).

So, why do we need another book on sports marketing?

Although the discipline has matured, it nevertheless needs to abandon the transactional analysis, now a little outmoded, which is usually employed in traditional works, and to move on to a more 'neo-marketing' approach, as described by Badot and Cova (1992) and Cova and Badot (1992).

Accordingly, this book presents a new paradigm in the field of sports marketing, with a truly international flavour. Its authors share a dual culture, both European and North American, which is the common theme of this publication.

From the standpoint of its contents, the conceptual or theoretical dimension forms the core of the book, but the case studies that punctuate the chapters also give it a managerial dimension, and make it easier to read.

To have the most complete and international approach possible, the two editors of this publication, Michel Desbordes and André Richelieu, have chosen to include colleagues from Germany, The Netherlands, China and France.

The first part, comprising four chapters, addresses the management of the brand and its internationalization.

Chapter 1, written by André Richelieu, discusses the strategic construction of a brand in the world of sport.

Chapter 2, also by André Richelieu, concerns the impact of globalization on the internationalization of sport, its organizations and its brands.

Chapter 3, written by Christoph Breuer, Tim Pawlowski and Christopher Rumpf, looks at sponsorship and the sports brand from an economic perspective.

Chapter 4, written by Guojun Zeng, Frank Go and Christian Kolmer, is devoted to the creation of a country's image via its sporting events, using the example of China during recent years. In this respect, a country may also be regarded as a brand.

The second part of the book concerns events, and their experiential dimension.

Wladimir Andreff has written Chapter 5, entitled 'Sports events, economic impact and regulation'. He seeks to add an economic dimension to sports events, and addresses the institutional and regulationist context in which they interact.

Chapter 6, written by Michel Desbordes, concerns the strategy of manufacturers of football equipment and the internationalization that results, in a relationship among three actors (club, equipment maker and sponsor).

Boris Helleu has written Chapter 7, entitled 'Be ready to be excited'. This chapter, which makes the connection between sport and spectacle, is applied to the World Wrestling Entertainment (WWE).

Chapter 8, written by Michel Desbordes, concerns the management of sporting venues. When seeking to optimize the event and the distribution strategy, the stadium or arena constitutes one of the key factors in the success of a sporting event.

Finally, Chapter 9, written by André Richelieu, looks back on what has been learned and then forward to what the future holds for sports marketing.

Now read on!

Michel Desbordes and André Richelieu

Notes

1 Lisa Ukman was the chair and co-founder of IEG (International Events Group), and editor of the *IEG Sponsorship Report.*

2 Additional information on the concept of ambush marketing is included in Chapter 6 of this publication.

3 Who can forget the Adidas advertising, using the famous 2*? This literally meant 'we're going to win our 2nd World Cup, it's in the bag.' It was a disaster in terms of public opinion because it was so conceited.

4 The same is true of cultural activities, which have their own particular marketing: see on this topic the work of Yves Evrard (Hautes Études Commerciales (HEC)) and Dominique Bourgeat (Université de Bourgogne).

5 On this subject the case of Andaska is instructive: a chain of sports stores specializing in outdoor products intended for a trendy urban clientele seeking an ambiance that offers escape through consumption (see Hetzel, 2002). Along the same lines we may cite the example of Niketown, also discussed by Patrick Hetzel, where the brand is unapologetically employed as part of the display at the place of sale.

6 The case of French football is particularly pertinent here, with reference to the sale of TV rights. These are now sold collectively by the LFP (Professional Football League), which has been delegated by the French Football Federation to organize professional football. The LFP then distributes this manna to the clubs. But it is possible to imagine other owners for these rights: the clubs themselves (as is the case in Spain and Italy), the clubs' majority shareholders, the players, the Sports Ministry, and so on.

7 On this subject Bernard Jeu has written that 'sport is perceived as a great story ... a veritable emotional force-field, a constant appeal to the imagination ... [where] the will to win is a passion'. For this author, 'sport has a poetic function' (Jeu, 1992, 20–21).

8 This is the goal of the regulations in the American leagues. The most profitable sports system is the one that is likely to maintain both fairness and uncertainty – at least on the face of it.

References

Amis, J. and Cornwell, B. (eds) (2005). *Global sport sponsorship*, Berg Publishers, London.

Arthur, D. and Chadwick, S. (eds) (2007). *International cases in the business of sport,* Elsevier, London.

Badot, O. and Cova, B. (1992). Des marketing en mouvement, vers un néo-marketing, *Revue Française de Gestion,* 136, 5–27.

Beech, J. and Chadwick, S. (eds) (2007). *The marketing of sport*, Financial Times Press, London.

Bourg, J.-F. and Gouguet, J.-J. (1998). *Analyse économique du sport*, Presses Universitaires de France, Paris.

Cova B. and Badot O. (1992). *Néo-Marketing*, ESF Editions, Paris.

Desbordes, M. (1998a). Management de l'innovation dans l'industrie du sport: variations autour du cas Salomon, *Annales des Mines – Gérer et Comprendre*, 53, 14–25.

Desbordes, M. (1998b). Facteurs clés de succès dans le management et la diffusion d'une innovation: analyse de cinq cas dans l'industrie du sport, *International Journal of Design and Innovation Research*, 1, 35–52.

Desbordes, M. (ed.) (2001). *Stratégie des entreprises dans le sport: Acteurs et management.* Editions Economica, Paris.

Desbordes, M. and Falgoux, J. (2007). *Les événements sportifs*, 3rd edition, Les Editions d'Organisation, Paris, preface by Michel Platini.

Desbordes, M., Ohl, F. and Tribou, G. (1999). *Marketing du sport*, 1st edition, Editions Economica, Paris, p. 507. (2000 prize from the Academy of Business Science for the year's best publication in management and marketing.)

Duchemin, R. (2002). *La médiatisation des événements sportifs: l'alternative innovante des partenariats médias*. DESS thesis '*Management international du sport*', Université Paris Sud-XI, France, Director: Michel Desbordes.

Hetzel, P. (2002). *Planète conso: marketing expérientiel et nouveaux univers de consommation*. Les Editions d'Organisation.

Hillairet, D. (1992). *Le système PISTE (Prospective et Innovation des Sports à Technologie Elevée)*. Doctoral thesis, STAPS, Université Paris Sud-XI, France, Director: Pr. Christian Pociello.

Jeu, B. (1992). Sport, philosophie, histoire, *Revue Française du Marketing*, 138, 19–26.

Meenhagan, T. (1994). Ambush marketing: immoral or imaginative practice. *Journal of Advertising Research*, 34, September, 77–88.

Meenhagan, T. (1998). Ambush marketing: corporate strategy and consumer reaction, *Psychology and Marketing*, July, 305–322.

Minquet, J.P.L. (1992). Le produit sport. *Revue Française du Marketing*, 138, 27–35.

Mullin, B.J., Hardy, S. and Sutton, W.A. (1993). *Sport Marketing*, Human Kinetics, Champaign, IL.

Ohl, F. (1995). Consommations sportives et interactions sociales, in *Sport, relations sociales et action collective*, Maison des Sciences de l'Homme d'Aquitaine, Talence, pp. 675–684.

Pigeassou, C. and Garrabos, C. coord. (1997). *Management des organisations de services sportifs*, Presses Universitaires de France, Paris.

Stotlar, D.K. (2001a). *Developing successful sport sponsorship plans*, Fitness Information Technologies, Morgantown, WV.

Stotlar, D.K. (2001b). *Developing successful sport marketing plans*, Fitness Information Technologies, Morgantown WV.

Part I

Management of the brand and its internationalization

1 Building sports brands

André Richelieu

Introduction

In the face of extremely competitive national and international markets, companies have found strategic and powerful leverages in the concepts of brand and brand equity (Aaker, 1997; Buil *et al.*, 2008; Kapferer, 2007). With a strong brand, companies are in a position to create positive images, to extend their brand into new product categories and to fuel customer loyalty (Brakus *et al.*, 2009; Keller, 2003; Wang *et al.*, 2009).

Brand equity, defined as 'the marketing effects uniquely attributable to the brand' (Keller, 1993, p.1), is the promise that a company makes to its consumers by responding to their expectations and continually offering them a quality product or service (Aaker, 1997; Kapferer, 2007; Lewi, 2005). In the service industry, brand equity is all the more important, for it is difficult to make a promise to clients by virtue of the intangibility and lack of consistency in the services rendered (Balmer *et al.*, 2009; De Chernatony *et al.*, 2005). The recent airline crisis caused by the volcano eruption in Iceland illustrated to what extent this was ignored by managers.

In recent years, professional sports clubs have viewed brand and brand management as ways to reinforce the emotional connection with their fans and to create a competitive advantage (Bauer *et al.*, 2005; Mullin *et al.*, 2007; Richelieu and Pons, 2009).

This chapter concentrates on the brand and its characteristics, analysing to what extent brand applies to sports. To do so, we will first look at the brand and its strategic importance. Second, we will see how sports organizations can be defined as brands in their own right. Third, we will introduce brand building strategies in sports, and illustrate their applications in a fourth section in this chapter. We will solidify the key elements of our discussion in the conclusion.

The strategic importance of a brand

By definition, a brand is 'a name, a word, a sign, a symbol, a drawing, or a combination of these' (Kotler *et al.*, 2000, p.478). A brand is made up of tangible elements, such as the logo and the colours, and intangible elements, like symbols and values, to which the consumer will often identify himself or herself and to justify his or her choice, especially in cases where the products are not really that different (for example, Coca-Cola and Pepsi). A brand allows for the identification of a company's products and services as well as its distinction from competitors, underlining its unique selling proposition (USP); in other words, the brand's unique characteristics that make the brand stand out from the competition and that are often incorporated in the brand slogan: 'Gillette, the best a man can get' or 'Munich loves you'.

Above all, a brand is a promise a company makes to its consumers (Lewi, 2005). This promise is built on the coherence and the continuity of products or services offered to consumers each time they come in contact with the product or service (Kapferer, 2007). Three types of brand objectives are attached to this promise: fundamental, intermediary and final. Fundamental objectives are linked to the external (competitors: Adidas versus Nike) and internal (other products or company brands in the same product category: Unilever with Persil and Omo for laundry detergent) positioning of the brand. Intermediary objectives deal with notoriety, penetration, brand diffusion, as well as consumer brand loyalty. Final objectives are related to the market share, revenue and profits generated by the brand (Kapferer, 2007; Lewi, 2005).

The value of a brand is measured by brand equity, which according to Kotler (2002, p.470), 'is based on the extent to which it has a high brand loyalty, name awareness, perceived quality, strong brand associations and other assets such as trademarks'. Generally, strong brand equity is the foundation of a successful brand strategy (Richelieu and Pons, 2006), with a positive impact on the buying intentions, prices and the loyalty to the brand (Raggio and Leone, 2009).

However, to remain strong and long-lasting, a brand must respect certain rules, such as the ability to maintain focus and to preserve quality and authenticity (Ries and Ries, 2002). In the opposite case, a brand becomes diluted and this potentially opens the door to its competitors. This was the case with Starbucks, which lost its status as 'The Coffee Authority', and paved the way for McDonald's to offer its premium coffee for one dollar. Toyota also lost its reputation for quality following a series of recalls of millions of vehicles in 2009–2010. One could say that the 2009 Tiger Woods sex scandal is a case of brand management, in which the promise of a quasi-perfect man, or a demi-God, or at least the example that the golfer projected, was betrayed. This case shows how the organizations and actors of the sporting world are seen as brands in their own right.

Sports teams as brands

It is now recognized that teams (Real Madrid, Olympique de Marseille, Stade Francais, etc.), players (Roger Federer, Tiger Woods, Lebron James, etc.) and sports organizations (CIO, NBA, UEFA, etc.) are brands (Mullin *et al.*, 2007; Séguin *et al.*, 2008). A brand constitutes the most important asset of clubs (Bauer *et al.*, 2005). In this respect, brand identity provides direction and meaning to the actors of the sport (Hill and Vincent, 2006). Brand and brand management allow the actors to create value (Mullin *et al.*, 2007; Richelieu, 2008a), as much on the marketing as the financial front (Mizik and Jacobson, 2008), in order to ensure their continued existence (Bauer *et al.*, 2005).

If we look at professional sports teams, they exhibit the characteristics of 'real' products, made up of tangible benefits, like the result of the game or even the derived products ('merchandising'), but also intangible benefits, like the emotions felt by the fans at the stadium or the feeling of pride and belonging (Bauer *et al.*, 2005). In this regard, a sports team has the potential to create and nourish its brand equity, amplifying the emotional connection that it shares with its fans, with the goal of reinforcing fan loyalty, of promoting positive word-of-mouth and of stimulating purchases of derivative products (Richelieu and Pons, 2009). The more a consumer identifies with a brand, the greater the chance that he or she will be loyal and will express his or her attachment by purchasing products with the brand logo, in addition to acting as an ambassador, such as Nutella lovers do (Cova and Pace, 2006; see www.mynutella.it).

Indisputably, with the exception of entertainment, religion and politics, professional sports teams generate an unmatched emotional response from their fans. Although still unharnessed, this connection of passion is very important, as the fans derive pride and self-esteem from their association with the team (Richelieu and Pons, 2006). While winning may be essential, it is not enough to nourish a team's brand equity (Ross, 2006). In fact, one could say that victory, tradition, championships and the hope of winning again represent the basis on which a sports team may depend to articulate a strong brand identity. It is a tangible asset that gives prestige to an organization and that allows it to get some mileage in the off seasons, and from which marketing actions (the 4 Ps: product, price, promotion and public relations (PR), and pipeline (distribution); Mullin *et al.*, 2007) can electrify the emotional connection in its supporters. While the team may not win every year, its legacy is present, and is remembered by its partisans, all in the hopes of winning again as soon as possible. This is what successful teams like FC Barcelona, Manchester United, the New York Yankees and the New Zealand All Blacks do. Others, unfortunately, seem to be prisoners of their glorious history, and have only marketing tools (mascots, promotional items, sound and light shows, etc.) to mask the long droughts on the field. Then, the inevitable happens, and fans gradually move away from the club that does not keep its promises and that cannot preserve its standing. This is the case of the Toronto Blue Jays baseball team that has not won a world series (play-off championship of Major League Baseball) since 1993, and that has been restructuring and unable to deliver on its promises since. Today, barely 10,000 people attend the Jays' home games, whereas in the first half of the 1990s the team used to play for sold out crowds of 46,000 spectators.

This being said, we have laid the groundwork for the next section in this chapter, in which we will consider the ways to build a brand in sports.

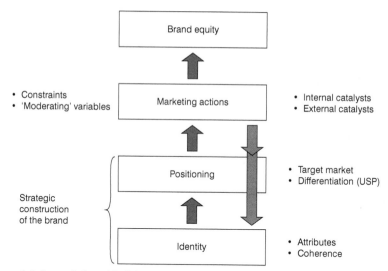

Figure 1.1 Strategic brand building in sports

Sources: Desbordes and Richelieu, 2011; Kashani, 1995; Richelieu, 2004; 2008a.

Strategic brand building in sports

Based on work done in brand management (Kapferer, 2007; Kashani, 1995), authors have articulated strategic brand building in professional sports, focusing mainly on sports clubs (Mullin *et al.*, 2007; Richelieu, 2008a; Ross, 2006).

Brand building goes through three stages (Figure 1.1):

1   Define the brand identity or personality.
2   Position the sports team in the market.
3   Develop marketing initiatives using the '4 Ps' that support the brand strategy.

Define the brand identity or personality

Brand identity or personality refers to two elements: 1) brand attributes or values; and 2) the relationship between the club's values, as communicated by leaders, and fan perception (Richelieu, 2004).

First and foremost, a club's brand identity is based on a number of attributes or values that make up its brand personality. In other words, how does a club want to be recognized: for its history and tradition, its victories, its game style, its conviviality, its proximity to its fans, its determination on the field, its humility, etc.? These values provide direction for the club brand; the starting point for a long-lasting brand strategy (Richelieu, 2008a). It is clear that the more history a team has, the more it is woven into the socio-economic fabric of its community, the more the team is in a situation to capitalize on the emotional connection of its fans, and, the stronger the brand. Consequently, old European soccer clubs (FC

Barcelona, Juventus of Turin, Olympique de Marseille) have an advantage over North American franchises that have been around for less than 30 years (Toronto Raptors in basketball, Colorado Rockies in baseball). However, North American clubs do not hesitate to use 'storytelling' to articulate a story of their myths, heroes and legends, especially if the team quickly becomes competitive on the field. This is the case of baseball's Miami Marlins who, though they started in 1993, have already won two world championships (1997 and 2003).

Secondly, once a brand's values have been well defined by the managers, it is necessary to ensure coherence with how fans perceive the club, using various techniques like focus groups and surveys. If necessary, the club must find ways to reconcile opposing points of view. As we know, perception is often more important than reality in marketing. For example, if the team continually touts their winning past, but does not manage to win any more titles, will the managers continue to bring these values to the fore? Are we not risking altering the brand image and promise made to fans, by communicating values that are no longer found in the product? The Toronto Maple Leafs have not won a Stanley Cup (play-off championship of the National Hockey League) since 1967: it is without a doubt why Toronto relies greatly on the entertainment experience at the arena (Richelieu and Pons, 2006), dissociating from their victorious past that does not appear to be returning any time soon.

Club managers must analyse the situation and then make adjustments along the way in order to reflect the brand identity that, without necessarily having to change with the seasons, evolves over time.

In summary, a strong brand identity has the potential to increase the emotions of fans and to reinforce their trust in and loyalty towards the brand; consequently, these fans will be more receptive to marketing efforts (the 4 Ps) put in place by the managers to attract fans (Richelieu and Pons, 2009), as we will investigate now.

Position the sports team in the market

In this regard, managers must examine the following questions: 1) Who are our fans, what category or profile do they fit into and what are they looking for from the club's brand? 2) How does our sports brand differentiate itself from other sports brands, and also from entertainment brands?

Identify the fans

It is important for managers to identify the consumers who have already developed or who are bound to develop a favourable tendency with regard to the club. In addition to the traditional sports fans that we often characterize as armchair sports fans, surrounded by beer bottles and bags of chips, studies have identified a number of other fan profiles, as well as their expectations (Pimentel and Reynolds, 2004; Richelieu and Pons, 2005).

With the advent of 'sportainment', or the fusion of sports and entertainment, different categories of fans have emerged:

1   Fans who go to the stadium to encourage their team ('it's my team!', emotional fans; Richelieu and Pons, 2005). These supporters often represent the club's hard core fans. They diligently follow their team, purchase derivative products and are, in some cases, ready to sacrifice their personal lives to help the club, especially in difficult times. When the feeling of belonging, appropriation and identification with the club are pushed to the extreme, these fans are one with their team: a victory of the club is their victory; inversely, the club's defeat is synonymous with personal failure (Richelieu and Pons, 2005). The expression of their allegiance can be displayed in many forms: attending all the club's games, even away games, planning vacations according to their team's calendar, collecting derivative products, transforming their rooms, or homes, into museums honouring the club (Pimentel and Reynolds, 2004). In the United States, Boston Red Sox fans might even buy toilet paper with the rival New York Yankees logo! In these cases, we're talking about 'super fans' or 'extreme fans', where the feeling of belonging to the club is literally unfailing (Pimentel and Reynolds, 2004). These fans can be very critical of management's decisions and the team's performances.

2   The fans who go to the stadium for the beauty of the game ('seeing Barcelona play, is the champagne of soccer!', cognitive fans; Richelieu and Pons, 2005). These fans love the sport itself. They see themselves as, and try to become known as, experts in the sport. If the local team wins, so be it, but in the opposite case, they don't make a big deal of it, wearing the expert hat, in contrast to the fan hat of the first group we presented. In some cases, they may become the target, verbal at least, of emotional fans that see them as 'vulgar', 'demagogues' and even 'traitors'. These cognitive fans do not welcome entertainment in the stadiums, underlining that it takes away from the sport. These fans may find themselves in a difficult position in North America since entertainment adds the final touch, and sometimes takes over the game, notably in the case where the team loses or is already eliminated from the play-offs, and the managers try to find ways of filling the stadium despite it all (Richelieu and Pons, 2005).

3   Fans who come to the game to socialize ('I go to the stadium to have fun with my family and friends', relationship fans; Richelieu and Pons, 2005). These fans demonstrate that sports, particularly professional sports, are a vehicle of social cohesion. Following the work of Holt (1995), these fans see the sport above all as a social platform, with family, friends or other fans. Without saying they are not interested in the sport or the local team, these supporters view the sport as an opportunity to get together and to have a good time with others. In this regard, these fans could be more open to entertainment than the cognitive fans, for example, insofar as going to the stadium is seen as an experience in itself (Richelieu and Pons, 2005).

4   Fans who go to the game to network ('I go to the game to help myself find a job via the contacts that I can make', calculated fans; Pimentel and Reynolds, 2004). Sports games, being rallying by nature, are not only an

occasion to socialize, but also to fill your address book or to find a job. Often practiced in the United States, this approach becomes apparent particularly during university football games. Through powerful 'alumni', it is possible to shake hands with sponsors and donors who may be looking for new talent. At the game, these encounters are very friendly thus making the contact easier. Moreover, companies do not miss out on the opportunity; they rent corporate boxes to invite clients and partners. This is very trendy in North America and allows teams to generate important revenue. The boxes can be rented for ten years at a time, for example; for the companies, this is almost equivalent to a game of golf, and does not require any exercise. In addition, calculated fans are also those who will support a team when and because they win: one always derives some satisfaction when identifying with winners!

5   Fans who go to the stadium in response to peer pressure ('if you don't support your local team, you are frowned upon', normative fans; Pimentel and Reynolds, 2004). This situation, however, is often found in, but not limited to, small communities. Take Université Laval's Rouge et Or football team, for instance. Beyond the feeling of belonging that we found in some respondents during our study in 2006 (Richelieu, 2008b), we noted that some had a moral obligation to support the local team, or risk being disparaged by their peers. This phenomenon also arises outside the stadium. In Europe, for example, during the Football World Cup, women can get together to watch the game, even if they are not really interested in it, to avoid being socially excluded.

We underline that these categories are not mutually exclusive and it is possible to have different combinations depending on the situation: one might be an emotional fan looking for the social aspect, or even networking; one could also be a calculated and normative fan at the same time.

It is important to remember the 'lifestyle' or 'fashion' fans. These are the consumers who will dress in the team colours and wear the team logo because their favourite rap or hip hop artist wore it at a concert or in a video; or even to show his or her allegiance to a street gang. This phenomenon began near the end of the 1990s, when Spike Lee asked New Era to make him a red New York Yankees cap with a white logo before a concert. This trend exploded into an industry of very lucrative 'lifestyle' sports dressing. Estimated revenues exceed US$12 billion per year in the United States for music and hip hop clothing, of which sports teams make up a large part: caps in a variety of colours, jackets, jerseys, chains, earrings and the list goes on (Manivet and Richelieu, 2008). Interestingly, this style has opened a royal path to vintage collections of major North American sports leagues, namely basketball ('Hardwood Collections') and baseball ('Cooperstown Collection'), which are extremely popular with the hip hop clientele. We could also say that today, thanks to rap and hip hop, the baseball cap has become, on a global scale, a symbolic denominator of cultural communion like jeans were in a certain era, expecially with youth.

Differentiate the sports brand

Brand identity or personality represents the foundations on which the club can position itself in relation to other sports teams or entertainment offers, via its USP, the goal being to convince the consumer to spend their money on the club. If a team is able to identify and highlight the uniqueness of its brand, it will be able to establish an enviable position in the market among its direct and indirect competitors. This is also a matter of survival, as mentioned by the former Vice President of Marketing for the Montreal Canadiens (National Hockey League; NHL):

> We need to justify to our fans why they are going to pay up to $200 a ticket to come to one of our games at the Bell Centre, even though they can very well stay at home, sitting comfortably in their living room in front of the high definition television, with a full fridge close by.... What we're selling is a unique experience, to share a special moment, a spectacular goal, a dramatic win, music, lights, white towels that fans wave together, etc. What we offer is an experience that we attempt to renew with each game.
>
> (Vice President of Marketing 2009)

Professional sports teams must distinguish themselves. What do they offer that is special enough to bring a consumer to choose a sports game over going to a restaurant, to the movies or to the museum or simply to save for a vacation in the sun?

This is the 'value proposition' offered to the consumer. Marketing has for a long time prided itself on wanting to satisfy the needs and desires of consumers. This is now an interesting challenge for professional sports teams who demand more and more money from their fans, without necessarily increasing the value proposition for their supporters.

That's how slogans like 'Mès que un club' (More than a club) of FC Barcelona take all their meaning. FC Barcelona is the symbol of a region and a people; it transcends soccer to become the standard bearer for Catalonia, since the Franco regime, when all independent symbols were banned with the exception of sports. Today, through its partnership with United Nations Children's Fund (UNICEF), FC Barcelona spreads its slogan even further into the societal sphere, with an image of responsibility, empathy and fraternity on an international level, which we will discuss in the second chapter.

Articulate coherent marketing initiatives

Once the fans are identified and the club's USP is defined, the managers must articulate a set of marketing initiatives that fall under the umbrella of the 4 Ps. These initiatives come from the identity and positioning of the club, all the while reinforcing them. The main objective of these marketing efforts is to ensure brand coherence while preserving brand authenticity. If a brand is to evolve, it should do so in continuity, rather than confusing the consumers (Ries and Ries, 2002).

For a sports team, the work is easy if there is a strong emotional connection between the fans and the club to begin with. It is in the team's best interest to use these marketing initiatives as leverage to reinforce the emotional connection: the more the fans feel valued, the more they will be attached to the club, and the more they will identify with it, the more likely they will be inclined to forgive their favourite team for their failures. Stephen Covey (1990) spoke of the 'emotional bank account' that needed to be replenished regularly in order to maintain a relationship. Some sports clubs have picked up on this already and started doting on their season's ticket holders, regular game attendees, the biggest fans of the team, the most colourful crowd leaders, etc. At a time when they still cared about their fans, the former Montreal Expos of Major League Baseball organized a yearly event dedicated to season's ticket holders, with a tour of the playing field and dressing rooms, games of skill, photo opportunities with the players, autograph sessions, etc. The Ottawa Senators of the NHL, on the other hand, started a loyalty programme in partnership with MasterCard called 'Sens Rewards' that allowed fans to accumulate points that were redeemable for products and activities, including a ride on the Zamboni! The Canadian Football League, Canada's equivalent of the NFL, organizes yearly contests that allow the most hard core fans of the eight teams to apply for the title of Extreme Fan of the Year, and to win a trip and a pair of tickets to the Grey Cup. These are all initiatives aimed at solidifying the sense of belonging, because fans feel that they are valued and involved.

For a long time, the emphasis and resources of sports organizations were placed on ticket sales. Today, the objectives have changed and are centred on the brand, through the reinforcement of the emotional connection between the club and its partisans, and, in turn, the trust and loyalty of the fans toward the club. In the same vein, the four elements of marketing must privilege the effects of synergy and coherence. This gave rise to the following, rather timely, questions:

1   Is it possible to be a prestigious club with corporate partners while presenting yourself as a friendly team that is close to its public? Particularly when the price of tickets is sky-high, to the point where parents have to practically take out another mortgage to take the family to the game?! Many European clubs, in particular the English teams from the Premier League, are faced with this dilemma. Even if the stadium is currently full, the problem cannot be ignored. Losing fans due to excessively high ticket prices will perhaps only be seen in a few years, but by the time the effects are visible, the fans will have already found other ways to spend their disposable income on other activities.

2   Can managers keep putting the history and tradition of the club at the forefront, and at the same time transform their stadium into a true circus where entertainment takes up the whole place, without diluting the club's brand? The Montreal Canadiens are between a rock and hard place: entertainment could damage the team's brand, but without the entertainment, the team will not be able to overcome the poor performance that has lasted since 1993, and continue to fill the arena. Is this similar to bandaging a wooden leg, which will not only have placebo effects but put the organization to sleep, eternally seen with a

mediocre product on their hands? We will see at the end of this section what solution the managers of the Canadiens came up with to remedy the situation.

3   Is it possible to sell a sport that has absolutely no cultural anchor while preserving its integrity? Or, does this call for creativity? At the end of the day, can we succeed at making a long-lasting club, league or sport, no matter the option selected? The North American Soccer League (NASL) hoped to sell soccer to North Americans from the 1960s to 1980s, by putting a spotlight on international stars, who were nearing retirement but who were still sufficiently admired (Pelé, Beckenbauer, Neeskens, Bettega, Best, etc.), and adapting the rules of the game to make it more entertaining (out of bounds lines in the opposing team's territory, similar to ice hockey, prolongation with penalty shots to take in a few seconds, etc.). To no avail; today, the Major League Soccer (MLS), tries to build more solid foundations, even though cultural adaptations do exist. For example, to reach out to the Mexican and American communities of Los Angeles, the club division from Guadalajara, Chivas USA, plays on its heritage of origin and the host culture. Mexican and American players make up the team, and the group of cheerleaders, called the Chivas Girls, was formed by recruiting candidates from the local community for a contest (see www.cdchivasusa.com/fans/chivagirls). In addition, a mascot and soccer schools were launched to attract families and young people talented in soccer, in a country where soccer is extremely popular on the participation level, falling short of the competitive level (Richelieu and Pons, 2009).

These questions and the discussion surrounding them illustrate the challenge that managers face when having to find a way to satisfy a clientele that can sometimes be very heterogeneous, not only in terms of their profile, but also because of their expectations of the team and its brand. In other words, how do we satisfy all our fans?

As mentioned earlier, this is all the more true today as we witness a sports appropriation on the part of rap, hip hop and urban communities. In this regard, what impact does seeing 50 Cent or Eminem wearing a New York Yankees cap, or an Oakland A's or Pittsburg Pirates cap have on the image of the club? Moreover, how do sports fans, deeply attached to a team, view the launch of 'lifestyle' collections in fluorescent colours to attract hip hop fans? Do we not risk alienating these fans who are the bread and butter of the sports team? These questions are worthwhile, for clubs may be tempted, unintentionally, to sacrifice the coherence of their brand in the long term, at the risk of diluting it, to generate revenues in the short term. The New York Yankees are familiar with this. In 2008, they decided to launch a cap where the logo smelled like pink chewing gum when you scratched it.

This is why the Toronto Maple Leafs NHL team work with the designers of New Era to introduce different cap models: those for hockey fans, which are sold at the club's arena (Air Canada Centre) and specialized sports stores, and those for 'lifestyle' fans, which are sold in trendy stores on Yonge Street and Queen Street West.

Indisputably, we now recognize that there exists a diversity of fans (fans who no longer only fall into the category of the typical sports fan, with beer and snack food) and this poses some challenges for the marketing managers of clubs. On the one hand, the managers hope to capitalize on these 'new' fans; on the other, they must do so tactfully, because a brand cannot be everything to everyone (authenticity!), even if the sport has the advantage of being a unifying social vehicle that few industries can boast of having.

The important thing for a team is to know who they are and what they represent as a brand, and then to articulate initiatives as a result. This is the case of the Montreal Canadiens, who have a vision articulated in five points, according to the club's documents provided by the Vice President of Marketing:

1 Mission: To be the best hockey organization in the world.
2 Promise: You will be proud to be a Canadiens fan.
3 Values: Authenticity, generosity, closeness, team work and performance.
4 Platform of Success: To build on our heritage, honour the brand, embrace change and invest in the sport.
5 All the above is supported by an organization who is 'passionate about hockey, committed to winning and inspired by its fans'.

However, the cultural context has its say as well, and the managers of the clubs are linked to that in certain ways. This is the point that we will make in the next section.

Brand and its application to sport

Culture influences sports marketing and everything that surrounds it. Take the case of the Nike advertisement, launched in April 2010, which used the voice of Tiger Woods' father, practically bringing us back to a scene from the movie *The Ten Commandments*. From the brand image management perspective, the commercial and its theme were very coherent, with the idea that Tiger Woods, who was in the midst of a scandal that tainted his image as a quasi-perfect man, almost a demi-God, needed to make amends, exercise humility and get both feet back on the ground. The controversy swirled around the message, whose meaning is anchored in the American culture: extremely puritan, very moralistic and where religious symbolism, especially in the southern United States, is very important. We need not discuss the entire saga, where the Hollywood hype surely made the European public smile. In Europe, moral affairs of celebrities were not so much the talk of the town (until the DSK scandal).

In addition, culture also influences sports marketing when the team operates in a non-traditional market: for example, a soccer team in North America, or a hockey team in the southern United States or in Europe. Can a sport be sold the same way from one region to another? If we rely on what was said earlier, and on what experience has shown us, the answer is no. In this case, does one alter the sport or use creativity to build up the product for consumers who, for the most part, are not experts in the area?

Although, we have illustrated a number of North American examples, there are many European ones as well. Take the case of the German hockey team, the Ice Tigers of Nuremberg. The ambiance in the arena suffices for us to understand that the product claims to be festive for fans and open to families, by virtue of scheduling matches on Friday evenings and Sunday afternoons. In adition, 'Pocki' the mascot is visibly present in the arena and during organized activities in the region. The Bavarian heritage is equally promoted, with a tour of the ice rink after each team victory at home, to the sound of traditional music, animated by the mascot. In this way, the Ice Tigers integrate 'modernity' of the idea of entertainment in a cultural context, following the example of Chivas USA with its Chivas Girls.

Entertainment, which is very much part of NBA basketball, is equally emphasized in the traditionally non-hockey cities of the southern United States in the NHL: 'Blue Land', an area laid out in Atlanta's Philips Arena by the former Thrashers, with cheerleaders and exciting and garish activities.

What can be said is that entertainment pervades in the stadiums around the world, through the North American influence (the power of accelerated acculturation in the context of globalization; see Chapter 2) and their success with the public. Even the teams of the KHL (Continental Hockey League, ex-USSR), have fallen in step, with sounds and lights on the giant screen, cheerleaders dance steps and the mascot, etc. (http://www.youtube.com/watch?v=JcGc3cHGwz0).

The essential thing here is not whether or not to subscribe to these practices for ideological reasons, but rather for brand logic. Once the brand identity and positioning are established, marketing initiatives are in some fashion an extension and a reinforcement of this brand identity and positioning. It is in fact a matter of brand coherence and not one of philosophy, even if culture may influence the response.

Conclusion

Throughout this chapter, we aimed to combine theory and practice, by illustrating our reflection of the various examples, through their national origin and their sport. The objective was to point out the inherent logic in the strategic building of the brand and its structure. This is by no means a recipe, but rather an approach, in three stages, which are represented in Figure 1.1:

1   Define the brand identity or personality.
2   Position the sports team in the market.
3   Develop coherent marketing initiatives via the 4 Ps, which will support the brand strategy.

Frankly, we leaned toward sports clubs, by choice, but also by pedagogical concern – sports clubs representing an increasingly articulated laboratory in the strategic building of a brand. However, this model can also be applied to players, which is why we discussed the case of Tiger Woods, for instance. These discussions will resume in the next chapter on globalization.

To build its brand, a team needs, above all, a vision. The managers have an asset in their hands, an asset at the foundation of the organization's durability. Sports managers often profit from an incomparable connection with their fans. Ideally, they should nourish it; the worst is to take it for granted. One cannot pretend to 'respond to the needs and desires of its consumers', following the example of too many companies today who find refuge behind 'low' prices or the economic crisis to sacrifice the product and service. It is necessary to sincerely value fans and involve them so that they identify more and more strongly with their favourite team. Fans will be more loyal to the club and will buy more merchandising products from the team.

If the stands are empty, it is rarely the fault of the fans. Perhaps it is because the sport is not adapted to the environment, as was the case of the NFL in Europe and ice hockey in the southern USA today (Miami, Tampa, Phoenix, in particular), because there are limits to what marketing can do to stimulate a demand that does not exist, beyond instigating the initial curiousity of the consumer. It could also be because the direction the club was taking contributed to breaking the emotional thread by betraying the emotions of the supporters, via doubtful exchanges, broken promises, continual mediocre performances and threats of moving (in North America, clubs can change cities), etc.

This is why brand management is important in professional sports. It is a beacon to the managers to help them reconcile the very rational financial objectives with the often emotional passion of their fans. We say that a brand is an asset, and this is true. The way to benefit from it is thanks to the fans and through a strategy of a coherent brand, which will keep its promise to its supporters. This is even truer in the context of globalization, such as we are presently living.

References

Aaker, J. L. (1997). 'Dimensions of brand personality'. *Journal of Marketing Research*, 34 (3): 347–356.

Balmer, J. M. T., H. Stuart and S. A. Greyser (2009). 'Aligning identity and strategy: Corporate branding at British Airways in the late 20th century'. *California Management Review*, 51 (3): 6–23.

Bauer, H. H., N. E. Sauer and P. Schmitt (2005). 'Customer-based brand equity in the team sport industry'. *European Journal of Marketing*, 39 (5/6): 496–513.

Brakus, J. J., B. H. Schmitt and L. Zarantonello (2009). 'Brand experience: What is it? How is it measured? Does it affect loyalty?'. *Journal of Marketing*, 73 (3): 52–68.

Buil, I., L. de Chernatony and E. Martinez (2008). 'A cross-national validation of the consumer-based brand equity scale'. *Journal of Product and Brand Management*, 17 (6): 384–392.

Cova, B. and S. Pace (2006). 'Brand community of convenience products: New forms of customer empowerment – The case "my Nutella The Community"'. *European Journal of Marketing*, 40 (9/10): 1087–1105.

Covey, S. (1990). *The 7 Habits of Highly Effective People*. New York: Simon & Schuster.

De Chernatony, L., S. Drury and S. Segal-Horn (2005). 'Using triangulation to assess and identify successful services brands'. *Service Industries Journal*, 25 (1): 42–54.

Desbordes, M. and A. Richelieu (2011). *Néo-Marketing du Sport*, Brussels, Belgium: De Boeck Publishers.

Hill, J. S. and J. Vincent (2006). 'Globalization and sports branding: The case of Manchester United'. *International Journal of Sports Marketing and Sponsorship*, 7(3): 213–230.

Holt, D. B. (1995). 'How consumers consume: A typology of consumption practices'. *Journal of Consumer Research*, 22 (1): 1–16.

Kapferer, J.-N. (2007). *The New Strategic Brand Management: Creating and Sustaining Brand Equity Long Term*. London: Kogan Page.

Kashani, K. (1995). 'Comment créer une marque puissante?' *Les Échos*, Available at: www.lesechos.fr (accessed February 2003).

Keller, K. L. (1993). 'Conceptualizing, measuring, and managing customer-based brand equity'. *Journal of Marketing*, 57 (January): 1–22.

Keller, K. L. (2003). 'Brand synthesis: The multidimensionality of brand knowledge'. *Journal of Consumer Research*, 29 (4): 595–600.

Kotler, P. (2002). *Marketing Management*, 11th edition. Upper Saddle River, NJ: Prentice Hall.

Kotler, P., P. Filiatrault and R. E. Turner (2000). *Le management du marketing*. Boucherville, Québec: Gaëtan Morin Éditeur.

Lewi, G. (2005). 'Branding management. La marque de l'idée à l'action'. Paris: Pearson Education France.

Manivet, B. and A. Richelieu (2008). 'Dangerous liaisons: How can sports brands capitalize on the hip hop movement'. *International Journal of Sport Management and Marketing*, 3 (1/2): 140–161.

Mizik, N. and R. Jacobson (2008). 'The financial value impact of perceptual brand attributes'. *Journal of Marketing Research*, 45 (1): 15–32.

Mullin, B. J., S. Hardy and W. A. Sutton (2007). *Sport Marketing*, 3rd edition. Champaign, IL: Human Kinetics.

Pimentel, R. W. and K. E. Reynolds (2004). 'A model for consumer devotion: Affective commitment with proactive sustaining behaviours'. *Academy of Marketing Science Review*, 2004 (5): 1–45.

Raggio, R. D. and R. P. Leone (2009). 'Chasing brand value: Fully leveraging brand equity to maximise brand value'. *Journal of Brand Management*, 16 (4): 248–263.

Richelieu, A. (2004). 'Building the brand equity of professional sports teams'. Chapter 1 in B. Pitts (ed.) *Sharing Best Practices in Sport Marketing*. Morgantown, WV: Fitness Information Technology Publishers, pp. 3–21.

Richelieu, A. (2008a). 'Creating and branding sport products'. Chapter 3 in S. Chadwick (ed.) *Sport Marketing*. London: Henry Stewart Talks. www.hstalks.com/sport/index.htm

Richelieu, A. (2008b). 'Combiner gestion de la marque et relations publiques dans une démarche stratégique: Le cas du Rouge et Or de l'Université Laval au Canada'. In C. Hautbois and M. Desbordes (eds) *Sport et Marketing Public*. Paris: Economica, pp. 237–253.

Richelieu, A. and F. Pons (2005). 'Reconciling managers' strategic vision with fans' expectations'. *International Journal of Sport Marketing and Sponsorship*, 6 (3): 150–163.

Richelieu, A. and F. Pons (2006). 'Toronto Maple Leafs vs. F.C. Barcelona: How two legendary sports teams built their brand equity'. *International Journal of Sports Marketing and Sponsorship*, 7 (3): 231–250.

Richelieu, A. and F. Pons (2009). 'If brand equity matters, where is the brand strategy? A look at Canadian teams in the NHL'. *International Journal of Sport Management and Marketing*, 5 (1/2): 162–182.

Ries, A. and L. Ries (2002). *The 22 Immutable Laws of Branding*. New York: Harper Collins.

Ross, S. D. (2006). 'A conceptual framework for understanding spectator-based brand equity'. *Journal of Sport Management*, 20 (January): 22–38.

Séguin, B., A. Richelieu and N. O'Reilly (2008). 'Leveraging the Olympic brand through the reconciliation of corporate and consumers brand perceptions'. *International Journal of Sport Management and Marketing*, 3 (1/2): 3–22.

Vice President of Marketing for the Montreal Canadiens (2009). Personal interview. Montreal, Canada, October 2009.

Wang, X., Z. Yang and N. R. Liu (2009). 'The impacts of brand personality and congruity on purchase intention: Evidence from the Chinese mainland's automobile market'. *Journal of Global Marketing*, 22 (3): 199–216.

2 The internationalization of sports teams as brands

André Richelieu

Introduction

In the context of today's globalization, very few countries or industries, if any, can exist in isolation from the rest. Described as the process of transformation of local phenomena into global ones, driven by economic, technological, sociocultural and political forces (Eitzen and Zinn, 2008), globalization has a major impact on the sports industry and its actors. As we shall see, globalization is a strong catalyst in the internationalization of sports actors, be they events (Formula 1 (F1) and Nascar races, Olympic Games, Football World Cup), leagues (English Premier League, NBA), teams (FC Barcelona, Manchester United, New York Yankees), players (David Beckham, Roger Federer) or equipment makers (Adidas, Nike, Puma, Reebok).

Begun in the late 19th century, the economic globalization accelerated in the 1990s with a series of events. The collapse of the former Soviet bloc, the emergence of newly industrialized countries and the birth of the World Trade Organization (WTO) opened doors to the integration of national economies into the international economy through an increase in trade, foreign direct investment (FDI), capital flow, migration and technological advances, thanks to a partial reduction or removal of trade barriers (Scholte, 2005).

Often compared to a 'tornado' (Valaskakis, 1990), globalization is a major phenomenon that brings both opportunities and threats. The purpose of this chapter is to analyse the internationalization of sports brands, especially sports teams' brands, in the context of globalization. Hence, we shall look at the following topics in their respective sections: 1) the globalization of sports, 2) the process of internationalization of sports teams' brands, 3) the relevant strategies for the internationalization of sports teams' brands, 4) the importance of the context and some determinants of success, and 5) a conclusion with the key knowledge we can extract from our reflection, from both a theoretical and managerial perspective.

The globalization of sports

In order to discuss the globalization of sports, we shall answer the following questions: Why? What? Who? How? and Where?

Why (the globalization of sports)?

Mainly for three reasons:

- An economic necessity. Sports teams and sporting events battle with a wide selection of other entertainment options for the disposable income of consumers. This competition is, first, local through cultural activities that abound in any decent size city. But it is also international, with satellite TV and the Internet, not to mention sophisticated home entertainment systems that are available to a growing number of households as technology drives prices down. Furthermore, we should not overlook the inflation in spending, as players' salaries increase, even, in the best of cases, with a salary cap, as is the case in the NBA, the NFL and the NHL.

   For instance, the average salary in Major League Baseball (MBL), in 1966, was US$17,000; in 1976, US$51,501; in 1980, US$143,756; in 1995, US$1.1 million; in 2008, it was over US$3 million (Bloom, 2009). MLB does not have and does not plan to have a salary cap in place even though disparities are alarming: prior to the 2010 season, the New York Yankees payroll was US$206 million, compared with US$35 for the Pittsburgh Pirates (see www.cbssports.com/mlb/salaries/teams).

   In the NHL, which installed a salary cap before the 2005–2006 season, the average salary was US$271,000 in 1990–1991, US$572,000 in 1994–1995, US$1.17 million in 1997–1998, US$1.83 million in 2003–2004, US$1.46 million in 2005–2006 and US$1.9 million in 2007–2008. Prior to the lock-out in 2004, 76 per cent of the League's revenues went to players' salaries (Bloom, 2009). With the new Collective Bargaining Agreement, players and teams share the revenues and the salary cap is correlated with the League's revenues. Prior to the 2009–2010 season, the salary cap was around US$55 million per team.
- New business opportunities. The sport industry is valued at over US$100 billion a year worldwide and growing, and it is expected to reach US$126 billion a year by 2011 (PriceWaterhouseCoopers, 2007). New streams of revenues appear, such as merchandising, exceeding US$19 billion a year in North America for all teams and all sports combined, as of 2008; this amount was estimated at US$7 billion for Europe, in 2008 (PriceWaterhouseCoopers, 2004). Capitalizing on a strong sports team brand can be extremely profitable for an organization, including, as we shall see, for some teams evolving in regional sports (baseball, rugby, etc.).
- The transformation of sports. Sporting events move from being solely a local activity to becoming a global one. Sports are moving away from what used to be comparable to a village circus, up to the 1980s, to become an activity similar in size and in its marketing machine to Walt Disney or Cirque du Soleil. In fact, sports seem to be merging more and more with the entertainment and communication industries to become recognized as 'sportainment' (Desbordes and Richelieu, 2011; Mullin *et al.*, 2007).

What (is globalization in sports)?

In line with what we have previously mentioned about globalization, there is an integration of sporting activities (events), leagues, teams, players and equipment makers at a global level. This happened thanks to the reduction and removal of barriers, be they legal, logistical or technological. Obviously, not every actor of the sports industry is moving at the same pace, but there is undoubtedly a movement in that direction, which we shall underline in the next section ('Who?').

What is interesting, when we refer to equipment makers, is that the old paradigm of the country of origin, the famous 'Made in ...', seems to be replaced by the concept of the country of association (Yasin *et al.*, 2007). Nike sneakers are made in Asia, but what matters most is the association with attributes such as lifestyle, coolness, endorsers of the brand (actors, singers, sportspeople, etc.) and the American image or way of life. At least brands seem to believe so when they ask their customers to pay a premium for their products: Nike sneakers, made in Vietnam, and sold at US$250 a pair, Levis' jeans, made in Bangladesh, and sold at US$125 each, Adidas soccer jerseys, produced in Thailand, and sold at US$100 a piece, etc. This is, in part, because customers build a relationship with brands, not necessarily with products, and also because symbolic dimensions, which we underlined in the previous chapter, resonate strongly in the heart of consumers (Kapferer, 2007; Lewi, 2005).

Furthermore, sports teams position themselves now as both a sports brand and a lifestyle brand. Consequently, they have the ability to transcend sports and the potential to become a global brand with mass appeal, such as Coca-Cola, Gucci, Louis Vuitton, etc. Just think about the New York Yankees or the New Zealand All Blacks: both compete in sports that have a limited regional appeal, at best, and nonetheless have managed to connect emotionally with fans around the world who proudly display their cap or their jersey. What's more, their strong brand has become the ambassador of the city (New York) or the country (New Zealand) they represent. This generates a natural co-branding spin-off, which strengthens the brand image of New York and New Zealand; in a way, it is as if New York and New Zealand had become 'cool' thanks to the Yankees' and the All Blacks' brands being showcased worldwide.

We should mention that sports apparel is increasingly becoming everyday wear. Thus, sports teams now have the possibility to capitalize on this social trend worldwide, with baseball caps, game jerseys, etc.

Who (is affected and potentially a winner of globalization)?

Essentially, five key categories of actors are concerned:

- Events (i.e. Formula 1 and Nascar races, Olympic Games, Football World Cup, etc.).
- Leagues (English Premier League, NBA, Spanish Liga, etc.).
- Teams (New York Yankees, Liverpool Football Club, Real Madrid, etc.).

- Players (David Beckham, Sidney Crosby, Roger Federer, Messi, Rafael Nadal, Cristiano Ronaldo, etc.).
- Equipment makers (i.e. Adidas, Nike, Puma, Reebok, etc.).

Obviously, neither the categories nor the actors display the same potential and challenge the same opportunities. For instance, equipment makers have been delocalizing their production since the second half of the 20th century. However, it is only recently that sports teams have started capitalizing on markets outside their immediate reach. Part of this is due to the nature of professional sports, which, for a long period of time, represented a local affair, limited, at best, to a national or continental event. However, owing to the progress of technology and the increasing exchange across countries and cultures, professional sports have taken a global dimension. All the more so, since some teams (FC Barcelona, Dallas Cowboys, Juventus Turin, etc.) and players (David Beckham, Roger Federer and Tiger Woods not so long ago) have achieved the status of international or even global brands, and are managed as such. Speaking of players, as they achieve the status of global icons, their global awareness, appeal and reach is now an integral part of their identity, no matter the sport in which they perform: David Beckham, Roger Federer, Lewis Hamilton and Cristiano Ronaldo sit side by side with Hollywood stars as 'sportainment' representatives.

How (do they go global)?

By making use of two sets of means: physical and virtual.

Physical

- Tours and exhibition games abroad, like some major European football teams do every year in Asia or America (Manchester United, FC Barcelona), but even less established ones (Newcastle United in Bangkok and Hong Kong) that believe it will generate additional brand exposure and fan support, which could then translate into additional TV viewership, team membership cards and merchandising sales.
- Increased association of athletes and coaches with foreign national teams in addition to local sports clubs. At the 2009 ice hockey world championship in Switzerland, Austria, Belarus, Denmark, France, Hungary and Switzerland were coached by foreign individuals. In the last decade, the English national football team, the country that gave birth to the beautiful game, has been managed by a Swede (Eriksson), then an Italian (Capello). In 1995, the European Court of Justice prohibited European football leagues from imposing quotas on 'foreign' European players. This explains why the top European teams often play with very few nationals, if at all. For instance, since 2005, it is not rare to see an Arsenal squad that does not include a single English football player, even though the team is based in London. However, it would be difficult to imagine Real Madrid without a single Spanish player on the field!

- In drastic contrast, some teams do their very best to include as many local players as possible. As a case in point, Atlétic Bilbao has only Basque players on its squad and Chivas Guadalajara's policy is to hire only Mexican players; the NHL Calgary Flames strongly favour Canadian players, which is a way to emphasize their Canadian identity in a League that counts only 7 teams from Canada out of 30.
- Stores in different countries, such as the Manchester United Megastore launched in Macao (China) in 2008 or through the equipment maker store that displays teams brands worldwide: Chelsea, Liverpool, Marseille, Milan AC, Real Madrid in Adidas stores in Paris, London or Montreal; Arsenal, FC Barcelona, Juventus Turin, Manchester United, Valencia in Nike stores in Berlin, New York or Toronto.
- Affiliated teams in promising markets, like the China Sharks, the Chinese affiliate of the NHL San Jose Sharks of the NHL (until 2009), the Ajax Cape Town (South Africa) affiliated to Ajax Amsterdam, the Urawa Red Diamonds (Japan) affiliated to Bayern Munich, etc. This gives a gateway to established teams in penetrating foreign markets and additional resources for local teams to develop.
- Relocation, which is a common practice with closed leagues in North America, contrary to European leagues that have a promotion and relegation system. Consequently, in the case where a franchise is not profitable enough anymore, teams are relocated in North America, which is the best way to tear apart the sense of belonging of fans. Hence, the Quebec Nordiques (NHL), the Winnipeg Jets (NHL) and the Vancouver Grizzlies (NBA) became respectively the Colorado Avalanche, the Phoenix Coyotes and the Memphis Grizzlies.
- Australia also follows this relocation model: in 2006, the Hunter Pirates of the Australian Basketball League became the Singapore Slingers, as League executives hoped to develop the Asian market.
- Endorsement of the brand by celebrities (actors, singers, etc.) giving sports teams the advantage of brand associations, image transfer and allegiance (Thomson, 2006) in order to reach consumers that do not necessarily feel attracted to sports in the first place. This relates to the market segment of the 'fashion fans' (Manivet and Richelieu, 2008; Richelieu and Pons, 2006), which we introduced in the first chapter.
- Product placement in movies, which has contributed in developing the awareness of some sports teams' brands. Examples are the Anaheim Mighty Ducks, Boston Red Sox and Miami Dolphins, which travelled beyond borders thanks to popular movies and initiated a group of followers worldwide; these fans could then crystallize their allegiance through games broadcast on TV or over the Internet, online fan communities, licensed products, etc.

Virtual

- Through the official team website, but also through online brand communities that are mostly launched and managed by fans around the world, but also social networks (Facebook, Twitter, etc.). For instance, online brand communities are formed by what some authors have called 'satellite supporters' (Kerr, 2009). This is how, for instance, Manchester United is estimated to have over 75 million fans worldwide (Hollenson, 2010). This is a phenomenon that is expected to grow for the most powerful sports teams' brands that can crystallize these emotions through several tangible points of contact, such as tours and exhibition games, but also through the introduction of a selection of merchandising products fans can proudly display in different aspects of their everyday life (at the stadium, in the office, at home, etc.).

Where (do they globalize)?

This globalization of sports is spreading all over the world. This being said, emerging markets are gaining a growing share at the expense of developed countries. With, on the one hand, industrialized but indebted and ageing countries (Canada, France, Germany, Great Britain, Italy, Portugal, Spain, the United States, etc.) and, on the other hand, emerging countries with growing middle and upper classes (Brazil, China, India, Malaysia, Russia, United Arab Emirates), teams and major events (Formula 1 races, Olympic Games, Football World Cup, etc.) are moving towards these emerging markets in order to finance their growth and perpetuate their respective brand. Thus, it is not by accident that we see a delocalization of Formula 1 races to Abu Dhabi, Kuala Lumpur, Shanghai and Singapore, and the organization of the Olympic Games and Football World Cup in Brazil, Qatar and Russia.

In the coming years, for economic, demographic and legislative reasons (i.e. less restrictive policy on tobacco and alcohol advertising, which are conducive to attracting major sports events in developing countries), the continuous growth of events, leagues and teams will be intertwined with emerging markets. In fact, these are already involved financially, directly or indirectly, with some European football teams (Arsenal, Hamburger SV, Manchester City, Paris Saint-Germain; Newcastle United might follow soon and FC Barcelona is doing so in the 2011–2012 season) being sponsored by the Qatar Foundation.

Now, within this new reality of globalization, how do/can sports teams' brands internationalize? Because in today's world, sports organizations need to develop and nurture their brand internationally, as the battle for fans' allegiance and disposable income is increasing. In this regard, we shall first introduce the concept of internationalization.

Internationalization as a process of brands and sports teams

The internationalization process of the firm

Internationalization is a process through which an organization or company increases its involvement abroad (Cateora and Graham, 2006). In order to do so, it can choose from four entry modes, namely exporting, licensing, joint venture (JV) and FDI. The internationalization requires a willingness from managers to go abroad; it is both a strategic mindset and a set of actions (Hollenson, 2010).

The literature on the internationalization process is very rich in international business. Some authors, affiliated with the Uppsala school in Sweden (Johanson and Wiedersheim-Paul, 1975; Johanson and Vahlne, 1977, 1990), have looked at the process as a sequential and linear one. As the company internalizes the learning of its internationalization, it gradually increases its involvement abroad by borrowing entry modes with a higher risk (from exporting to FDI) and by entering countries with which the cultural distance is more and more pronounced.

Other authors have identified ways to speed up the process, using the 'leapfrog model', for instance, where firms generally bypass exporting and enter culturally distant markets very quickly; this also relates to 'born global' firms that jump into foreign markets within the first two years of their inception in order to capitalize on opportunities in various countries (Luostarinen and Gabrielsson, 2006).

A firm could also internationalize through institutional levers, which is associated with an institutional approach (Miller and Lessard, 2000). In this case, companies, especially for larger projects or projects that take place in hostile environments, will combine their efforts with the support of international agencies (United Nations Development Programme (UNDP), World Bank), national export agencies (Export Development Canada, United States Agency for International Development (USAID) USA, Coface France) and private partners who possess a good knowledge of the local environment.

The contribution of the literature on the internationalization process of the firm lies in 1) determining how a company can increase its involvement abroad, 2) identifying the determinants of success in going international, and 3) assessing the impact of cultural distance on the internationalization of the firm.

The internationalization of brands

Inspired by the literature on the internationalization of the firm, some authors have reflected on the internationalization of brands, both as a process (Anderson *et al.*, 1998; Cheng *et al.*, 2005) and as a set of strategies (Kapferer, 1998; Van Gelder, 2002). Their contribution helps us to better understand how a brand can move along the 'brand equity pipeline' and identify the catalyst factors in the internationalization process of a brand (Richelieu *et al.*, 2008).

From a process perspective, Anderson *et al.* (1998) have identified five stages of internationalization for a brand:

1 Aspirational: the desire to internationalize the brand is born and communicated within the organization.
2 Procedural: the decision to internationalize the brand is implemented.
3 Behavioural: the company adjusts its brand according to cross-cultural requirements.
4 Interactional: the company creates, builds and maintains effective and meaningful relationships with new and existing stakeholders.
5 Conceptual: the company constantly re-evaluates its way of thinking and operating with its brand in foreign markets.

Cheng *et al.* (2005) have also contributed to the reflection on the internationalization process of a brand. According to them, companies can follow four progressive stages in order to build an international brand:

1   Pre-international: the company focuses on ensuring its survival, before building itself as a top tier brand in its home country.
2   Global lead market carrying capacity: the company develops a presence and a brand awareness in foreign markets, especially in lead markets (North America, Western Europe and Japan), mainly as a supplier to major brands.
3   International branding and market succession: the company works on developing an international brand of its own in lead countries.
4   Local climax: the company focuses on developing its brand in other markets, for example lead emerging markets (Brazil, China, India, Russia, etc.).

In terms of the strategies that a brand could follow when going international, Kapferer (1998) underlined three main avenues:

1   Think local, act global. This strategy is especially well suited for standardized products and consists of a gradual implementation abroad based on the success in the local market. This enables the brand to increase its chances of acceptance abroad and to reduce the financial risk. This is the case of Campbell's tomato soups, which are sold with a different taste and under a different brand name in Europe (Liebig in France, Délisoup in Belgium, Bla Band in Sweden) in order to take into account local preferences.
2   Think global, act global as much as possible. This provides the brand with better chances of acceptance abroad and a lower financial risk. Firms that follow this option generally have a global mindset. This strategy is well suited for brands that can capitalize on a strong positive predisposition from consumers because of the myth associated with their respective brand: watches, perfumes and other luxury goods (think Hermès, Gucci, Louis Vuitton, for instance).
3   Unifying local brands. This occurs when a firm buys another one and two different organizational and country cultures need to be integrated (Schuiling and Lambin, 2003). An example is the acquisition, by the Brazilian mining company, Rio Tinto, of the Canadian aluminum company, Alcan, which gave birth to Rio Tinto Alcan in 2007.

Moreover, Van Gelder (2004) elaborated four strategies:

1   The brand domain specialist. This strategy enables the brand to influence the development in a specific domain, such as in technology, and consumers' preferences (Apple's iPhone).
2   The brand reputation specialist. This strategy emphasizes authenticity, credibility and reliability (Volvo with safety).

3   The brand affinity specialist. This strategy aims to outperform the competition by building relationships with consumers and by offering a memorable experience (Walt Disney).
4   The brand recognition specialist. This strategy increases the brand's spontaneous notoriety, which can make it top-of-mind (Nestlé's Nescafé).

The internationalization of sports teams' brands

As in many industries today, the brand represents the most important asset of a sports club (Bauer *et al.*, 2005). This brand is composed of 1) intangible benefits, such as the emotions fans experience at the stadium and the sense of belonging to the team, as well as 2) tangible benefits, such as the result of the game and team's merchandise (Boatwright *et al.*, 2009; Holt, 1995). Accordingly, in professional sports, along with entertainment, religion and politics, the emotional response from fans is stronger than in any other industry (Couvelaere and Richelieu, 2005; Desbordes and Richelieu, 2011).

A professional sports team has the potential to build its brand equity by capitalizing on the emotional relationship it shares with its fans. This is all the more important considering that customer loyalty and long-term association are often sacrificed by teams for short-term revenue growth (McGraw, 1998). A global brand needs to find a way to provide relevant meaning and experience to people in various markets (Van Gelder, 2002). A global brand creates perceptions of brand superiority, quality and preference among consumers (Steenkamp *et al.*, 2003), but also expectations towards the promise it communicates. As symbols of cultural ideals and ways of life, global brands are generally sought after by consumers (Holt *et al.*, 2004).

In this regard, and by referring to the existing literature, we are able to introduce Figure 2.1, which is a synthesis of our work on the process of internationalization of sports teams and their brands. This figure is of sequential inspiration (Cheng *et al.*, 2005; Johanson and Wiedersheim-Paul, 1975; Johanson and Vahlne, 1977, 1990), without being deterministic. A sports team brand generally goes through a sequential approach. But it can also borrow a leapfrog or an institutional approach through tours abroad and co-branding, for instance. The nature of the international opportunity, the financial means of the sports team and the cultural distance it faces are among the factors that influence the choice of the strategic expansion the team might undertake. Furthermore, strong foundations are needed before a sports team can expect some international success: indeed, time is necessary to build a record, one's history, one's own brand. North American observers will probably recall the strong ascension and spectacular decline of the New York Cosmos and Montreal Manic of the defunct North American Soccer League (NASL).

In order to move along the 'brand equity pipeline', a sports team could choose from four strategies, which appear to be the most relevant in the sports arena. The reader should note that these strategies are not mutually exclusive and as such, teams are able to combine them (Table 2.1; Richelieu *et al.*, 2008).

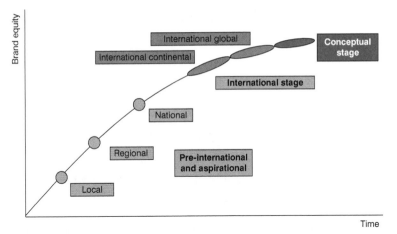

Figure 2.1 The internationalization process of a sports team brand

Sources: Couvelaere and Richelieu, 2005; Richelieu, 2008; Richelieu *et al.*, 2008.

Table 2.1 The four main (relevant) strategies in order to establish a sports team as a global brand.

Strategy	Description
Brand reputation (think local, act global/the brand reputation specialist)	The team capitalizes on its reputation to go abroad. It gradually enters foreign countries thanks to the results and the history of the team (Chicago Bulls, New Zealand All Blacks, New York Yankees, Real Madrid).
Brand affinity (think local, act global/the brand affinity specialist)	The team builds a strong fan base through the unique emotional experience it offers to its fans, at both the local and international level. Fans identify strongly with the team, the players, and often unite within brand communities (Liverpool Football Club, Manchester United).
Brand challenger (think local, act global/the brand recognition specialist)	The team favours promotion and high investments in players as the first step toward (re-)establishing the sport team brand. But results, history and fans are needed: the team may realize, sooner or later, that there is no shortcut in establishing a strong international sports team brand (Chelsea, Manchester City).
Brand conquistador (unifying local brands/the brand recognition specialist)	The team pairs with another team across continents. The local team benefits from an image transfer and brand associations; the foreign team borrows a springboard to enter one or many promising markets (Ajax Amsterdam/Ajax Cape Town, Bayern Munich/Urawa Reds, Real Madrid/Beijing Guoang). This strategy can also take the form of co-branding between the sports team and its official equipment maker, especially through stores around the world (i.e. Adidas and Nike megastores).

Source: Inspired by Richelieu *et al.*, 2008.

Let's now have a look at the importance of context and some success factors when a sports team wants to make its brand international or global.

The importance of the context and some determinants of success

As stated before in the literature on the internationalization of the firm (specifically Johanson and Vahlne, 1990), and in international marketing in general (Cateora and Graham, 2006), the context can have a decisive impact on the success of the firm's endeavours in foreign markets.

When we look at sports, three elements, namely 1) the nature or type of sport, 2) the management system of the league and 3) the concept of experience at the game, can influence the potential for and the success of a sports team brand's internationalization:

- The nature of the sport involved. Not all sports are born equal and, thus, do not share the same global appeal and media coverage (football, F1, basketball versus ice hockey, baseball, curling, for instance). Unless team managers are able to position the brand as both a sport and lifestyle brand (see Chapter 1), a club evolving in a regional sport could well be limited to a regional/niche expansion abroad.
- The management of the league. Most if not all North American leagues are highly centralized, which limits their autonomy to initiate marketing actions of their own and slows down their internationalization. In comparison, European leagues are generally highly decentralized and allow dynamic teams to introduce aggressive marketing actions, nationally and internationally, with huge discrepancies between the top teams and the rest of the pack, though.

  Indeed, it is the league that goes international in North America, not really the clubs. Teams often end up playing a support role for the internationalization of the league, for example NBA exhibition games in France, the opening of the NHL season in Sweden, Finland or Czech Republic, etc. Teams for such international promotional activities are chosen by the respective league. Same for licensed products: in the NHL, teams can initiate marketing actions within a 150 km radius of their local market; beyond that, the NHL decides what is being sold and where, according to its priorities.

  In the European system, the strongest team brands evolve in a non-regulated universe and can reach a very high level of brand equity, such as Real Madrid and Manchester United. In contrast, team brands that are not as well equipped or that are more fragile cannot thrive in such a free market environment.

  Consequently, in North America, team brands are levelled at the bottom in order to feed the League brand, which operates a very tightly regulated and controlled system; in Europe, the most resourceful and creative teams can leverage their brands, while the others are left out, trying to survive, in a non-regulated, extremely competitive market. Some observers would say that this is an irony, as the North American system appears to be more 'socialist' than the European one!

- The experience of the game. Whereas the beauty of the game still seems to prevail in Europe, the entertainment experience is a key selling point in North America. With a few exceptions, such as the Stade Français rugby team shows at the Stade de France, Europe focuses on the game. However, in North America, entertainment prepares the game, feeds it and even replaces it in the event the product on the field is not good enough, because managers still need to sell tickets to fill in their stadium. A major difference exists between Europe and North America, which is culturally driven.

The North American marketing manager must constantly try to renew the experience fans will enjoy in order to make it appear unique, especially for season ticket holders. Hence, in 2002, the minor league hockey team Indianapolis Ice hired a former Sudanese basketball player, Manute Bol (at 2.30m in height), who did not know how to skate. Needless to say, the buzz created by this event attracted a huge crowd to the arena!

But these differences also relate to the promotion and relegation system in European championships, as there is something at stake until the end of the season. Whereas the play-offs system in North America, which limits the number of teams that take part in the second season, sometimes drastically as in MLB, forces managers to reposition their offering into a family-friendly and/or an entertainment activity during the season. In terms of internationalization, this entertainment approach can make a regional product more attractive to foreign audiences, at least when it comes to capturing occasional fans (Kerr, 2009).

Moreover, we should mention that our research on the topic (Richelieu and Pons, 2006; Richelieu *et al.*, 2008) enabled us to highlight a set of 'winning conditions', both internally and externally, that could also serve as a guideline for other sports team brands (Table 2.2).

In order to state our case from Table 2.2, let's look at FC Barcelona. Internally, we could mention:

- An impressive record on the field. Twenty-one Spanish Leagues, 25 Spanish Cups, 10 Spanish Super Cups, 4 European Champions Cups, 4 European Super Cups and 4 European Cup Winners' Cups (as of February 2012).
- A well-developed system of communications. A website in various languages (English, Chinese and Japanese), a team magazine (launch of the FC Barcelona magazine for the Chinese, Japanese and Singaporean markets), a TV channel (broadcasting FC Barcelona games in China), but also online communities launched and managed by fans themselves, which help nurture the passion of fans and build the team's brand. Barcelona can also count on *socios* clubs around the world, called *penyes* (over 1300), which act as ambassadors of FC Barcelona worldwide and contribute in expanding and

Table 2.2 The key determinants in successfully internationalizing a sports team brand

Internal determinants
An impressive record on the field.
A well-developed system of communications (team website, team TV, team publications, presence on social networks, etc.).
A strong community involvement.
A series of tours in promising markets (i.e. Asia and North America for football).
A good range of team merchandise.
The hiring of some star players and/or local players.
External determinants
Fans taking possession of the team and its brand through supporters' websites and social networks.
The support of a major equipment maker (i.e. Adidas, Nike, Reebok).
A strong rivalry between teams (i.e. Real Madrid versus FC Barcelona).
The association with a renowned country in the sport the team represents (i.e. Brazil or Spain for football; Canada or Russia for hockey; Japan or USA for baseball; Australia or New Zealand for rugby).

Sources: Inspired by Richelieu and Pons, 2006; Richelieu *et al.*, 2008.

crystallizing the brand in foreign markets. FC Barcelona is also present on Facebook, Twitter and YouTube.

- A strong community involvement. In 2006, the club decided to give up a lucrative sponsorship shirt deal, worth an estimated 15 million euros a year, and chose to pay 1.5 million euros a year to support UNICEF; a way to reinforce the image of the club as generous, socially responsible, close to its fans and making it truly 'més que un club' (more than a club) in the eyes of public opinion worldwide. It would be interesting to see what happens now that the club has signed a sponsorship deal, worth 33 million euros a year, with the Qatar Foundation, starting with the 2011–2012 season, until 2016.
- A series of tours in promising markets. This is especially true for FC Barcelona, which visits markets where the club wants to showcase and expand its brand (China, USA), and thus increase its global reach.
- A good range of team merchandise. From traditional team kits to baby products to merchandise for women, which are gaining in popularity in all sports and leagues (European football, but also in the NHL, for example). In the case of FC Barcelona, having UNICEF as its main sponsor, at least until the end of the 2010–2011 season, provided a competitive selling advantage that made its jersey even more attractive to mums who would be tempted to offer a soccer jersey to their son, in comparison with teams that promote a beer or a betting company, for example.
- The hiring of foreign and local star players. These players act as emotional anchors for teams that can then strengthen fans' allegiance to the club through

these players. This is definitely an advantage for FC Barcelona, which, throughout its rich history, has seen some of the greatest players wear the *blaugrana* jersey (foreign: from Cruyff, Deco, Kocsis, Koeman, Krankl, Kubala, Laudrup, Macedo, Maradona, Neeskens, Ronaldinho, Ronaldo, Rivaldo, Schuster, Stoichkov to Eto'o, Henry, Keita, Messi; local: from Amor, Asensi, Begiristain, Guardiola, Migueli, Quini, Suarez, Torralba, Zubizarreta to Bernabeu, Puyol).

As for the external determinants of success, we could underline:

- An appropriation by fans who have taken possession of the team even more. There is a plethora of online fan communities, launched and managed by FC Barcelona fans worldwide, such as: www.fanclubbarcelona.nl, www. fcbarcelona.ch, www.fcbarcelonaclan.com, www.fcbarcelonaweb.co.uk, www.fc-barcelone.com, etc. These communities have their own code of conduct and reward system for the most committed fans. This is an opportunity for fans to get involved in the life of the club, to be able to speak up and participate in the co-creation of FC Barcelona life as 'consumactors'. This can only reinforce the sense of belonging of these very committed fans towards FC Barcelona outside the stadium.
- The support of a major equipment maker. FC Barcelona can count on Nike. Thus FC Barcelona can capitalize on the distribution channel of its equipment maker to grow its brand internationally. Nike stores worldwide showcase the FC Barcelona brand, in addition to the team stores, when those exist abroad, such as the one opened in 2007 in China.
- A strong rivalry between teams. What are referred to as *classicos*, the games between local rivals, FC Barcelona and Real Madrid, generate increased media coverage when compared to a regular league game. They also contribute in the construction of iconic brands, in the home country but also in foreign markets, because these rivalries crystallize team allegiance via the 'us against them' confrontations.
- The association with a renowned country in the sport the team represents: FC Barcelona can benefit from the fact that Spain is known as a 'football country', even though Catalan nationalists might not like this brand association! Furthermore, like many other sports teams, the denomination of the team includes the name of the city: according to Kapferer (1998), this reminder is a way to reinforce the identity of the club throughout the world and make the internationalization of the brand easier.

This being said, not every team has the potential of a Real Madrid or New York Yankees, for instance. In fact, we could add that even lower division sports teams do not share the same potential among them. This is why, Richelieu *et al.* (2011) conducted a study in order to understand and explain how managers can build a football team brand at different levels of competition, at the minor league as well as at the champions league level.

What comes out of both Richelieu *et al.* (2011) and Couvelaere and Richelieu (2005) is that a minimum of sporting success is required, as well as some resources, in order to climb up the ladder of international expansion (Table 2.3). In fact, the idea behind Figure 1.1, as well as Tables 2.1, 2.2 and 2.3, is to underline how a sports team can achieve its full potential as a sports brand, be it at a local, regional, national or international/global level.

Table 2.3 Objectives and means sports teams could use in order to go through the different stages of internationalization

Stage of internationalization	Objectives	Means	Examples
From a local to a regional brand	Build and perpetuate the brand. Work on the brand image, build fan loyalty and increase regional presence.	Strategic construction of the brand, CRM system, advertising campaigns, distribution partnerships in order to increase the regional presence, leverage the social identity of the brand.	Hoffenheim (football), Nashville Predators (NHL), Oklahoma City Thunder (NBA), Memphis Grizzlies (NBA), Jacksonville Jaguars (NFL).
From a regional to a national brand	Reinforce the national positioning. Increase brand recognition and presence.	National strategic partnerships (equipment makers, distributors, media, foreign clubs), new design for team jersey or launching of a vintage collection, website, hiring of star players.	Anderlecht (football), Aston Villa (football), Calgary Flames (NHL), Ottawa Senators (NHL), Baltimore Ravens (NFL).
From a national to an international brand	Export and globalize the brand. Increase brand recognition and presence worldwide.	International strategic partnerships (equipment makers, distributors, media), tours or tournaments abroad, hiring of international stars, website tailored for different countries and languages, opening of stores abroad.	FC Barcelona (football), Juventus Turin (football), New York Yankees (MLB), Los Angeles Lakers (NBA), Toronto Maple Leafs (NHL).

Source: Inspired by Couvelaere and Richelieu, 2005.

Because of a lack of sporting record, limited resources, a constraining league system (very centralized in North America) or the nature of the sport in which the team evolves, managers might realize they have reached a plateau for their club's brand. When such a situation arises, what can managers do? Work in order to strengthen the brand and make it a reference in its category, be it local, regional or national. Otherwise, the brand can be diluted to abysmal level. Suffice to look at Nottingham Forest Football Club, two times European Champions (1979 and 1980) under the reign of Brian Clough, and now in the English second division ('Championship') after spending some time in third division (2005–2008). And what about the NHL Edmonton Oilers: winners of five Stanley Cup trophies between 1984 and 1990, they have been unable to reach the play-offs since the 2006 season.

It should be said that the ambition to make the sports brand grow is necessary in order to bring it to its full potential. But this is no smooth process and growing pains occur: just ask the German football club Hoffenheim. Gone from the amateur lower divisions to the top Bundesliga league in about ten years, Hoffenheim even challenged for the title in its first year in first division, in 2008–2009. This was before disappearing in the anonymity of the middle of the table since then.

Conclusion

The purpose of this chapter was to analyse the internationalization of sports brands, especially sports teams' brands, in the context of globalization. Thus we looked at the following topics: 1) the globalization of sports, 2) the process of internationalization of sports teams' brands, 3) the relevant strategies for the internationalization of sports teams' brands and 4) the importance of the context and some determinants of success.

We positioned our reflection in the context of the globalization phenomenon, which has a major impact on the sports industry and its actors. As we have seen, globalization is a strong catalyst in the internationalization of sports actors, be they events, leagues, teams, players or equipment makers. Starting with the view of well-known experts in international marketing and international business, we analysed the internationalization of sport through the lenses of established paradigms; these provided us with some guidelines in sports. This approach also enabled us to articulate four strategies, as a sports team tries to expand its brand across markets: brand reputation, brand affinity, brand challenger and brand conquistador.

In addition, Table 2.3 underlined some strategic leverage for sports teams that can accompany their chosen strategy. Gradually, a sports team can capitalize on its brand asset and reinforce the emotional connection it shares with its fans. Emotions are intangibles and very fragile; by enlarging its circle of influence, a sports team brand assumes new responsibilities, which forces its managers to deliver on the brand promise, across borders and cultures (see Table 2.4). If becoming an international or a global brand increases the revenue and value potential, it also requires special efforts to strengthen and perpetuate the brand. Indeed, who remembers Arthur Andersen, Compaq, Enron, Pan Am, Steinberg, Woolworth, etc.?

Table 2.4 A sample of sport brand value and revenues among the Top 50 Forbes ranking in 2010

Team	Value (billion US$)	Revenues (million US$)
1. Manchester United	1.83	459
2. Dallas Cowboys	1.65	280
3. New York Yankees	1.60	441
6. Real Madrid	1.32	563
8. Arsenal	1.18	369
16. Ferrari	1.05	308
25. FC Barcelona	1.00	513
35. Boston Red Sox	0.87	266
41. Liverpool FC	0.82	304
48. Chelsea	0.65	340

Source: *Forbes*, 2010.

In a period of great economical transformation, professional sports teams have realized the power that branding encapsulates in marketing their club beyond their local market, making brand the most important asset of a sports club (Bauer *et al.*, 2005). What we call globalization offers both opportunities and threats to sports teams. They can no longer hide behind what used to be a very local activity.

The third chapter will look at how sport sponsorship can contribute to the branding strategies of both large and small corporations. In this regard, we shall take the case of the SpVgg Vreden 1921 e.V., an amateur soccer club in the north-western part of Germany

References

Anderson, V., S. Graham and P. Lawrence (1998). 'Learning to internationalize'. *Journal of Management Development*, 17 (7): 492–502.

Bauer, H. H., N. E. Sauer and P. Schmitt (2005). 'Customer-based brand equity in the team sport industry'. *European Journal of Marketing*, 39 (5/6): 496–513.

Bloom, H. (2009). 'The good news a new MLB labor accord, the bad news a new MLB labor accord II'. http://sportsbiznews.blogspot.com/2006/10/good-news-new-mlb-labor-accord-bad_24.html (accessed April 2009).

Boatwright, P., J. Cagan, D. Kapur and A. Saltiel (2009). 'A step-by-step process to build valued brands'. *Journal of Product and Brand Management*, 18 (1): 38–49.

Cateora, P. R. and J. L. Graham (2006). *International Marketing*, Canadian edition, Homewood: Irwin.

Cheng, J. M.-S., C. Blankson, P. C. S. Wu and S. S. M. Chen (2005). 'A stage model of international brand development: The perspectives of manufacturers from two newly industrialized economies – South Korea and Taiwan'. *Industrial Marketing Management*, 34 (5): 504–514.

Couvelaere, V. and A. Richelieu (2005). 'Brand strategy in professional sports: The case of French soccer teams'. *European Sport Management Quarterly*, 5 (1): 23–46.

Desbordes, M. and A. Richelieu (2011). *Neo-Marketing du Sport. Regards Croisés entre Europe et Amérique du Nord*. Brussels: De Boeck Publishers.

Eitzen, D. S. and M. B. Zinn (2008). *Globalization: The transformation of social worlds*. Belmont, CA: The Wadsworth Sociology Reader Series.

Forbes (2010). 'The world's most valuable sports teams'. www.forbes.com/2010/07/20/most-valuable-athletes-and-teams-business-sports-sportsmoney-fifty-fifty-teams_slide_51.html (accessed February 2011).

Hollenson, S. (2010). *Global Marketing: A decision-oriented approach*, 5th edition, London: Prentice Hall.

Holt, D. B. (1995). 'How consumers consume: A typology of consumption practices'. *Journal of Consumer Research*, 22 (1): 1–16.

Holt, D. B., J. A. Quelch and E. L. Taylor (2004). 'How global brands compete'. *Harvard Business Review*, (September): 68–75.

Johanson, J. and F. Wiedersheim-Paul (1975). 'The internationalization of the firm – Four Swedish cases'. *Journal of Management Studies*, 12 (2): 305–322.

Johanson, J. and J.-E. Vahlne (1977). 'The internationalization process of the firm – A model of knowledge development and increasing foreign market commitments'. *Journal of International Business Studies*, 8 (1): 23–32.

Johanson, J. and J.-E. Vahlne (1990). 'The mechanism of internationalization'. *International Marketing Review*, 7 (4): 11–24.

Kapferer, J.-N. (1998). *Les marques, capital de l'entreprise: Créer et développer des marques fortes*, 3rd edition. Paris: Éditions d'Organisation.

Kapferer, J.-N. (2007). *The New Strategic Brand Management: Creating and sustaining brand equity long term*. London: Kogan Page.

Kerr, A. K. (2009). *You'll never walk alone. The use of brand equity frameworks to explore the team identification of the 'Satellite Supporter'*. PhD thesis. School of Leisure, Sport and Tourism, Faculty of Business, University of Technology, Sydney Australia.

Lewi, G., (2005). *Branding management. La marque de l'idée à l'action*. Paris: Pearson Education France.

Luostarinen, R. and M. Gabrielsson (2006). 'Globalization and marketing strategies of born globals in SMOPECs'. *Thunderbird International Business Review*, 48 (6): 773–801.

Manivet, B. and A. Richelieu (2008). 'Dangerous liaisons: How can sports brands capitalize on the hip hop movement?' *International Journal of Sport Management and Marketing*, 3 (1/2): 140–161.

McGraw, D. (1998). 'Big league troubles'. *US News and World Report*, 125 (2): 40–46.

Miller, R. and D. Lessard (2000). *The strategic Management of Large Engineering Projects: Shaping institutions, risks and governance*. Cambridge, MA: MIT Press.

Mullin, B. J., S. Hardy and W. A. Sutton (2007). *Sport Marketing*, 3rd edition, Champaign, IL: Human Kinetics.

PriceWaterhouseCoopers (2004). 'Global outlook for the sports market'. *Global Entertainment and Media Outlook Report: 2004–2008*. New York.

PriceWaterhouseCoopers (2007). 'Global outlook for the sports market'. *Global Entertainment and Media Outlook: 2007–2011*. New York.

Richelieu, A. (2008). 'Creating and branding sport products'. Chapter 3 in S. Chadwick (ed) *Sport Marketing*. London: Henry Stewart Talks. Spring 2008. www.hstalks.com/sport/index.htm

Richelieu, A. and F. Pons (2006). 'Toronto Maple Leafs vs. F.C. Barcelona: How two legendary sports teams built their brand equity'. *International Journal of Sports Marketing and Sponsorship*, 7 (3): 231–250.

Richelieu, A., S. Lopez and M. Desbordes (2008). 'The internationalization of a sports team brand: The case of European soccer teams'. *International Journal of Sports Marketing and Sponsorship*, 9 (4): 29–44.

Richelieu, A., T. Pawlowski and C. Breuer (2011). 'Football brand management: Minor League vs. Champions League'. *Journal of Sponsorship*, 4 (3). In press.

Scholte, J. A. (2005). *Globalization: A critical introduction*. 2nd edition. New York: Palgrave Macmillan.

Schuiling, I. and J. J. Lambin (2003). 'Do global brands benefit from a worldwide unique image?' Reprinted with permission from Global Markets and Marketing Research, Symphonya: *Emerging Issues in Management*, www.unimib.it/Symphonya-Emerging-Issues-in-Management (accessed September 2006).

Steenkamp, J. B. E. M., R. Batra and D. L. Alden (2003). 'How perceived brand globalness creates brand value'. *Journal of International Business Studies*, 34 (1): 53–65.

Thomson, M. (2006). 'Human brands: Investigating antecedents to consumers' strong attachments to celebrities'. *Journal of Marketing*, 70 (3): 104–119.

Valaskakis, K. (1990). *Canada in the Nineties: Meltdown or renaissance*. Ottawa, Canada: World Media.

Van Gelder, S. (2002). 'General strategies for global brands'. *Global Brand Strategy, Brand Meta*, www.brand-meta.com (accessed September 2006).

Van Gelder, S. (2004). 'Global brand strategy'. *Journal of Brand Management*, 12 (1): 39–48.

Yasin, N. M., M. N. Noor and O. Mohamad (2007). 'Does image of country-of-origin matter to brand equity?'. *Journal of Product and Brand Management*, 16 (1): 38–48.

3 Sponsorship and branding

*Christoph Breuer, Tim Pawlowski and
Christopher Rumpf*

Adapted by André Richelieu

Theoretical framework

Introduction

The importance of branding in the contemporary marketing environment is undisputed (Esch and Langner, 2001; Keller, 2003). Adamson (2006, p. 226) defines branding as 'the process of creating and managing the associations that generate images and feelings about the brand'. In order to link exchangeable products and services to distinctive brands, effective marketing activities need to be arranged. Whereas in the past marketing communication tools like advertising, sales promotion and public relations were mainly utilized to strengthen brand associations and brand meaning, the expenditure on sponsorship has increased by over 10 per cent annually during the last two decades (Pilot Group, 2008). Hereby, corporate sponsors create a link with an external issue, particularly sport, art or social activities, hoping to influence the consumers by this connection (Koo *et al.*, 2006). Today large corporations such as T-Mobile or BMW are allocating a formidable share of their annual marketing budgets to sponsorship. But also small businesses on a regional level are interested in the capabilities of sponsorship. In view of this, the goal of this chapter is to investigate how sport sponsorship can contribute to branding strategies of both large and small corporations.

Sport sponsorship

Over the last two decades, sponsorship has evolved from a small-scale activity to a major business sector (Cornwell, 2008; Walliser, 2003). Whereas in 1990 the financial volume of sponsorship in Germany accounted for only 750 million euros per year, it is estimated to increase up to 5.2 billion euros per year until 2010 (Pilot Group, 2008). The major part of sponsorship investment goes to sport entities like federations, clubs, events and athletes. From their perspective sponsorship means a fundamental source of income in order to assure competitiveness.

Since traditional communication vehicles such as advertising and promotion suffer from information overload in commercial environments (Bruhn, 2003), sponsorship is more than ever vital to achieve favourable publicity for a brand within a target group (Cliffe and Motion, 2005). Meenaghan (1983, p. 9) defines sponsorship as 'the provision of assistance either financial or in kind to an activity by a commercial organization for the purpose of achieving commercial objectives'. This definition points out clearly that modern sponsorship has moved from being a philanthropic approach to a marketing tool that focuses increasingly on its commercial potential and its contributions to corporate profits (Gwinner and Swanson, 2003). Using this indirect persuasion technique, corporate sponsors hope to increase brand awareness and to build strong brands by transferring the image of highly popular sport entities (Gwinner and Eaton, 1999; Quester and Farrelly, 1998).

At this point it must be mentioned that sponsorship works differently in relation to the consumer than do other forms of marketing communication, though advertising and sponsorship, for instance, partly share the same objectives. While advertising messages are communicated directly and explicitly, sponsorship works below the line and is therefore able to overcome certain communication barriers (Walliser, 2003). In contrast to advertising and promotion, sponsorship addresses the target group in a sport activity with which the consumer has an intense emotional relationship. Furthermore, the belief that the sport activity benefits from the sponsor's investment can create goodwill and positive attitudes towards the company and its brands (Meenaghan, 2001). Therefore sponsorship is highly accepted in society as it supports the financial foundations of very popular issues like sports. While classical advertising is often perceived as disturbing in the media environment, 74 per cent of the German public has a positive reception of sponsorship (Sportfive, 2003).

The emotional power of sports

The relevance of sport as a vehicle for implementing branding strategies has grown at an increasing rate. This is a consequence of the fact that sport represents significant human needs in modern societies like fun, pleasure, entertainment, excitement, wellness or even self-fulfillment (Hermanns and Marwitz, 2008). Thus, sports-related sponsorship provides the opportunity for companies to leverage brand experiences by presenting their logo in a sport context (Cliffe and Motion, 2005). Whereas in the past primarily sport outfitters used the platform of sport to give a more emotional touch to their brands, nowadays a large variety of non-sport brands try to associate themselves with sports.

In today's consumer markets most products and services are characterized by their replaceable functions. Hence, the competition between brands for the consumer's preference often lies in staging experiences. Sport works as a suitable scene to mediate these experiences. In almost no other sphere do victory and tragedy appear so close to each other, heroes can be born overnight and fascinating legends are written by just one brilliant play. The emotional power of sports can create an atmosphere of excitement that serves to create a world of emotions around the brand (Kiendl, 2007). Thus, added value can be put on the brand, which helps to differentiate it from competitors (Pine and Gilmore, 1998). Furthermore, brands have the chance to address consumers in their leisure time, when they might be spending time with friends or family. This favourable condition, either in a stadium or at home, leads consumers to be relaxed and receptive to brand messages (Nicholls *et al.*, 1999). Therefore more and more brands see the value of sponsorship activities as a means to connect with the audience in a more direct and empowering way. In this manner peerless touch points can be set up in order to build long-lasting brand equity (Jackson, 2009).

But this, of course, is only half the story. Some critics claim that the enthusiasm, excitement and enjoyment in a sports environment preoccupy the spectators. Thus they might fail to absorb the sponsor's message (Dolphin, 2003). Many sport fans that are highly involved with a sports team or athletes simply lack additional capacity to perceive marketing stimuli. Another critical aspect about the reception of sponsorship messages lies in the overstimulation of sponsors within many sport events. Hence, it seems questionable whether a recipient is able to absorb ten or even more different brands that are frequently exposed at the same time. These general threats lead to the need of a differentiated sponsorship strategy and a meaningful evaluation in order to gain the whole impact of sports facilities rather than going down in a jungle of billboards.

Sponsorship objectives

The first step to a sophisticated sponsorship strategy is about defining reviewable objectives. Sponsorship falls into the set of strategic marketing communication options that are compared with each other. A rational marketing executive will only then invest in a sponsorship programme if it achieves the overall objectives more efficiently than its alternatives. For meaningful consideration, a deeper insight into how sponsorship activities can benefit a brand is critical. Therefore this section will deal with the objectives and the way they can be achieved by the adoption of sponsorship. Research findings have suggested that most companies invest in sport activities with the following objectives:

- Raising brand awareness (e.g. Bennett, 1999; Hoek *et al.*, 1997; Nicholls *et al.*, 1999; Tripodi *et al.*, 2003).
- Enhancing brand image (e.g. Chien *et al.*, 2005; Gwinner and Eaton, 1999; Quester and Farrelly, 1998).
- Increasing sales and market share (e.g. Dean, 1999; Madrigal, 2001).
- Obtaining corporate hospitality opportunities (e.g. Collett, 2008).

Below, these objectives are briefly analysed as they are part of most corporate sponsorship strategies and were found to be generally noticed in sponsorship literature.

Raising brand awareness

In today's cluttered media markets, sport sponsorship provides the opportunity to increase and stabilize brand awareness (Hermanns and Marwitz, 2008; Nicholls *et al.*, 1999). Especially in very specific and hard to reach target groups, sponsorship is favoured compared to traditional advertising due to its integrated character. By the pure presence in proximity to popular figures like athletes, marketers pursue more attention for their brand, which might result in a first trial of the product. Once a trial has occurred, sponsorship can also work as reinforcement of this purchasing behaviour (Hoek *et al.*, 1997). Beyond, sponsorship serves the purpose of affecting traditional advertising campaigns as it can simply draw attention to a brand logo that might be then taken on by a TV spot. But how does this awareness shift actually occur in the consumer's mind? According to Kroeber-Riel and Weinberg (2003) and their model of effects, the following process can be used to explain awareness increase: due to situations with low attention towards the sponsor, sport viewers remember only short and simple information. Therefore, a high repetition of sponsorship stimuli is necessary in order to activate cognitive processes. If the exposure rate is on a sufficient level the company's name or a brand's logo is stored in the mind. This memorization can later be relevant for purchase behaviour if the consumer recognizes the sponsor's product in a buying situation and prefers it to competing offers (Hermanns and Marwitz, 2008).

However, the chance to raise brand awareness by means of sponsorship depends on several factors. Since there are plenty of different possibilities of placement in the venue or on the jersey, awareness is strongly influenced by the location of the signage (e.g. Miloch and Lambrecht, 2006). Not surprisingly, the average visibility of sponsors on a TV broadcast differs enormously depending on location. Johar and Pham (1999) found that brands that are perceived to be more prominent in the marketplace are more likely to be identified than brands that are less prominent. As further research indicates, consumers do not solely identify sponsors from their memorization but start contingent processes of source identification (Pham and Johar, 2001). This effect can be moderated by another critical aspect, called relatedness. Relatedness draws on the fit of the relationship between a brand and the event. Consequently, brands that are perceived as fitting to an event are identified more often as a sponsor than brands lacking this advantage (Johar and Pham, 1999).

Enhancing brand image

In order to differentiate products and services from the competitors, a well-elaborated brand identity is a critical factor of business success (Bruhn, 2003). Thus, brand identity should be the initial point for a sophisticated branding strategy. In this context sponsorship can contribute to the process of transferring this brand identity to the consumer's mind (Keller, 1993). While brand identity reflects the self-perception of the brand within the company, the external perception by the target group is termed brand image (Kiendl, 2007). Brand image is a multidimensional construct that is 'reflected by the brand associations held in consumer memory' (Keller, 1993, p. 3). In order to enable consumers to link specific associations with a brand, awareness is, initially, a necessary constraint. Hence, brand awareness can be seen as the anchor for the fastening of brand associations (Keller, 1993).

In order to investigate image effects scholars use various theories drawing on consumer behaviour research. At this point, only two theoretical concepts are briefly introduced: balance theory and meaning transfer. Heider's (1958) balance theory argues that individuals seek consistency and avoid unbalanced situations. If there is no balance in a certain situation, psychological tension arises. Therefore, in a sponsorship context, the individual will strive for a balanced relationship in the perception of the event and the sponsor. To give an example, an imbalance occurs if a positive attitude towards a soccer club and a neutral or even negative attitude towards a brand are combined in a sponsorship. In order to find harmony, the recipient will reconsider his attitude towards the brand and adjust it in a positive direction. Another approach attempting to explain image shifts of sponsors considers meaning transfer. In brief, this theory implies that 'meaning' moves from the sport event to the sponsor, when their brands are exposed simultaneously (Cornwell *et al.*, 2005).

Increasing sales and market share

More and more frequently sponsors not only aim for communicative objectives but also detect the broad fan community as a sales platform. Therefore some clubs devise certain business models with their sponsors, who aim to use the club's brand to increase sales. One good example for such a strategic partnership was evolved by FC Bayern Munich with a bank sponsor who supplies an 'FC Bayern saving card'. Depending on the amount of scored goals and the overall success of the club, clients obtain extra interest rates for their savings. In general, however, the impact on sales assigned to sponsorship is difficult to evaluate and therefore questionable. It was shown that frequency of attendance and education are significant predictors of purchase intentions concerning sponsor products. Though it has not yet been proved, it is believed that sales figures for sponsor products are actually higher than for competitive products (Walliser, 2003).

Obtaining corporate hospitality opportunities

The establishment, maintenance and fostering of business contacts is an important field in relationship marketing. Therefore in many cases corporate hospitality arrangements are negotiated within a sponsorship contract. Generally, hospitality activities apply to the key corporate target audience, who are invited and then treated preferentially. For this purpose VIP boxes and business seats are provided at the venue. Due to their informal and exciting atmosphere, sport events offer attractive entertainment opportunities for business-to-business (B2B) contacts. However, the business value of corporate hospitality is hard to evaluate because of its emphasis on personal contacts and the wide range of possible outcomes (Collett, 2008).

Sponsorship evaluation and certain barriers

Since marketing managers have the same accountability for their spending on sponsorship as for other marketing communication tools, it is essential to evaluate the business value of each sponsorship activity. The ultimate question, in this context certainly, is whether €1 invested in a sponsorship campaign pays back more than that €1. Answering this question is a complex task facing plenty of potential influences that are hard to isolate and often not under direct control (Green, 2008). Right holders and suitors in sponsorship markets have to fix an adequate price in order to reach an agreement.

Market prices evolve from the coincidence of supply and demand. Following the neoclassical approach, a sponsor would invest the maximum amount of money for a sponsorship that assures a positive cost–benefit ratio. Moreover, the investment should be also cost-effective, i.e. there should be no other investment that equals the same objectives in same quality at less cost. But there are two crucial problems for a rational decision by the sponsor. Firstly, they are not aware of the economic benefits of their sponsorship. Instead of that they act in an atmosphere of uncertainty. Thus, a rational decision is not possible. Secondly, they are not aware of the effects of alternatives such as investing in an advertising campaign instead of a sponsorship deal.

Therefore most players in the sponsorship market rely on surrogate evaluation methods, such as media monitoring and market research that provide indicators in a comparatively easy way. By using media monitoring, the quality and quantity of media exposure can be determined. Relevant and widely utilized parameters in this context are on-screen visibility and frequency. Most sponsors seek for shifts in terms of brand awareness and image achieved by their sponsorship investment. Therefore the more traditional market research is used, capturing the impact of a campaign among sport fans by recall, recognition or image tests (Hermanns and Marwitz, 2008). In order to compare the efficiency of a sponsorship activity to alternative communication tools, various outcome measures can be employed. Below, some prevalent methods are presented and briefly discussed.

Comparative advertising space (CAS)

'Comparative advertising space' is calculated from the column inches devoted to an event in the print media, multiplied by the number of readers of each publication. Similarly, broadcast time on TV or radio can be used to determine the media value of a sport event. The next step is to estimate the cost of an advertising campaign that would have generated the same level of exposure (time or column inches) (Jeanrenaud, 2005). This method is primarily suggestive for title sponsors, for example BMW hosting the BMW International Open.

Cost per thousand (CPM)

The 'cost per thousand' indicator is adapted from advertising evaluation and reveals the cost of reaching 1000 viewers by 30 seconds of on-screen time within a sport broadcast. CPM can determine whether sponsoring a particular event, team or athlete is cost-effective, or whether some other communication tools would be more economical (Dinkel and Seeberger, 2007). However, both indicators (CAS and CPM) have their drawbacks. Firstly, the effective visibility is not considered (e.g. share of brand logo on screen, but advertisement is 100 per cent). Secondly, the viewer's gaze spot is variable (even if the board is on-screen it is not clear whether the viewer looks at it or not). Furthermore, these indicators say nothing about the effect of the sponsorship on the target group (Tripodi *et al.*, 2003). Lastly, both CAS and CPM can only be employed for ex post measurement.

Event study method (ESM)

The 'event study method' relies on the judgement of financial markets. Here the focus is on changes in the value of a company's shares after the announcement of a new sponsorship. ESM draws on the assumptions that financial markets act efficiently and investors are able to value ex ante the future benefits likely to be generated by a sponsorship deal (Jeanrenaud, 2005; see also Agrawal and Kamakura, 1995). Miyazaki and Morgan (2001) found out that by employing ESM, sponsoring the Olympic Games created a remarkable added economic value for the sponsors. However, it is questionable whether stock market behaviour is rational so that this could be a precise measurement.

Impact on sales

From a sponsor's perspective, it is mostly desirable to evaluate the impact that a sponsorship investment has on sales (Crompton, 2004). Though sponsorship can create a specific climate conducive to the development of extra sales, only very rarely is it the direct means of achieving them. Therefore sales growth achieved by the use of sponsorship is difficult to be estimated precisely (Jeanrenaud, 2005). In addition, the possible influences of collateral marketing communications, carry-over effects of past activities and changing economic conditions make it highly problematic to use sales figures as an indicator of sponsorship success (Bennett, 1999). Though sponsors can gain some tangible parameters that help to evaluate their activity, they often overlook the specific benefits and the relative advantages of a sponsorship compared to traditional forms of corporate communication (O'Reilly, 2008). These lie in staging brand experiences, transferring image associations in an emotional surrounding as well as pinpointed targeting (Preuss, 2009). At the same time, sponsorship's disadvantages have to be taken into account as most sponsors lack an exclusive appearance and viewers usually show low involvement with sponsorship messages due to their focus on sport action.

However, the main problem of sponsorship evaluation lies in the fact that sponsorship in the majority of cases is utilized simultaneously with other forms of corporate communication. Hence, an appropriate research design has to take this difficulty into account. Therefore a control group has to be inserted that was not exposed to the examined sport event in order to discount the effects of other communications. Another approach would be a two-part survey with assessments immediately before and after the event (Crompton, 2004). As a result of the demonstrated complexity of sponsorship evaluation, a consistent and universally accepted methodology is yet to be developed. To date, most research companies have designed their own methods and indices to determine the success or failure of a sponsorship investment. But in times of increasing sponsorship fees, corporations are demanding legitimate, consistent and meaningful measurement techniques. This results in a need to evaluate multiple sponsorships in different sports with each other as well as comparing sponsorship to other marketing communication tools.

Choice of the right sponsorship

Companies harnessing the emotional power of sport to strengthen brand perception face an immense number of potential linkages. The various associations between a brand and non-product elements such as sport teams or athletes can influence the perception of the brand. In fact, a well-chosen sponsorship has the capacity to drive particular brand values (Dolphin, 2003). Therefore, the choice of an appropriate sponsorship deal should be made from defined strategic considerations rather than a gut feeling.

Firstly, brands can either associate with an athlete, a team, an event or a venue. Secondly, they can choose from a wide variety of sports, e.g. extreme sports, premium sports or motor sports, which all symbolize different images and values (Raynaud and Bolos, 2008). Consequently, the congruence between the perception of a brand and a sponsorship must be considered as an important success factor of sponsorship effectiveness (Gwinner and Eaton, 1999; Koo *et al.*, 2006). As research identified, sponsorships are more successful in terms of awareness increase and image transfer if the consumer perceives either a functional-based or an image-based similarity (Gwinner and Eaton, 1999). Accordingly, a high fit can be emphasized as a critical factor in terms of the attention paid to the sponsor, the sponsor's image as well as increasing purchase intentions of the sponsor's products (Koo *et al.*, 2006). Good examples for a high level of congruence are Rolex's long-time engagement in golf or Mercedes-Benz in motor sport, whereas a cigarette brand sponsoring a track and field event might be seen as a disputable linking. Figure 3.1 shows a semantic network of image associations based on an automobile brand X engaged in a golf sponsorship. Whereas the dashed ellipse represents the fit due to a congruent image association (here: expensive) the wider, solid lines imply the possible image transfer (luxury and exclusive).

However, a sponsorship that fits might not turn out as a lucrative investment if the sponsor trusts on mere brand exposure during sport competition. In fact a sponsorship has to be seen as a close relationship between brand and sport with a sophisticated strategy and analogous messages. A lack of synergy between sponsor and sport entity limits the return on investment. In this context, it is essential to devise common objectives for the sponsorship to ensure they act together. While sport events, teams or athletes usually focus on fundraising in order to improve their performance, corporations primarily seek to increase brand awareness and image. But beyond that, corporations and sport often have congruent objectives in terms of an attractive appearance or the increase of media coverage. The more

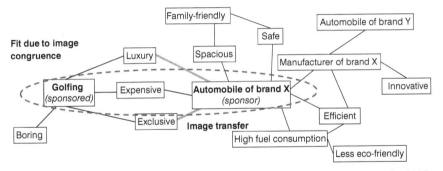

Figure 3.1 Semantic network of image associations (according to Baumgarth, 2000; Drenger, 2003)

both sides can contribute to these common objectives, the more positive outcomes a sponsorship can achieve (Adjouri and Stastny, 2006).

Whereas most research focuses on the management of nationwide or even international sponsorships, only few contributions examine local or regional activities. However, these so-called grass roots sponsorships reach fewer consumers but the return on investment for small businesses can be much greater. On this most basic level of sport involvement, local or regional organizations target both spectators and participants. In doing so sponsors take the opportunity to address their local target groups by associating their brands with the culture of a sports club. The decisive factor is that most participants and spectators of these events are more identified and passionate about their sport than the average mass-sport consumer. Often the participation is a fundamental part of their everyday life, which might result in higher awareness shifts and image enhancements concerning sponsors. Furthermore, spectators and participants in grass roots sport events are typically more homogenous than audiences of major events, which allow a more targeted audience for corporations (Miloch and Lambrecht, 2006).

Case study: SpVgg Vreden 1921 e.V.

Introduction

Even though fees in a grass roots sport sponsorship are obviously lower, local sports clubs can no longer pass on developing attractive arrangements that include the specific motives of corporate partners. From the opposite perspective, businesses should consider if they have a logical tie to the activity of interest. If this is the case, a sustainable and long-lasting sponsorship can be developed. In this section we will introduce a middle size soccer club that set up an interesting concept to attract local sponsors. After some detailed explanation about the marketing and branding strategy from the club's perspective, the perspective of local businesses that might use sponsorship for branding purposes will be considered.

SpVgg Vreden 1921 e.V. is an amateur soccer club in the north-western part of Germany. With more than 1000 members and more than 30 junior teams with kids and youth aged 5–19 organized in the competitive system, the club has one of the biggest junior sections in the region. The biggest challenge for the club is the financial situation since it is hard to acquire sponsors on amateur sport level. Since this is a task most amateur clubs are faced with, the German Sport University Cologne approached this problem with a pilot study. The main idea was to build a new brand image of the club to attract new sponsors. This image shift would be realized by a strong focus on quality in youth training and youth work.

The measures implemented already are promising and quite successful. Regarding quality improvement of training, all coaches received individual instructions for training in techniques and tactics specially designed for the target group of children and adolescents. In the area of youth self-development, a commitment to preventing alcohol and nicotine abuse was implemented in the statutes of the club. In a broader pedagogical context, on-the-spot support (e.g. for homework) for young students as well as a kid's club concept was developed.

Since all measures are quite expensive, a detailed sponsoring proposition has been developed and implemented. With the financial support of several companies it was possible to build two mini soccer courts and hence improve the training conditions for club members. In addition, publicity about the club was extended to a regional and supra-regional level via modified internal and external print media, as well as via regional broadcasting. Another strength is that the club is located in a region with financially healthy businesses, which means a widespread area of potential sponsors.

Marketing and branding strategies of the club

The first proper marketing strategy was developed in 2007 with the start of the pilot project. Before this project, the people in charge recognized that many companies were interested in fostering the youth and not the senior team playing in a bush-league. Therefore it was assumed that the youth should play the central role in the strategic marketing concept. A brand strategy was firstly developed at that time. This strategy is based on two components: on the one hand the club tries to capitalize on the city's image (small but financially strong, traditional). Hence, the club's colours and parts of the club's logo are based on the city logo (co-branding). On the other hand, fostering youth training and young people's self-development are two of the main objectives, mainly as a result of the big junior section. The club's mission statement 'strong partners for youth' emphasizes this philosophy. This image is of importance for sponsors.

The infrastructure of the club might be really an asset for the club's brand. The club is proud of recently building dressing cabins and two mini-courts with artificial turf. Also the little 'stadium' has got a new look with a new perimeter advertising board structure. The logo of the club changed from a soccer player to the basic structure of the city logo. The second logo 'strong partners for youth' was recently developed (see Figure 3.2).

At the amateur level, the game jersey is less important as a sponsoring tool compared to professional sports. Still, the club avoided putting only one

Figure 3.2 Club logo and mission statement 'strong partners for youth'

sponsor on the jersey. On the contrary, the club's mission statement is printed on the front, with which all sponsors identify. Furthermore, the club developed a corporate design appropriate for all internal and external communications. Thus, for instance, the letterhead, the club's magazine, the year book and the website are consistent. This is seen as an important factor for leveraging the club's brand.

As mentioned before, the financial situation is a constraining factor as the implementation of the above mentioned measures are costly. Therefore it was essential to improve the existing sponsorship strategy. With the objective of fostering the youth and the general marketing focus on the youth, the club could increase its sponsoring success, even though the first senior team was relegated, and the sponsorship structure of the club was completely revised. There are now three sponsor categories: 'classic partnerships' include conventional sponsoring tools, whereas 'business partners' and 'premium partners' receive individually designed sponsorship propositions.

In summary, the club is trying to become a regional brand due to their extraordinary quality proposition based on boosting social responsibility. The club's mission statement and logo 'strong partners for youth' is positioned on the perimeter advertising board, on the website, the club's van and on the jersey of the first senior soccer team.

Sponsorship implementations of local businesses

After having presented the innovative marketing and branding strategy of the club, the following paragraphs deal with the objectives local businesses try to exploit by sponsoring SpVgg Vreden. Generally, the goal for local businesses is to increase revenues through a shift in brand awareness, the enhancement of brand image and the fostering of relationships with the local community (Miloch and Lambrecht, 2006). However, the 19 partners of this club are motivated to engage in their sponsorship for a variety of specific reasons, which will be analysed by reference to three examples.

One of the club's premium partners is Fliesen Lepping, a local tiling service provider. When SpVgg Vreden planned to build new dressing rooms, Fliesen

Lepping decided to support this project by its work input. Though this effort was not financial but in kind, the club benefited significantly from this input. In return, the business obtained space for its logo on the new perimeter advertising board at the venue as well as a prominent position for its link on the club's website. For Fliesen Lepping, this sponsorship gives them the chance to raise local awareness with both club members and spectators. Especially in a local context, a generous sponsorship is usually well communicated via word of mouth. Besides raising awareness for the tiling service, the sponsorship provides the opportunity to testify to the handcrafter's high quality as many club members enter these new, tiled dressing rooms.

Another interesting sponsorship was implemented by a local paper mill called Papierfabrik. Since this company suffers from an outmoded image, the relationship with the ambitious and innovative soccer club could assist the external communications in breaking new ground. Therefore the company funded two mini-courts with artificial turf. These courts are considered to give an ideal playing surface for the youth for daily practice. From the company's perspective, this sponsorship serves as credible proof of its social responsibility as these courts are primarily intended to support the young generation.

Teka is a manufacturer of filtering systems with a sales market all around the world. Since the company's claim is 'We set air in motion', the association with sport seems logical. The corporate communication therefore focuses entirely on sport marketing activities including various sponsorships both on performance and at the grass roots level. One element in this strategy is the premium partnership with SpVgg Vreden. In this context Teka offers a special service for the club's talents to allow them to do their homework on the spot and under professional supervision. This so-called 'Teka-homework support' is well established in the club because parents know their children are in good hands. Furthermore, the young soccer players are assisted in balancing school and sports. Teka utilizes this sponsorship to show responsibility for the region in general and the education of the next generation specifically. This message fits perfectly into the company's overall marketing communication programme.

The fostering of regional business contacts is an often mentioned objective of grass roots sponsors. To meet this requirement, the club frequently invites all its sponsors to a sociable get-together; sponsors of grass roots sport sometimes not only target current stakeholders but also try to recruit qualified personnel from the club. This is highly remarkable as it reveals another interesting field of sponsorship implementation.

Conclusion

The sponsorship of sports offers a broad variety of opportunities for leveraging branding strategies. The aforementioned case was supposed to illustrate these multi-sided capabilities. In this final section, the state of the art in both managerial procedure and scientific research are briefly summarized in order to reveal further fields of interaction.

On the managerial side, the strategy, implementation and evaluation of sponsorship activities has experienced professionalization during the last decade. Most sponsors have some kind of sponsorship strategy at least regarding the amount of investment and predefined objectives. Concerning the implementation of such activities, companies have employed people who deal with sponsorship and its activation in the media; there are plenty of sport marketing agencies that provide full-service implementations. As sponsorship expenses grow, the number of corporations who employ evaluations such as media ratings and response tests has increased. However, there are many sponsors who do not check their activity at all due to inappropriate measurement categories or cost cutting. In general, it must be stated that the evaluation of sponsorship activities is far behind compared to other disciplines such as advertising. To date there is no standardization achieved and the return on investment depends ultimately on the accounting policy. But since companies need rational criteria for their investments, this gap might lead to a decrease of sponsorship investments in the future, which would be a problem for the financial situation of professional sports. Thus, the pursuit of a systematic approach to weigh the odds with alternative communication instruments goes on. Specifically, management suffers from a lack of both a clear understanding of how sponsorship works in the consumer's mind and comprehensible performance indicators in order to back up the investment.

Scientific research on sponsorship has advanced significantly over the past ten years. In this process, the strategic use of sponsorship, the perception of sponsorship stimuli and the evaluation of sponsorship activities received the main attention. In his extensive literature review, Walliser (2003) identified more than 230 studies about sponsorship. Thus, this specific field of research can no longer be claimed as sparse. Early contributions focused on strategic aspects dealing with the management of associations and the way sponsorships could be integrated into the overall marketing programme. These findings, without doubt, helped management practice to evolve professionalism in order to leverage sponsorship investments. However, a widely established theoretical framework for sponsorship effects is lacking. In fact, the most urgent research gap lies in the explanation of sponsorship information processing. In order to provide meaningful guidelines, a clear understanding of the internal processes related to the activity is necessary. Thus, a deeper insight into the effectiveness of sponsorship bears a two-fold benefit: firstly, it provides a more efficient implementation of sponsorship for corporations; secondly, it gives substantial information for the evaluation of these activities. As there are similarities between advertising and sponsorship, models of how advertising works are often applied to sponsorship. However, there is no consensus among researchers about the relationship between advertising and sponsorship, which is an essential premise for the transferability of advertising models. In order to nurture a meaningful sponsorship model both more empirical evidence about the internal information processing and the relationship between advertising and sponsorship is needed.

In this context, the interest group S20, representing the most powerful sponsors in Germany, in cooperation with the German Sport University Cologne

(Institute for Sport Economics and Sport Management) drew up an extensive research project. The overall goal is to introduce generally accepted standard metrics concerning the evaluation of sport sponsorship. To date, most research consultants employ their own measurement metrics that are mostly descriptive in nature and hard to compare. In order to develop a transparent standard that enables all market actors to evaluate their sponsorship consistently, the specific value of contacts with target customers as well as the value of diverse sponsorship tools have to be identified. This benefits both right holders who are dependent on obtaining sponsorship revenues, and sponsors who require standard metrics for a sophisticated branding strategy.

The fourth chapter will look at how a city and a country can capitalize on a major sporting event in order to improve their brand image. In this regard, we shall take the case of the 2008 Beijing Olympic Summer Games.

References

Adamson, A. P. (2006). *Brandsimple: How the Best Brands Keep it Simple and Succeed.* Houndmills: Palgrave Macmillan.

Adjouri, N. and P. Stastny (2006). *Sport-Branding. Mit Sport-Sponsoring zum Markenerfolg.* Wiesbaden: Gabler.

Agrawal, J. and W. A. Kamakura (1995). The economic worth of celebrity endorsers: An event study analysis. *Journal of Marketing*, 59 (3): 56–62.

Baumgarth, C. (2000). Methoden zur Markenfitanalyse. *Planung und Analyse*, 27 (5): 48–52.

Bennett, R. (1999). Sports sponsorship, spectator recall and false consensus. *European Journal of Marketing*, 33 (3/4): 291–313.

Bruhn, M. (2003). *Kommunikationspolitik: systematischer Einsatz der Kommunikation für Unternehmen*, 2nd edition. Munich: Vahlen.

Chien, P., T. Cornwell and R. Stokes (2005). A theoretical framework for analysis of image transfer in multiple sponsorships. ANZMAC 2005 Conference Proceedings: 17–25.

Cliffe, S. and J. Motion (2005). Building contemporary brands: A sponsorship-based strategy. *Journal of Business Research* 58 (8): 1068–1077.

Collett, P. (2008). Sponsorship-related hospitality: Planning for measurable success. *Journal of Sponsorship*, 1 (3): 286–296.

Cornwell, T. (2008). State of the art and science in sponsorship-linked marketing. *Journal of Advertising*, 37 (3): 41–55.

Cornwell, T., C. Weeks and D. Roy (2005). Sponsorship-linked marketing: Opening the black box. *Journal of Advertising*, 34 (2): 21–42.

Crompton, J. (2004). Conceptualization and alternate operationalization of the measurement of sponsorship effectiveness in sport. *Leisure Studies*, 23 (3): 267–281.

Dean, D. (1999). Brand endorsement, popularity, and event sponsorship as advertising cues affecting consumer pre-purchase attitudes. *Journal of Advertising*, 28 (3): 1–13.

Dinkel, M. and J. Seeberger (2007). *Planung and Erfolgskontrolle im Sportsponsoring. Die Medianalayse in Theorie und Praxis.* Heidelberg: abcverlag.

Dolphin, R. (2003). Sponsorship: Perspectives on its strategic role. *Corporate Communications: An International Journal*, 8 (3): 173–186.

Drenger, J. (2003). *Imagewirkungen von Eventmarketing: Entwicklung eines ganzheitlichen Messansatzes.* Wiesbaden: DUV.

Esch, F.-R. and T. Langner (2001). Branding als Grundlage zum Markenaufbau. In: F.-R. Esch (ed.), *Moderne Markenführung*, 3rd edition. Wiesbaden: Gabler: 573–586.

Green, A. (2008). Planning for effective evaluation: Are marketers really doing it? *Journal of Sponsorship*, 1 (4): 357–363.

Gwinner, K. and J. Eaton (1999). Building brand image through event sponsorship: The role of image transfer. *Journal of Advertising*, 18 (4): 47–57.

Gwinner, K. and S. Swanson (2003). A model of fan identification, antecendents and sponsorship outcomes. *Journal of Services Marketing*, 17 (3): 275–294.

Heider, F. (1958). *The psychology of interpersonal relations*. New York: John Wiley & Sons.

Hermanns, A. and C. Marwitz (2008). *Sponsoring. Grundlagen, Wirkungen, Management, Markenführung*, 3rd edition. Munich: Vahlen.

Hoek, J., P. Gendall, M. Jeffcoat and D. Orsman (1997). Sponsorship and advertising: A comparison of their effects. *Journal of Marketing Communications*, 3 (1): 21–32.

Jackson, K. (2009). Influencing behaviour towards a brand through experiential marketing and sponsorship. *Journal of Sponsorship*, 2 (2): 164–169.

Jeanrenaud, C. (2005). Sponsorship. In: W. Andreff and S. Szymanski (eds), *Handbook on the Economics of Sport*, Cheltenham: Edward Elgar: 49–58.

Johar, G. and M. Pham (1999). Relatedness, prominence and constructive sponsor indentification. *Journal of Marketing Research*, 36 (3): 299–312.

Keller, K. L. (1993). Conceptualizing, measuring, and managing customer-based brand equity. *Journal of Marketing*, 57 (1): 1–22.

Keller, K. L. (2003). Strategic brand management process. In: F.-R. Esch (ed.), *Moderne Markenführung*, 3rd edition. Wiesbaden: Gabler: 83–102.

Kiendl, S. (2007). *Markenkommunikation mit Sport – Sponsoring und Markenevents als Kommunikationsplattform*. Wiesbaden: Gabler.

Koo, G., J. Quarterman and L. Flynn (2006). Effect of perceived sport event and sponsor image fit on consumers' cognition, affect, and behavioral intentions. *Sport Marketing Quaterly*, 15 (2): 80–90.

Kroeber-Riel, W. and P. Weinberg (2003). *Konsumentenverhalten*, 8th edition. München: Vahlen.

Madrigal, R. (2001). Social identity effects in a belief attitude – intentions hierarchy: Implications for corporate sponsorship. *Psychology and Marketing*, 18 (2): 145–165.

Meenaghan, T. (1983). Commercial sponsorship. *European Journal of Marketing*, 17 (7): 5–73.

Meenaghan, T. (2001). Understanding sponsorship effects. *Psychology and Marketing*, 18 (2): 95–122.

Miloch, K. and K. Lambrecht (2006). Consumer awareness of sponsorship at grassroots sports events. *Sport Marketing Quaterly*, 15 (3): 147–154.

Miyazaki, A. D. and A. G. Morgan (2001). Assessing market value of event sponsoring: Corporate Olympic sponsorships. *Journal of Advertising Research*, 41 (1): 9–15.

Nicholls, J., S. Roslow and S. Dublish (1999). Brand recall and brand preference at sponsored golf and tennis tournaments. *European Journal of Marketing*, 33 (3/4): 356–386.

O'Reilly, N. (2008). Sponsorship evaluation. *Journal of Sponsorship*, 2 (1): 8–10.

Pham, M. and G. Johar (2001). Market prominence biases in sponsor identification: processes and consequentiality. *Psychology and Marketing*, 18 (2): 123–143.

Pilot Group (2008). *Sponsor Visions*. www.pilot.de.

Pine, J. and H. Gilmore (1998). Welcome to the experience economy. *Harvard Business Review*, 76 (4): 97–105.

Preuss, H. (2009). Sponsoring im Spitzensport. In: C. Breuer and A. Thiel (eds), *Handbuch Sport-Management*, Schorndorf: Hofmann-Verlag: 282–299.

Quester, P. and F. Farrelly (1998). Brand association and memory decay effects of sponsorship – the case of the Australian Formula one. *Journal of Product and Brand Management*, 7 (6): 539–556.

Raynaud, J. and G. Bolos (2008). Sport at the heart of marketing: The integration debate. *Journal of Sponsorship*, 2 (1): 31–35.

Sportfive (2003). *Affinitäten_2. Wertigkeit, Sympathie und persönliche Nähe von Marken und Sport. Wirkungsvoraussetzungen für erfolgreichen Imagetransfer im Sportsponsoring*. Hamburg: Sportfive.

Tripodi, J., M. Hirons, D. Bednall and M. Sutherland (2003). Cognitive evaluation: Prompts used to measure sponsorship awareness. *International Journal of Market Research*, 45 (4): 435–454.

Walliser, B. (2003). An international review of sponsorship research. *International Journal of Advertising*, 22 (1): 5–40.

4 The impact of the 2008 Summer Olympics on Beijing's and China's image

Guojun Zeng, Frank Go and Christian Kolmer

Adapted by André Richelieu

Introduction

National reputation affects perceptions and various spatial decisions made by three groups: the general public, decision makers on the national level and the place's inhabitants (Avraham, 2000). A country's position in global competition might be affected by its national image. Special events, including sports events, are now playing an integral role in image change and many destination marketing strategies (Hede, 2005). Some destinations are using sports events as a constant, and core, component of their destination marketing strategies (Hede, 2005). In this process, the media is the key intermediary between the mega-events and the national image of destination (Rivenburgh, 1992).

Despite an increasing academic interest in mega-events and place image in the global marketplace, China has not received significant attention despite its emerging economy and rising profile. There have been very few attempts to examine how mega-events work on the national image in Chinese cultural and economic contexts. Coverage plays a key role in the implications of media processes in relation to cultures and modern identities, and the inter-cultural barriers in such processes that are likely to cause confusion and misunderstanding on the part of the message recipients. China represents a culture with a history that spans several millennia. The IOC's decision in 2001 to give the Olympic Games to Beijing was a political signal and a contribution to China's gradual opening to the world, which was supposed to be helpful for China to promote their international image. The Chinese government consciously chose to stage the Beijing Olympic Games 2008, in part, to send a message across the world that the country has joined modernity.

Mega-events such as the Beijing Olympic Games 2008 are designed to impact the perception of a worldwide public, via the media. Namely, the interactions between media practices and tourist imagination are becoming increasingly important in shaping public perception. That is important, because, in turn, the media shapes decision making, both in the choices of consumers and at business-to-business level. Accordingly, business, government leaders and the public at large need insight into the meaning of the news items. How can countries be considered as brands and how can they leverage themselves by hosting sport events? What news items affect the image of China and the Chinese people based on the Olympics? This study explores the persistent image of China that lingers in the minds of many people. Next, it chronicles the growing role of international TV media telecasts in relation to mega-events as a lever to build positive attitudes towards China to the world before, during and after the Olympic Games in 2008.

The relationship of sport events, national branding and media coverage

Place branding

Since 1850 places, towns, cities and regions have been involved in promotion and the use of publicity to sell place, which subsequently evolved into contemporary place marketing (Gold and Ward, 1994). In recent years the terms place brand and place branding have become a fundamental part of the marketing of nations, regions and cities. Presently, brands are seen to add value for countries, regions, cities and their stakeholders.

The difficulty in labelling the overlap between the areas linked to the study place branding caused Anholt (2005, p. 117) to distinguish between three definitions of place branding: first, 'a popular and least precise way referring to buzz words and vague marketing terms; second, a simple understanding, which refers to a designed visual identity – name, logo, slogan, corporate livery', third, the advanced definition covering 'a wide area of corporate strategy, consumer and stakeholder motivation and behavior, internal and external communications'. The latter affords countries or cities a window for embarking 'on conscious branding', choosing 'some industries, personalities, natural landmarks and historical events that could provide a basis for strong branding and storytelling' (Kotler and Gertner, 2002, p. 258).

Olins (2002, p. 241) presents historical evidence suggesting that nation branding may face a significant impediment, because 'many detest the word brand'; which appears for some 'to have trifling and superficial implications unworthy of the national idea'. Yet, 'the need for collective understanding and appreciation of place marketing, the achievement of wide cooperation and clear role allocation, the implementation of marketing as a long-term process and the expansion of marketing understanding to fields other than tourism development' were identified as significant issues in relation to the future marketing (Kavaratzis and Ashworth, 2008, p. 150). In turn, a collective understanding and appreciation of place marketing resides in a paradigm. For framing and synthesis purposes we must, therefore, look beyond place branding antecedents to the evolving marketing discipline and cognate disciplines within a temporal–spatial context.

Mega-events and place branding

Geographic events may result in strong touristic implications (Gunn, 1989), which can be taken as the actions of place branding. As Lee *et al.* (2005) pointed out, mega sports events such as the World Cup and the Olympics receive a great deal of international attention and contribute to increased interest in sports tourism. Mega-events increase recognition of the host country (Brown, Chalip, Jago and Mules, 2004). An artificial demand rise of accommodation, transport and hospitality is created in host destinations whilst mega-events are being staged (McManus, 1999). One important aspect of strategic action is to utilize the event to improve the image of the host destination. During the post-staging period benefits of mega-events are realizable for host destinations. Indeed, this aspect of mega-events can represent a large legacy for host destinations, but media is a crucial component in promoting the image of destination. Destinations often seek to change their images through hosting events (Brown *et al.*, 2004).

Some researchers focus on the impacts of events on place branding (Xing and Chalip, 2006; Giffard and Rivenburgh, 2000). Roche (1994, p. 7) notes that 'mega-events are short-term events with long-term consequences'. The benefits of staging mega-events for host destinations, in the long term, are repeat visitation of spectators, and increased investment and tourism, as a result of the related media exposure the host destination is afforded. After the staging of the special event, some of the expenditure associated with the staging of mega-events can be recouped through new income from tourism, particularly in non-peak periods (Chalip *et al.*, 2003). Indeed, this is the goal of many event-related national branding strategies. Hede (2005) explored the efficacy of the Australian telecast of the Athens 2004 Summer Olympics in developing positive perceptions and attitudes of Greece as a tourist destination and was origin-based – in that a survey was undertaken of a sample of Australian residents. They report 39 per cent of respondents indicate that their overall attitudes toward Greece as tourist destination improved as a result of their consumption of the telecast.

Given the phenomenal potential that has been attributed to this aspect of event-related place branding there is a dearth of literature on this topic. Chalip *et al.* (2003) noted that very little empirical evidence has been gained with regard to the role of mega-events in developing positive impressions of host destinations. Smith (2005) explored the role of sporting-related initiatives in developing domestic tourism in three cities that have used sport as a means of 'reimaging' their host destinations. While this study focused on domestic tourism, there has been little research undertaken to specifically explore the role of mega-events in developing national image in international media. As Xing and Chalip (2006) stated, we know very little about changing a destination's image or brand.

At the same time, according to a study by the Third World and Environment Broadcasting Project, two thirds of mainstream international news coverage about developing countries concentrated on conflicts and disasters. Coverage tends to focus on a few protagonists: governments, major politicians and politics in general (Blay and Alabi, 1996). And international media tends to focus on events rather than a continuous analysis of progress. Although some researchers witness a slight increase in process news, it is still marginal compared to the overall coverage.

The role of sport events to leverage a national brand in media coverage

In the formation process of destination image, media plays a very important role (Martin and Bosque, 2008). Telecast is an increasingly important aspect of event-related destination marketing strategies. Because of their global reach, the media are active in defining, shaping and changing the national image around the world (Rivenburgh, 1992). A televised national image portrayal will not simply become the image of each audience member. But one can infer that repeated national images, as a component of mainstream media content, will influence the understanding of audiences by setting limits on the quality and quantity of information (Rivenburgh, 1992). The audiences may have no other or direct experience with that nation.

When destinations host mega-events, they gain publicity and advertising opportunities, which may be helpful to national branding. The telecasts of the Summer Olympic Games were popularized as a result of the success of the telecast of the 1968 Summer Olympic Games (Chalip *et al.*, 2003). The Olympics, a typical and important mega-event, have allowed viewers throughout the world to share in the pageantry of the opening and closing ceremonies and the victories and achievements of outstanding athletes. It has, in many ways, been responsible for the strategies of national branding.

The telecasts of Olympic Games not only report on the sports, but they increasingly provide coverage of the host country – its landscape, attractions, culture and people (Hede, 2005). As Dong *et al.* (2005) pointed out, the 2008 Beijing Olympics is a good opportunity to build China's image. The components of national image include visibility, valence, breadth and attribution (Rivenburgh, 1992). Visibility refers to the quantity of media coverage of another nation (Manheim and Albritton, 1984; Rivenburgh, 1992), as well as the location or placement of image exposure. Valence refers to the degree to which a news item reflects favourably or unfavourably on the nation as derived by some assessment of cues within the content (Manheim and Albritton, 1984). Breadth, which tends to cluster around political or economic issues, is about the content themes or topics of other nations (Rivenburgh, 1992). And attribution focuses on how another culture's behaviour is being interpreted for home television audiences. The analysis of it can often be accomplished by looking at source characteristics (Rivenburgh, 1992). These dimensions can be taken together to explore the national reputation.

Event media coverage increases recognition of the host country (Brown *et al.*, 2004), however, impacts of mega-events on destination images prove to be an important yet understudied topic. The core of the telecasts of mega-events is the coverage of the sports in focus; the telecasts also provide opportunities for images and communication about the host destinations to be projected to audiences all around the world. Mega-events provide destinations with unique, and substantial, opportunities for promotion through the media attention that they attract. Therefore, marketers of the host destination have the opportunity to develop positive impressions of the host destinations. One strategy used by nations to enhance their image is to host global media events (Giffard and Rivenburgh, 2000).

The role of sport events to leverage a national brand proves to be an important yet understudied topic. Based on the analysis framework of national reputation, this case study seeks to understand the implications of media representation and processes in relation to the Beijing Olympic Games 2008 and tourism, particularly, whether the Beijing Olympics 2008 may, or may not, transform the image in TV media that foreign publics have of China's national image. The main aim of this case study is to analyse how the process of the foreign TV media telecasts of Beijing 2008 affects the worldwide perceptions about China. The media set used, represents nine different countries and provides results that are interpreted and discussed. Finally, the conclusions and implications are drawn and study limitations and suggestions for further research are proposed.

The database of news coverage about the Beijing Olympics was retrieved from Media Tenor International. As Berelson (1971) points out, although there is no strict dividing line between qualitative and quantitative analysis, the qualitative form is only roughly quantitative and, as such, is not numerical; the data are less precise and interpretations are made as part of the analysis, rather than after the analytical procedure (Rivenburgh, 1992). Our case study is different from Xing and Chalip's (2006) study. They investigate the individuals and this chapter uses the information of international media in nine countries. So their study reveals the opinions of public agenda. In this study, the results of media agenda are shown.

Methodology and data collection

Methodology

The method of case study is suitable for explaining the effect of mega-events on place branding. The case study approach is appropriate when the research to be conducted focuses on contemporary situations and does not require control over behavioural events (Yin, 2008). These assumptions were relevant to this study, as they have been to other studies on mega-events (Arthur and Andrew, 1996; Persson, 2002). Eisenhardt (1989) described the process of inducting theory using case studies from specifying the research questions to reaching closing. The process of case study is highly iterative and tightly linked to data. The logic of case study is unique to the inductive, case-oriented process. And the resultant theory of case study is often novel, testable and empirically valid (Eisenhardt, 1989). While the case study method was employed for this study, it was used in conjunction with other research methods.

One of the world's most spectacular and widely covered mega-events is the Olympic Games (Bernstein, 2000), which China was hosting in 2008. The case used for this study was the international telecast of Beijing 2008. The Beijing Olympic Games were performed in seven places. The majority of events were held in Beijing. But events that required specific facilities were performed away from the Chinese capital. For instance, the sailing event was held in Qingdao, equestrian events in Hong Kong; men and women's football matches were played in the following four cities: Tianjing, Shenyang, Qinghuangdao and Shanghai. Based on the case of 2008 Olympics, there are multiple factors that have impacts on the image of China, including international broadcasts that have an important influence on how worldwide audiences perceive China. Case study helps us gain insights into the various layers that represent the determinants.

The international TV coverage of the 2008 Olympics serves as an excellent case study on the importance of sport events to leverage the national brand for several reasons. Firstly, the broadcast before, during and after the Olympic Games 2008 is a meticulously planned media event. One can generally assume that the network gave audiences the best it was willing and able to offer in terms of coverage. Secondly, according to the Olympic Charter, the modern Olympics are intended to promote international understanding and cooperation, and television coverage is acknowledged as an important means to this end (Rivenburgh, 1992). This includes a focus on the host country. Thirdly, China had an explicitly stated desire for its positive national images to be portrayed to the rest of the world, allowing some insights into television as a tool of international relations. And finally, Chinese culture, in particular, had been victim of some of the most over-simplified, misunderstood, and fascinating images to be formulated by western minds, which in conjunction with China's growing assertiveness in world economic and political affairs, complicates the image of China and makes it an interesting and important issue to study. So there is a need for a systematic framework to comprehend the multitude of concepts, theories and examples in relation to the TV coverage of the Beijing Olympics 2008, including the cultural, political and social issues.

Any mega-event starts before the actual event starts, so we can distinguish three stages: (1) before the mega-event, (2) during the mega-event and (3) after the mega-event. There are different news reports on what happens, with whom and why throughout these three stages. The Opening Ceremony of the Beijing Olympics was on 8 August 2008, and the Closing Ceremony of the Beijing Olympics was on 24 August 2008. During the period of the Olympics, international media mainly focused on the games per se, while before and after the period of the Olympics, international media decentralized their focus to all kind of topics, including political, economic, social and cultural environments. With the aim of investigating the possible change of China's image, it is appropriate to compare the broadcasts one year before and one year after the Olympics. The two comparative periods are from 8 August 2007 to 7 August 2008, and from 25 August 2008 to 24 August 2009, respectively. News items before and after Olympics in nine countries are compared paired-sample t-test with the help of SPSS 11.5 (Statistical Package for the Social Sciences).

Data collection

Content analysis method is adopted in this study. Content analysis is a research technique for the objective, systematic and quantitative description of the manifest content of communication (Berelson, 1971). This methodology has very often been defined as 'quantitative content analysis', whereas techniques developed in the hermeneutic or linguistic tradition are labelled as 'qualitative'. In contrast to other analysis methods, which try to identify and analyse the characteristic and defining elements of media content, quantitative content analysis in the first step establishes the numerical distribution of the variables and in the second step makes inferences from these findings.

Media Tenor International supports journalists, scientists, politicians and managers. This case study uses Media Tenor International's content analysis as a methodological approach and qualitative data gathering method, particularly a sophisticated coding system to gain insight into the qualitative and quantitative volume of coverage in the media. Everyday more than 250 Media Tenor analysts all over the world scrutinize each contribution in the major German, American, Czech, South African, British and other daily and weekly newspapers and monthly journals, as well as TV news and magazines. Sentence by sentence the analysts ask what topics, from what originator and source, the journalists selected for print or broadcast. Following a set of criteria, established in cooperation with the universities of Mainz, Munich, Leipzig, Berlin and the partner institutes in Media Tenor International, the contents of the media are subject to a scientifically approved analysis. This offers the opportunity of measuring – beyond personal bias – what matters to the media and what does not. Based on Rivenburg's (1992) research, media name and country of origin relate to visibility. Results of content analysis provide data on image valence. Thematic structure can be used to analyse image breadth. And publishing date and the relation to the Olympics connect to attribution of image. Thus a database is created that contains media name, country of origin, the results of content analysis, thematic structure (sports, foreign affairs, etc.), telecasting date, and so on.

Media play a significant role in the presentation of national images (Rivenburgh, 1992). TV is selected as the main media type. Because satellite technology allows diverse cultural groups to view each other on the screen of a box, for many, television is the primary source of information concerning the world 'out there' and, in turn, has introduced new ways in which nations and cultural groups perceive and deal with each other.

An analysis of the reports on US, UK, Germany, France, Italy, Switzerland, Spain and Arabic satellite TV and South African television news over two comparative periods can show the change in China's image. The media set is as follows. US: NBC Nightly News, ABC World News Tonight, CBS Evening News, Fox News. UK: BBC 1 10 o'clock news, ITV News at Ten, BBC 2 Newsnight. Germany: ARD Tagesschau, ZDF heute, RTL Aktuell, ARD Tagesthemen, ZDF heute journal. France: TF1 Le Journal. Italy: RAI Uno. Switzerland: SF DRS Tagesschau. Spain: TVE 1. South Africa: SABC 3 News @ One, SABC 2 Afrikaans News, SABC 3 English News, SABC 3 Africa News Update, E-TV News, SABC Zulu/Xhosa News, SABC Sotho News. Although every endeavour has been made to collect the news from the important neighbouring countries of China, such as Japan, India and Australia, Media Tenor International cannot afford them without several years of preparation.

Although the tone of coverage relates to the main protagonist of the news story, as opposed to one of countries listed, news items such as 'British athlete wins the gold medal in China' influence viewers' perception around the world of China. All news stories analysed were broadcast in the respective programmes, out of which 7261 news stories focused on China as the dominant location of Olympic events. These stories have been collected in the database of Media Tenor International by content analysis from 8 August 2007 to 24 August 2009.

In order to organize the coding of valuations in a stringent way, only valuations of subjects – persons and organizations – are coded. The valuation only refers to the description of the coded subject, not to the event covered in the news. In addition, there is continuous coding of the state of the nation in terms of economic, social and value-based developments. Valuations can be expressed in two ways: either by the use of clearly positive or negative terms. The explicit rating can be contrasted with an implicit rating that embeds the description of the protagonist in a positive or negative context. The other kind of implicit valuations are those that refer to facts or issues that are perceived in a positive or negative way in a certain society. Rising unemployment figures constitute negative information, even when the journalist does not assess this development in explicit terms. In some cases, when this cannot be decided unequivocally, media analysts are required to code the valuation as 'ambivalent'. Most often, each segment possesses some sense of balance by mixing negative themes among neutral or positive themes. This practice is a familiar international news reporting norm where a 'two sides to every story' approach offers the appearance of journalistic balance.

Media Tenor distinguishes between manifest and latent valuations and measures both dimensions separately on a six-point scale: 0 (neutral), 1 (positive), 2 (rather positive), 3 (ambivalent), 4 (rather negative) and 5 (negative). It also combines two six-value variables into one variable so as to improve valuation (*wertung*). Next, it applies the following three-step strategy in an attempt to achieve such balance. Step 1 concerns the recoding of the tone of neutral (0) into ambivalent (3). Step 2 recodes the valuation rating by adding relevant values of explicit and implicit valuation (*wertung* = (explicit + implicit) / 2). Step 3 recodes valuation into the three-level format (-1 / 0 / +1). For example, if the valuation is lower than 2.5, then the value is recoded into 1. In the case where the valuation represents a value higher than 3.5, it is recoded into -1. Finally, if the value is between 2.6 and 3.4, it is recoded into 0.

Results

The period can be divided into three stages. The three stages examined amounted to a total of 7261 international TV news stories. The first stage amounted to 3969 TV news stories, almost double the 2094 TV news stories in the third stage. And during the Olympics, the amount of news coverage was 1198. Based on news data, the change of visibility, valence, breadth and attribution of the internationally televised Chinese image are analysed.

The role of the Olympics in leveraging China's visibility

In media analysis, visibility provides a quantitative measure related to exposure. As an image dimension, visibility is important because it often speaks to the salience of one nation to another nation, although salience can also result from meeting other media format characteristics such as drama, conflict, disaster and the like. Visibility can be measured by the share of stories about China in foreign news. In China, Tibet riots, an earthquake in Sichuan Province and the Olympics drove reporting. Unexpected events can disrupt structures of reporting: While in 'routine coverage' the share of China varies between 0.9 per cent and 4 per cent of all foreign news, dramatic events like the Tibet riots or the Sichuan earthquake boosted the visibility of China significantly.

Attention to Chinese affairs varies markedly between the analysed media markets. US TV focuses the most intensively on China. In the US, 7.99 per cent of the TV news about foreign countries focuses on China. TV news in France and South Africa also pays significant attention to China, with 6.05 per cent and 5.91 per cent, respectively, while Arabic, Swiss and Italian TV show less interest in China (see Figure 4.1). The ratio of China news to all foreign news is lower than 3.5 per cent in these three countries.

The coverage about destination often mounts up sharply before the mega-events, and issue perceptions used to change after the media coverage. There has been considerable discussion about the appropriate time lag between coverage in the media and subsequent changes in issue perceptions (Stroud and Kenski, 2007). Answers have ranged from lags of one and two months (Behr and Iyengar, 1985) to a lag of a few days (Watt and Berg, 1978). The appropriate time lag differences probably depend on the issue and the medium (Wanta and Hu, 1994). These studies all focused on the time lag between media coverage and

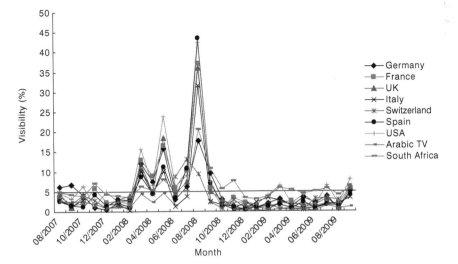

Figure 4.1 Share of foreign news stories

issue perceptions. But the time lag between mega-events and media coverage was seldom studied. Theoretically, this time lag is very much connected to the proposed mechanism. Though there is little agreement in the literature about the mechanism, one proposed explanation is that the Olympics covered in the international TV media become more accessible before and during the Olympics. This enhanced accessibility leads reporters of TV news programmes to concentrate on the Olympics. At the same time, the audiences of international TV news often watch the news reports before the Olympics and lose interest after it. So the TV news programmes will have no impetus to cover the Olympics 2008 because of weariness of audience and media.

The role of the Olympics in leveraging China's valence

As an aspect of image analysis, visibility ignores the quality of the portrayal. Valence becomes one of the most important aspects of national image. The origins of national image research are mainly based on opinion and attitude surveys concerning domestic and foreign policy. As such, the data collected are primarily concerned with how favourably (positive) or unfavourably (negative) a respondent views another nation as reflected in the common usage of evaluative scales (like/dislike, friendly/unfriendly, etc.) and semantic differential approaches (lazy/industrious, peace-loving/aggressive, etc.). When used in the analysis of media content, valence refers to the degree to which an article or item reflects a positive or negative view on the nation as derived by some assessment of cues within the content. This affective aspect of image content is judgemental and evaluative, often based on ethnocentric notions of what is right, good or valued by one culture when looking at another. Similarly, an assessment of image valence is subjective in both measurement and application (Rivenburgh, 1992).

News is the recording unit for valence. In the first stage, more than 35 per cent of segment themes were found to be negative, 48.39 per cent neutral and 16.27 per cent positive from the value perspective of the audience in nine countries. During the Olympic Games, only 17.44 per cent of segment themes were found to be negative, 39.15 per cent neutral (which decreased compared with that of the first stage), and 43.42 per cent positive (which is far higher than that of the first stage). In the third stage, 44.77 per cent of segment themes were found to be negative, 5.43 per cent higher than in the first stage; 26.39 per cent neutral, decreasing by 22 per cent; and 32.84 per cent positive, double that of first stage in nine countries. The data are mixed. The results of data analysis cannot prove that China has a more positive international televised image around the world after the 2008 Olympic Games.

Arabic and South African TV reported the most positively in the first stage. Positive coverage in South African and Arabic TV, far higher than the average level in the first stage, was strongly driven by business news. While generally low coverage is strongly connected to negative news, reporting in France, the UK, Italy and Switzerland, which showed scant interest in China, was more negative than in other markets. In the third stage, the positive tone percentage in South Africa remained the highest in the nine countries. TV reported more positively during the third stage in Germany, France, the UK and Spain. China's image has been improved in these countries since the Olympics.

The valence of the international televised image of China has been polarized since the Olympics. With the paired-samples test, the percentages of negative tone, positive tone and the tone of no clear rating have been compared. The percentages of positive and negative tone in international television about China increased significantly (percentage of negative tone, $t = -2.960$, Sig. = 0.018; percentage of positive tone, $t = -4.151$, Sig. = 0.003; see Table 4.1). The TV reports in the nine countries understand and cover China more clearly, which is due to the power and influence of the Olympic Games.

The role of the Olympics in leveraging the breadth of China's image

Breadth (thematic structure) of national image refers to the cognitive complexity of an image as defined by the range and character of knowledge areas presented or recalled about a nation or culture. Real understanding can only occur through a grasp of norms, values, beliefs and communication styles relating to a wide variety of behavioural areas, including homework, leisure, politics, religion, etc. National image research reveals that people, rather than acquiring or retaining a diverse range of knowledge from which to better explain cross-cultural behaviour, instead tend to perceive other nations rather narrowly, based on political alignment, economic development and, to a lesser degree, geography and population factor (Perry, 1985).

While open to refinement, this study derived the following exhaustive categories list from a survey of multicultural communication literature for use in this study (e.g. Rivenburgh, 1992): political values, party politics, crime/domestic security, domestic policy, foreign affairs, economy/public policy, business: companies, media, business: other aspects, society/education/arts, religion/church, environment/transport, energy, science/technology, history, sports, human interest and other topics. For television analysis, verbal associations with a nation can be identified and analysed using the same categories. The inclusion of the category 'Olympics', of course, pertains directly to the case chosen for this study.

Olympic messages were well placed in advance: sport was the most important message in the second half of 2007. After the unrest in Tibet, discussion of the Olympic Games, especially about the merits of a boycott, drove up the share of sports-related coverage again. Enthusiasm decreased late in 2007: although the evaluation of protagonists in sports coverage from China was less positive in 2008, it was nevertheless notably better than in the other reports from China. The international media emphasized the positive impact of the Olympics on the development of China.

Table 4.2 shows the main themes broadly categorized. Sports news plays a significant role in international TV coverage. This holds true for the media image of China. At a glance, sports were the number 1 message before and after

Table 4.1 Positive, negative and unclear reports of China in the three stages in nine countries

Country	Negative No	Negative %	No clear rating No	No clear rating %	Positive No	Positive %	Total
8 August 2007–7 August 2008							
Germany	405	38.50	509	48.38	138	13.12	1052
France	116	32.58	216	60.67	24	6.74	356
UK	168	43.52	196	50.78	22	5.70	386
Italy	53	34.19	88	56.77	14	9.03	155
Switzerland	45	32.85	78	56.93	14	10.22	137
Spain	56	18.73	203	67.89	40	13.38	299
USA	187	36.74	263	51.67	59	11.59	509
Arabic TV	42	16.41	153	59.77	61	23.83	256
South Africa	318	40.61	197	25.16	268	34.23	783
Total	1390	35.34	1903	48.39	640	16.27	3933
8 August 2008 –24 August 2008							
Germany	29	18.83	69	44.81	56	36.36	154
France	32	19.51	67	40.85	65	39.63	164
UK	46	17.90	79	30.74	132	51.36	257
Italy	6	10.17	21	35.59	32	54.24	59
Spain	6	5.45	58	52.73	46	41.82	110
USA	23	9.79	110	46.81	102	43.40	235
South Africa	66	30.84	63	29.44	85	39.72	214
Total	208	17.44	467	39.15	518	43.42	1193
25 August 2008 –24 August 2009							
Germany	199	48.54	108	26.34	103	25.12	410
France	30	30.00	47	47.00	23	23.00	100
UK	63	46.67	41	30.37	31	22.96	135
Italy	39	49.37	31	39.24	9	11.39	79
Switzerland	58	48.74	36	30.25	25	21.01	119
Spain	32	25.60	57	45.60	36	28.80	125
USA	98	53.55	61	33.33	24	13.11	183
Arabic TV	36	36.73	40	40.82	22	22.45	98
South Africa	293	35.26	128	15.40	410	49.34	831
Total	848	40.77	549	26.39	683	32.84	2080
Paired samples test before and after Olympics							
T		–2.960		11.391		–4.151	
Sig (2-tailed)		(0.018)		(<0.001)		(0.003)	

Table 4.2 Reports of different topics on China before and after the Olympics

Theme group	8 August 2007 – 7 August 2008		25 August 2008 – 24 August 2009	
	Total	Order	Total	Order
Political values	54	12	9	16
Party politics	42	13	7	17
Crime/domestic security	270	6	158	6
Domestic policy	332	5	95	9
Foreign affairs	352	4	173	4
Economy/public policy	92	10	175	3
Business: companies	103	9	98	8
Media	78	11	10	15
Business: other aspects	358	3	436	2
Society/education/arts	160	8	140	7
Religion/church	34	14	15	13
Environment/transport/energy	181	7	36	10
Science/technology	23	16	31	11
History	7	17	13	14
Sports	1147	1	503	1
Human interest	32	15	23	12
Other topics	668	2	158	5
Total	3933		2080	

the Olympics about China on international TV. Apart from the Olympic focus, China was very much framed as an important business spot in some markets as well. Business, foreign affairs, accidents and natural disasters generally play a significant role in foreign news. The top six coverage themes in the first stage were 'sports', 'other topics', 'business: other topics', 'foreign affairs', 'domestic policy' and 'crime/domestic security'. After the Olympic Games, the coverage of other topics dropped from second in the first stage to the fifth in the third stage, while the other five themes listed in the top six in the first stage still stayed in the same order. Although the sum of coverage has declined significantly since the Olympics, the breadth of the internationally televised image of China experienced no significant change before and after the Olympic Games.

With the paired-samples test (Table 4.3), the tone percentages of different topics in international TV coverage of the first and third stages are compared. The percentages of positive and negative tone in international television about China increased significantly (percentage of negative tone, $t = -2.579$, Sig. $= 0.020$; percentage of positive tone, $t = -2.099$, Sig. $= 0.052$). From the perspective of breadth of image, the valence of the international televised image of China also has been polarized since the Olympics.

Table 4.3 Paired-samples test of topics' ratios before and after the Olympics

Paired samples	Mean	t	Sig. (2-tailed)
Negative tone	−0.114747	−2.579	0.020
Unclear tone	0.173676	4.166	0.001
Positive tone	−0.058935	−2.099	0.052

The role of the Olympics in leveraging the attribution of China's image

The concept of attribution from the inter-cultural communications literature refers to the interpretation of another behaviour (Burriss, 1988). When one involves people from the same culture, their attribution confidence increases as they discover that they share the same meanings for most behaviours (Gudykunst, 1988). In the international context, few shared meanings are found to exist and attribution confidence is low. The natural tendency is to project one's own cultural perspectives and assumptions onto the behaviour of the other. This results in misunderstandings, misperceptions and even conflict (Albert and Triandis, 1988; Rivenburgh, 1992).

The source characteristics can be selected to determine whether cross-cultural attributions are being excessively guided by a western-centred approach. Table 4.4 shows that the source 'political section' controlled and dominated the narrative about China before, during and after the Olympic Games. After the 2008 Beijing Olympics, the coverage from the political section went down sharply, while the coverage from the economic section rose. News from the sports section also declined in the third stage compared with the first stage. Therefore, the attribution of the internationally televised image of China experienced no change before and after the Olympic Games.

Conclusion

According to our case study, countries can be considered as brands. And they can leverage these brands by hosting sport events. As Go and Govers (2010) pointed out, place brand strategy probably leads to a conversation and co-creation of place identities, imagination and sustainment of a competitive place brand advantage. Such conversation and co-creation of place identities may indeed be structured as 'area brands'.

Based on the TV database of content analysis from Media Tenor International and the analysis framework of visibility, valence, breadth and attribution, this case study of the Beijing Olympic Games 2008 provides insights into the role of mega-events to leverage the brand China. This case study extends a framework of national branding to explain the change of China's image with the impacts of the Beijing Olympic Games 2008. The Olympics cannot improve the national image of China directly. It can only interest the international media in China and make the international image of China clearer after the Olympics than before.

This case study brings forward the complexity of effects of mega-events on national branding. The Beijing Olympics 2008 enhanced the visibility of China in

Table 4.4 Attribution of the internationally televised image of China in different phases

Stage/Source	8 August 2007 – 7 August 2008	8 August 2008 – 24 August 2008	25 August 2008 – 24 August 2009	Total
Editorial staff – political section	2987	815	1351	5153
Editorial staff – economic section	458	33	468	959
Editorial staff – sports section	334	327	252	913
Editorial staff –other section	160	0	1	161
Other sources	30	23	22	75

international TV media before the Opening Ceremony. But it is worthy of further study how the news coverage of mega-events can improve the brand image of the host country, and in what conditions the news coverage of mega-events cannot improve the brand image of the host country. More often than not, special events will cast a spotlight on a country without creating a sustainable image. The press departments of the host country need to provide a variety of topics even in 'good' times, in order to continuously find the media's ear. The function of mega-events for the host country is mainly to let people all around the world know and understand the country.

Using the construct of national branding, it is appropriate to question whether any sense of real understanding of this nation could be derived from the image constructed in the international media as demonstrated through an analysis of the component concepts of image visibility, valence, breadth and attribution. Although the stated intent of many segments was to reveal to audiences facets of China, the attempt to do so was both limited and shallow. The results of this study partially revealed how international media work on the image of China. It also raised some critical issues and barriers.

The results that have been presented are only based on one case study – as such they cannot be generalized. They do, however, provide insights into the contemporary phenomenon of event-related media and destination image. Further, it cannot be determined from this study whether the relationship between event-related media and change of national image of the host country is a causal one. The study was not an experiment and it must be remembered that other variables may have come into play within this context. That is to say, it is necessary to separate the influence of mega-events on national image because of the complexity of influencing factors.

Constraints on data, time and participant availability means that the study has only discussed media in nine countries. TV news in several other countries, such as Japan, Australia and India, should be taken into account in content analysis because they are not only important countries around the world, but also the big neighbouring countries to China. Further research on the change of national image with data from more countries, especially neighbouring countries, with more comprehensive techniques, is recommended.

A continued study of place image is also suggested. There is especially a need to do research on countries' public relations and discover how a country can improve its image in international news media. In addition, there is a lack of knowledge about the connection between the media image of countries and their perception among the general public. It is necessary to investigate the relation of media agenda and public agenda when considering the impact of mega-events on national image. And to what extent does a media image affect the decisions of multinational corporations and governments around the world? The answers to these questions are likely to further advance the study of national image in the international media.

References

Albert, R. D. and H. C. Triandis (1988). 'Intercultural education for multicultural societies: Critical issues' in Samovar, L. A. and R. E. Porter (eds), *Intercultural Communication: A Reader*, 5th edition. Belmont, CA: Wadsworth Publishing Co: 373–383.

Anholt, S. (2005). 'Some important distinctions in place branding'. *Place Branding*, 1 (2): 116–121.

Arthur D. and J. Andrew (1996). 'Incorporating community involvement in the management of sporting mega-events: An Australian case study'. *Festival Management and Event Tourism*, 4 (1/2): 21–28.

Avraham, E. (2000). 'Cities and their news media images'. *Cities*, 17 (5): 363–370.

Behr, R. L. and S. Iyengar (1985). 'Television news, real-world cues and changes in the public agenda'. *Public Opinion Quarterly*, 49: 38–57.

Berelson, B. (1971). *Content Analysis in Communication Research*. New York: Hafner Pub Co.

Bernstein, L. (2000). 'Things you can see from there you can't see form here – globalization, media and the Olympics'. *Journal of Sport and Social Issues*, 24 (4): 351–369.

Blay, A. K. and N. Alabi (1996). *State of the Media in West Africa 1995–1996*. Accra, Ghana: Friedrich Ebert Foundation, Ghana Office.

Brown, G., L. Chalip, L. Jago and T. Mules (2004). 'Developing brand Australia: Examining the role of events', in Morgan, N., A. Pritchard and R. Pride (eds), *Destination Branding: Creating the Unique Destination Proposition*, 2nd edition. Oxford: Butterworth-Heinemann: 279–305.

Burriss, L. L. (1988). 'Attribution in network radio news: A cross-network analysis'. *Journalism Quarterly*, 65 (3): 690–694.

Chalip, L., C. Green and B. Hill (2003). 'Effects of sport media on destination image and intentions to visit'. *Journal of Sport Management*, 17: 214–234.

Dong, X., Q. Li, Z. Shi, Y. Yu, W. Chen and Z. Ma (2005). 'Beijing Olympic Games and building national image: Subject analysis of the foreign media's reports on four Olympic holders'. *China Soft Science*, 2: 1–9.

Eisenhardt, M. K. (1989). 'Building theories from case study research'. *Academy of Management Review*, 14 (4): 532–550.

Giffard, C. A. and N. Rivenburgh (2000). 'News agencies, national images, and global media events'. *Journalism and Mass Communication Quarterly*, 77 (1): 8–21.

Go, F. and R. Govers (2010). *Place Branding*, Unpublished paper.

Gold, J. R. and S. Ward (eds) (1994). *Place Promotion: The Use of Publicity to Sell Towns and Regions*. Chichester: Wiley.

Gudykunst, W. B. (1988). 'Uncertainty and anxiety' in Kim, Y. Y. and W. B. Gudykunst (eds), *Theories in Intercultural Communication*. Newbury Park, CA: Sage Publications: 123–156.

Gunn, C. A. (1989). *Vacationscape: Designing Tourist Regions*, 2nd edition. New York: Van Nostrand Reinhold Publishers.

Hede, A. (2005). 'Sports-events, tourism and destination marketing strategies: An Australian case study of Athens 2004 and its media telecast'. *Journal of Sport Tourism*, 10 (3): 187–200.

Kavaratzis, M. and G. Ashworth (2008). 'Place marketing: How did we get here and where are we going?'. *Journal of Place Management and Development*, 1 (2): 150–165.

Kotler, P. and D. Gertner (2002). 'Country as brand, product and beyond: A place marketing and brand management perspective'. *Journal of Brand Management*, 9 (4–5): 249–261.

Lee, C., Y. Lee and B. Lee (2005). 'Korea's destination image formed by the 2002 World Cup'. *Annals of Tourism Research*, 32 (4): 839–858.

Manheim, J. B. and R. B. Albritton (1984). 'Changing national images: International public relations and media agenda setting'. *The American Political Science Review*, 78 (3–4): 641–657.

Martin, S. and I. Bosque (2008). 'Exploring the cognitive–affective nature of destination image and the role of psychological factors in its formation'. *Tourism Management*, 29: 263–277.

McManus, G. (1999). 'Making the most of mega-events'. *New Zealand Management*, 46 (2): 30–35.

Media Tenor International (2006). *Media Tenor Profile Analysis Codebook 2006*. Unpublished.

Olins, W. (2002). 'Branding the nation – The historical context'. *Journal of Brand Management*, 9 (4–5): 241–248.

Perry, D. K. (1985). 'The mass media and inference about other nations'. *Communication Research*, 12: 595–614.

Persson, C. (2002). 'The Olympic Games site decision'. *Tourism Management*, 23: 27–36.

Rivenburgh, K. N. (1992). 'National image richness in US-televised coverage of South Korea during the 1988 Olympics'. *Asian Journal of Communication*, 2 (2): 1–39.

Roche, M. (1994). 'Mega-events and urban policy'. *Annals of Tourism Research*, 21: 1–19.

Smith, A. (2005). 'Reimaging the city: The value of sports initiatives'. *Annals of Tourism Research*, 32 (1): 217–236.

Stroud, J. N. and K. Kenski (2007). 'From agenda setting to refusal setting: Survey nonresponse as a function of media coverage across the 2004 election cycle'. *Public Opinion Quarterly*, 71 (4): 539–559.

Wanta, W. and Y. Hu (1994). 'Time-lag differences in the agenda-setting process: An examination of five news media'. *International Journal of Public Opinion Research*, 6: 225–240.

Watt, J. H. and S. A. Berg (1978). 'Time series analysis of alternative media effects theories' in Brent, D. (ed.) *Communication Yearbook*, 2nd edition. New Brunswick, NJ: Transaction Books: 215–224.

Xing, X. and L. Chalip (2006). 'Effects of hosting a sport event on destination brand: A test of co-branding and match-up models'. *Sport Management Review*, 9: 49–78.

Yin, K. R. (2008). *Case Study Research: Design and Methods*. London: Sage.

Part II
Events and their experiential dimension

5 Sport events, economic impact and regulation

Wladimir Andreff

Economic globalization has spread throughout all the various markets of the sports economy during the past two decades or so. Sport mega-events have become entirely global, whether they are contests between opposing national squads, sports teams in a league or individual athletes. And any sports event may go global as soon as it is televised. In this context, some crucial relationships have been increasingly tying the media-exposed and commercialized part of the sports economy on the one hand with, on the other hand, marketing, and communication and sport management.

The first relationship is that a sports show may be viewed by a crowd of maximal size, in the range of millions or billions of spectators (in a cumulative audience), in order to provide an excellent basis for communication, marketing and sponsorship. Reaching such magnitude is only possible when a sports event is broadcast to millions of TV viewers. Televised sport that previously was a derivative product of sport attendance in a stadium or arena has become the core product while attending the event around the pitch has become a secondary product. This is obvious when one compares the relative shares of TV rights and gate receipts in the budgets of media-exposed sports contests, sports leagues and sports teams. The second relationship ties a sports event and its image with trade brands, specific products and those firms producing them. Here, not only the media-exposed character of sport is significant but, in addition, the quality of sports shows and their images sold to sponsors and spectators is absolutely crucial.

Following economic common sense, one might believe that market competition by itself would screen and select the best sports events (shows) to offer them to viewers and would provide sufficient incentive to each sports event organizer to endlessly improve the quality of its show in view of coping with competitors. An in-depth economic analysis (see later) shows that it is not so, and this opens some room for regulation. The latter is necessary to guarantee that supplied sports events are of high enough quality to attract the demand of sports fans, sports spectators,[1] sports TV viewers, sponsors and other economic agents likely to pay for sports shows.

After presenting some evidence about sports economic globalization, this chapter deals with the most significant drivers of a sports event's quality – outcome uncertainty, unpredictability, attractiveness[2] – since quality directly impacts on finding purchasers for the sports event, on product sales looked for by sponsors and, finally, on sports finance. Various regulations are at work depending on the type of sports contest (single sport or multi-sport, knock-out or round robin), its organization (in a sport league or not), revenue sharing across teams or individual athletes, recruitment and transfers of sporting talents, in particular in professional sports, and the current rules of the game prevailing in a specific sport. The real impact of regulatory tools is heavily determined by the nature of each sports event.[3] At a global level, a sport event may convene (nearly) all sports of different nations in the world (Olympic Games), all the national squads in a given sport discipline (the Soccer World Cup) or the best clubs' teams of all participating nations (UEFA Champions League). A national sport contest – though strictly domestic – can also be turned into a global event through broadcasting (for instance, the championship of major professional soccer leagues in Europe). We show, with a few examples, that there is a need for regulation with regards to the (sporting) rules of the game, financial disparities between sporting competitors, and allocation of sporting talent – labour – in the face of current issues met by the four global sport contests mentioned above.

Globalization of the sports economy

There is not such a thing as an economic accounting of sports at a world or international level (Andreff, 2010a). A 'guesstimate' of the major global sport markets is, for 2004:

- Global market for all sporting goods and services: €550–600 billion.
- Soccer global market (all goods and services related to this sport discipline): €250 billion.
- Global market for all sports goods: €150 billion.
- Overall international trade in sporting goods: US$30 billion (Andreff and Andreff, 2009).
- Global market for TV broadcasting rights of sports events: €60 billion.
- Global market for sport sponsorship: €18 billion.
- Global market for doping: €6 billion (in 2006).

Globalization of the sports economy is partly determined by the extension of paid holiday leaves and the increase in free time in most developed countries of the world economy and, more recently, in some emerging countries. The swift development of markets for leisure activities in these countries encompasses an increasing number of sports events shown as sports shows. A second tendency that has pushed the sports economy towards globalization is TV broadcasting of sports events in the past half-century, starting with Eurovision and then world broadcasts. With this trend, developed market economies ceased to be the only privileged markets for spreading sport images since an access to sport mega-contests has been made available for anyone in the world. A last significant evolution is the emergence of new information and communication technologies – from the Internet to webcam and mobile phone – thanks to which sport images can be instantly transferred to any point of the globe.

A first dimension of a globalizing sports economy is the organization of international sport mega-events. Modern Olympic Games have become more and more internationalized if we measure it by the endless increase in the number of participating countries and athletes in the past decades (Table 5.1). International sports federations have taken their share in globalizing most sport disciplines through organizing world championships. International sports contests bringing together sports clubs, such as the European soccer Champions League, have also contributed to the globalization trend. One witnesses a rapid growth in the number of international sport mega-events in the long run: the number was 20 in 1912, 315 in 1977, 660 in 1987 and 1,000 in 2005 (Bourg and Gouguet, 2005). That is about three international sports events per day on average.

When it comes to the market for sport events' TV broadcasting, it is definitely global. Global sport mega-events are broadcast in many countries: the Soccer World Cup and Summer Olympics in 220 of them, Motorcycle World Championship in 208, the whole circuit of Formula 1 Grand Prix in 206, the Athletics World Championship in 200, the Roland Garros international tennis tournament in 195, the Rugby World Cup in 180, and the cycling Tour de France in 170. The cumulative audience goes up from about 1 billion TV viewers of the Tour de France to 5 billion TV viewers of Summer Olympics, 25 to 30 billion for the Soccer World Cup, and over 50 billion for a whole Formula 1 season. TV broadcasts deepen the differentiation between sport disciplines: soccer is the most exposed to TV media (and its exposure is increasing), and this is the reason why we focus on it in the present chapter. Globalization of televised sports shows has opened up the sport sponsorship market, i.e. it is now global. Sponsors of global sport mega-events are usually multinational companies (MNCs) from the sport equipment industry and other industries. Those sports clubs regularly qualifying for European contests have transformed into MNCs as well (Andreff, 2010b).

Production of high-quality events by sports clubs, and not only by national squads, has entailed globalization of the (labour) market for high level sporting talents through an increasingly extensive process of international athletes (players) transfers. This transfer market is entirely deregulated since the Bosman case in 1995. Deregulation has spread throughout all sports and all continents due to the Malaja, Kolpak and Simutenkov cases and the Cotonou agreement (2001) between the European Union and Asian–Caribbean–Pacific (ACP) countries. In some countries, one sports discipline governing body can lose control over the transfer balance – the difference between the number of domestic players transferred abroad and the number of players transferred from abroad – as happened in French professional soccer on the eve of the 2000s. A parallel (illegal) market for teenage players (below 18) has also become global, circumventing FIFA rules adopted in 2001 that forbid player transfers below the age of 18.[4]

International transfers of techniques also happen in globalized sports. For instance, in the long run, different techniques (tactics) happened to emerge with

Table 5.1 Globalization of Summer Olympics and Soccer World Cup

Summer Olympics						Soccer World Cup			
Year	Number of countries	Number of athletes	Number of sport disciplines	TV rights (million US$)		Year	Number of countries	Cumulative audience (billion TV viewers)	TV rights (million €)
1984	140	6797	221	287		1986	109	13.5	31
1988	159	8465	237	403		1990	103	26.7	66
1992	169	9368	257	636		1994	129	32.1	77
1996	197	10310	271	898		1998	163	24.8	94
2000	199	10321	300	1332		2002	187	28.8	908
2004	202	10500	301	1493		2006	181	26.3	1048
2008	204	10942	302	1737		2010	204	26.0	2100

Sources: IOC and FIFA.

regards to how to distribute soccer players across the pitch, such as 4.2.4, then 4.3.3 and, nowadays, 4.4.2 and 4.5.1. When Brazil's national squad introduced 4.2.4 and won the Soccer World Cup, these tactics were adopted by (transferred to) other countries and eventually prevailed during the 1960s. In 1962, Brazil won the World Cup playing 4.3.3 and this technique was adopted later on by a number of teams and prevailed during the 1970s. Since then even more defensive tactics have come into being. Kuper and Szymanski (2009) show with the case of Guus Hiddink, and some other famous coaches in international soccer, how they have propagated the most elaborated technique of playing soccer[5] from big European clubs' teams where it was implemented to different countries such as South Korea, Japan, Greece, Turkey, China, Australia and Russia. All the latter countries have markedly improved their performances in global soccer thanks to this technology (know-how) transfer.

Finally, globalization of the sports economy is utilized by those who are involved in a sort of underground sports economy based on accounting and financial rigs, embezzlements, fixed matches, corruption, money laundering, etc. As more sports drift towards these bad practices, they are becoming globalized (Andreff, 1999 and 2007a). In the present chapter, we shall not stress these financial misdoings in sport that are enabled by globalization allowing the avoidance of controls. More than any other dimension of sport economic globalization this raises the issue of regulation to maintain an ethical quality of sports events.

Global sport mega-events: uncertainty, predictability, attractiveness

Global sport mega-events are now examined with regards to the building blocks on which quality is based: a) the sport contest's format and its organization are important for outcome uncertainty; b) revenue sharing is crucial for the competitive balance and athletes recruitment (thus the squads' quality); c) the rules of the game enforced in a specific sport discipline are decisive for show quality, sporting contention and scoring. Within the limits of this chapter, we cannot avoid selecting a few sport mega-events. We have retained the Summer Olympics, FIFA World Cup, UEFA Champions League and the five major national soccer leagues in Europe (England, France, Germany, Italy and Spain). All these sport mega-events contain the above-mentioned dimensions of globalization. On the other hand, they differ as regards to regulation.

The Summer Olympics is a worldwide confrontation of the best performing athletes and, de facto, of all nations in about 300 different Olympic sport disciplines.[6] This is precisely the major source of Olympics' attractiveness to (TV) spectators and sponsors as well as their multi-sport character, bringing together the most significant sport disciplines. Therefore the Olympics are sometimes used to assess the relative might of a nation (remember the political and media use of the Olympic Games by the German Democratic Republic and the Union of Soviet Socialist Republics in former times). Though outcome uncertainty is real for each participating athlete, the multi-sport character of the Games makes the nations' sporting performances rather predictable in so far as they are heavily dependent on country size (population) and level of economic development. The Summer Olympics' format combines knock-out contests and, namely in team sports, qualifying round robin stages in which each team plays all the seeded teams. In the first case, outcome uncertainty is guaranteed and evolves when a contestant is knocked out. In the second case, how the opponents are seeded (at random or oriented by a preselection of top-seeded contestants) influences outcome uncertainty, competitive balance and thus the attractiveness to spectators.

Witnessing the deep unevenness in the Olympic medals distribution between national squads exhibits that it is detrimental to developing countries. A first econometric model (Andreff, 2001) has shown that two variables are extremely significant in explaining such distribution, i.e. population and gross domestic product (GDP) per inhabitant. A standard model (Bernard and Busse, 2004) has introduced two other variables that improve the explanatory power of medal wins per nation: one is the benefit drawn from hosting the Games, the other one is the nation's political regime – in particular being a former communist country increases the number of medal wins. In a further model, we have added another variable that aims at capturing the differences in sporting culture between various regions of the world economy (Andreff *et al.*, 2008); the estimation of medal wins by nation has been further improved and this model has been able to correctly predict 88 per cent of total medal wins at Beijing Olympics (Andreff, 2009a). Thus, Summer Olympics are only 12 per cent unpredictable so they do not encompass a high outcome uncertainty for each nation. Outcome uncertainty only pertains to each athlete and each sports discipline in the Olympic Games. It is because when a number of different sports are taken together in a world contest, demographic and economic variables determine national sporting results since these variables express the economic (demographic) capacity of each country to mobilize resources to win medals.

Should one imagine a regulation that would increase the share of developing countries in the overall number of medal wins? The response is as unlikely as the question because the only radical tool would be to transform developing countries into developed and rich nations, a target that has never been reached by any regulation so far, whatever the motivation. Therefore, a competitive balanced contest is impossible at the Olympics as long as global economic development is uneven. On the other hand, it is quite normal (and in tune with Coubertin's objectives) that each country in the world must be able to participate in the Olympics even if it has no chance of winning even one medal. Some of the least advanced and poorest countries even lack the economic resources necessary to participate in the Games. They usually receive financial assistance from IOC's Olympic Solidarity and may benefit from an invitation if none of their athletes has reached the required minimal performance to qualify for the Olympics. Such regulation aims at levelling the chances of all countries of participating in the Summer Olympics but it remains without any effect on the concentration of medal wins on about 40 countries, the most developed and a few emerging ones. Other regulations (Chappelet and Kübler-Mabbott, 2008) have the purpose of guaranteeing that Olympic Games operate exactly under the conditions foreseen with regards to the relationships between athletes and their national federations (the Court of Arbitration for Sport; CAS), anti-doping tests (the World Anti-Doping Agency), and preserving the Games ethics (the IOC Ethics Commission[7]). If one regulation is really missing in the Olympics, it is to be looked for in the area of athletes' transfers (40 per cent of the cases dealt with by CAS) and their naturalization (see later).

The FIFA Soccer World Cup is the archetype of mono-sport world cups and championships bringing together national squads. It starts with a qualifying knock-out stage within each of FIFA's geographical zones (UEFA, CONMEBOL (the South American Football Confederation), CONCACAF (Confederation of North, Central American and Caribbean Association Football), etc.). Then teams are convened into seeded groups during the first round of the final tournament where each team plays all other seeded teams in the group. From the last 16 on, qualification is obtained through knock-out games. FIFA organizes group seeding in such a way that major favourites (potential finals' winners) do not meet, the favourites being the top seeds. It has been demonstrated (Monk and Husch, 2009) that being top seeds improves a team's sporting results – its ranking gains 5 places on average in the ranking of all the 32 teams participating in the final tournament (the winner is ranked 1, the finalist 2, and the other teams according to their relative performance down to 32). Thus, the format of Soccer World Cups diminishes the competitive balance of the first round seeded groups in order to augment outcome uncertainty in further games, which must be more balanced between the favourites in a second (knock-out) round of the final tournament. However, this does not exclude some surprises (surprising sporting results) such as France and Italy's early elimination during the first round of the 2010 World Cup.

Despite the deliberately unbalanced seeded groups, The Soccer World Cup delivers more uncertain outcomes and contains more surprising results than the Olympic Games (Torgler, 2004; Paul and Mitra, 2008). We have recently verified this empirical evidence for the 2010 Soccer World Cup (Andreff and Andreff, 2010). A prediction model derived from our econometric estimation of the determinants of making it to the semi-finals has not performed well – correctly predicting only two semi-finalists out of four.[8] Two basic reasons for such lower predictability compared with the Olympics are: a) for a nation, there is the possible compensation of unexpected Olympic medal 'losses' in some sporting disciplines and unexpected medal wins in other disciplines, a reality that is often observed for major sporting nations; this is not possible with FIFA World Cup since it is a mono-sport contest; b) the performances of a national squad in the world championship of a single sport discipline are not – or not primarily – determined by economic variables. A country may allocate all its economic and human resources to only one sport, for instance soccer (or any other sport discipline) while another country may allocate no resource to soccer, independently from its level of economic development, population or political regime. Here, a country's sports policy has a significant impact, though it has not been empirically (econometrically) tested by economists[9] so far.

Apart from the FIFA division into geographical zones, the choice of top seeded nations and a not exactly random distribution of nations across the seeded groups for the second round of the final tournament, does Soccer World Cup call for more regulation? A priori, it does not seem to be the case since its sporting outcomes are rather uncertain and unpredictable due to a good number of surprising (unexpected) results, which contribute to the higher TV attractiveness of Soccer World Cup than the Summer Olympics. In the last World Cups, the qualification of African and Asian national squads for the second round of the final tournament demonstrates an improving competitive balance that is not only due to new geographical rules of allocating the Cup to different hosting continents (it is not South Africa, the host country, but Ghana that qualified for the second round in 2010).

Regulation issues are to be found elsewhere as regards to FIFA World Cup: do national squads succeed in having their selected players released by foreign clubs after their transfer on the international labour market for soccer players? Even though all (including foreign) clubs are compelled by FIFA rules to release players selected in a national squad, it is not always that easy. Are the players released by the clubs for free, or at what rate? Is the authenticity of a sport contest opposing national squads consistent with a mass selection of naturalized players? For example, there is no one original Qatari in Qatar's soccer squad, only naturalized neo-Qataris from Brazilian, Moroccan, African, etc., origins.[10] Since international athlete transfers and naturalizations are issues that go far beyond the case of the Soccer World Cup, the question of how to regulate the labour market (and nationality) for athletes is discussed further below.

The European Soccer Champions League has the same contest format as the Soccer World Cup, starting with a qualifying knock-out stage, then a seeded groups stage and finally qualification through home and away knock-out games. It is even more attractive to TV viewers over a whole season.[11] However, the two sports events are different as far as regulation is concerned as the Champions League is a contest of opposing sports clubs' teams and not national squads. After the Bosman case, there are no longer nationality rules enforced on players fielded in the teams participating in the Champions League, which is not as concerned as much as the Soccer World Cup with the effects of international player transfers and naturalizations. In 2008, among the players involved in the Champions League, 107 were Brazilian, 34 Argentine, 72 French (but not all registered in French clubs) … and only 30 English despite the domination of English Premier League teams (including the winner, Manchester United) over the Champions League.

Static outcome uncertainty related to each game as well as to the whole season is rather comparable or slightly higher in the Champions League when compared to the rugby Heineken Cup and the men's and women's basketball Euro leagues (Scelles, 2009). On the other hand, in a dynamic perspective of the whole Champions League existence, the chance of unpredictable results are not very high. Since 1993, four clubs have won the Champions League ten times over the past 18 years: Manchester United, Real Madrid, FC Barcelona and AC Milan. They have 56 per cent of all possible wins. Three of them are the three richest soccer clubs in the world (Manchester United, Real Madrid and AC Milan) and FC Barcelona is the seventh richest. Other indexes confirm the high concentration of participation by a few teams. From 1999 to 2007, two clubs from the English Premier League (Manchester United and Arsenal) have participated nine times each in the Champions League, two others (Chelsea and Liverpool) six times; three Spanish clubs have participated respectively nine times (Real Madrid), eight times (FC Barcelona) and six times (Valencia); in Italy, AC Milan eight times, Juventus and Inter Milan six times; in the *Bundesliga*, Bayern Munich eight times and in French *Ligue* 1, Olympique Lyonnais eight times. Moreover, 80 per cent of clubs participating in the Champions League are the same from one season to the next, which turns it into a somewhat quasi-closed league in practice though it is an open league (see below) on institutional grounds.

Given the redistribution rules of TV rights revenues between participants in the Champions League,[12] each year the richest European clubs receive revenues from UEFA that further increase the financial gap between them and less rich clubs.[13] Financial gains drawn each year from the Champions League by Manchester United, Arsenal, Chelsea, Liverpool, Real Madrid, FC Barcelona, Valencia, FC Sevilla, AC Milan, Inter Milan, Juventus, AS Rome, Bayern Munich, Werder Brême, Schalke 04, Olympique Lyonnais, FC Porto, PSV Eindhoven are in the range of 20 to 50 million euros. This entails a virtuous circle for these rich clubs: they can recruit more, thus improve their chance of qualifying again for the Champions League next season, therefore becoming even richer and again recruiting more and more, and so on and so forth. But for the majority of European clubs, this translates into a vicious circle of no qualification for the Champions League, less revenue increase and less recruitment (Andreff, 2009a).

Thus, two issues call for possible additional regulation: a) financial revenue concentration on a few clubs has become the clear determinant of Champions League's sporting outcomes, and the wealth unevenness between European clubs is a concern so that it does not destroy outcome uncertainty at the end of the day; b) clubs' good performances in the Champions League deteriorate competitive balance in national leagues, deepen financial inequalities and, therefore, the more unbalanced a national league the higher the chance for its top clubs to perform well in Champions League again and again (Andreff and Bourg, 2006). The big five – those usually best ranked clubs – together receive 50 per cent of English Premier League revenues and 10 per cent of all revenues distributed by the Champions League. A similar concentration is observed in smaller leagues such as in Belgium and Portugal (Gouguet and Primault, 2008). The French *Ligue* 1 is the most balanced among the five biggest national European soccer leagues because the French clubs (Lyon aside) are not winning so much at the European level of soccer contest. Thus they do not earn those financial gains that would enable them to continuously dominate their national championship. How far will TV viewers follow this leap forward in the financial concentration of sporting wins? A regulation that the Champions League urgently needs pertains more to clubs' finance than to sporting issues per se, namely because of the Champions League financial interference with national leagues.

Box 5.1 North American closed leagues

Institutional rules that fix how major professional team sports leagues such as the MLB, NFL, NBA and NHL are organized, regulated and managed can be encapsulated in 11 'stylized facts' (Szymanski, 2003; Andreff, 2007b):

1   A North American professional team sports league is an independent organization and it is *closed* by an entry barrier created by franchise sales. Entry in a closed league is only possible by purchasing an expansion franchise, when the new team's market and its assigned location are assessed profitable by the league commissioner. Moreover entry in the league cartel must be voted by a qualified majority of incumbent teams.

2   In a closed major league the number and identity of teams are fixed. There is no economic competition through entry and exit in the league (industry). A bottom-up route from a lower to a higher league (division) cannot happen in a closed league system since the major league is closed downwards; a top-down route to lower divisions cannot either. The only competitive threat that a closed league may face comes from the creation of a rival major league in the same sport by club owners disappointed with the entry barrier in the existing league. Thirteen rival leagues have emerged since the inception of the four North American major leagues, seven to compete against NFL, three against MLB, two against NBA and one against NHL. The US Congress usually facilitates, after some years of economic competition between two major leagues, their merger into a new league exempted from anti-trust law enforcement.

3   In a closed league, a team enjoys absolute exclusivity over an urban area where it is the only one (in a given professional sport) allowed to organize major league's games. Thus each team has a monopoly on the local market for its sports shows. If the local market ceases to be profitable, a team can move to another urban area with the league's agreement. From their inception up to 2005, 48 team relocations have occurred in the four North American major leagues (7 in NFL, 9 in NHL, 12 in MLB and 20 in NBA). Thus, club mobility is horizontal and geographical and not vertical between higher and lower divisions as in European leagues.

4   Competitive balance is looked for through labour market regulation. A closed league can restrict recruitment rules and players' labour mobility since it enjoys a monopoly in the labour market for talent. This occurred for the first time in baseball as early as 1879 when a reserve clause was introduced to prohibit any player moving from one team without the team owner's agreement. Since the 1970s, after several labour conflicts (strikes and lockouts), veterans have obtained a free agent status that prevails after a defined number of years playing

in a major league. However, newcomers (young and foreign players) in the league are picked up from a rookie draft on which experts rank them according to their sporting performance.

5 A rookie draft also functions as a reverse-order-of-finish draft. Thus, professional team sports is the only industry in North America where firms (teams) have a restricted right to choose who they will hire. Team owners in North American major leagues argue that such restriction is a must for balancing team sports contests. Hiring players is also quantitatively restricted by roster limits.

6 Player mobility in closed leagues is all the more limited in that trading for cash is restricted or forbidden (since 1960 in NFL and 1976 in MLB), especially for superstars. Inter-team player transfers are not so frequent, so team competition for hiring the same player is practically nil.

7 Player working conditions and salaries result from collective bargaining between club owners and player trade unions in closed leagues. Some leagues (NBA 1983, NFL 1994) have succeeded in negotiating a salary cap, which is advocated by club owners as a means to avoid superstar concentration in rich teams and to maintain competitive balance. But it is also a lever for keeping a league monopoly over the labour market as the reserve clause has been abandoned. A luxury tax completes this payroll regulation in some leagues.

8 Pooling TV rights sales at the league level with revenue redistribution across teams is common practice in closed leagues. A monopoly is thus ensured in the league on the market for its derived product, i.e. televised sport. Professional team sports are the only US industry where such cartel behaviour is exempted from anti-trust law enforcement since the enactment of the Sports Broadcasting Act (1961). Revenues obtained from gate receipts, sponsorship and merchandising are also pooled and redistributed. Local TV revenues are the only exception to pooling and redistribution.

9 Most American sports teams are not stockholding companies whose shares are floated on the stock exchange. Flotation is even absolutely forbidden in NFL. Club owners do not want to be exposed to the risk of being merged or acquired by an outsider on the stock market (another entry barrier in a closed league).

10 Being a cartel of teams, a closed league maximizes its profit and shares it across teams. Thus it is assumed that the objective function of North American professional sports teams is profit maximization. When a team is no longer in the race for play-offs, this financial objective eventually prevails over winning games.

11 Due to profit maximization in closed leagues, investment in sporting talent is only undertaken if it increases revenues more than costs. Small market teams lack profit incentives to build up competitive teams that will maximize league revenues; this justifies big market teams subsidizing small market teams.

Regulation of sports events organized into a professional league

Renown and TV audience in North American major leagues of professional sports spread far beyond the US and Canada geographical territory: their games are broadcast in many countries in the world. This is also seen with some European professional sports leagues, namely: the English Premier League, the Spanish *Liga de Futbol*, the Italian *Lega Calcio*, the German *Bundesliga* and the French *Ligue* 1. An economic theory of professional team sports leagues sheds some light on regulation issues. This theory has been encapsulated in a Walrasian equilibrium model since El Hodiri and Quirk (1971) with regards to North American closed leagues (see Box 5.1). Here we look at the question of how the theory has been adapted to European open leagues, such as the five leagues mentioned above.

The organization of an open league in European professional team sports leagues, such as in soccer, can be described with 11 'stylised facts' (Szymanski, 2003; Andreff, 2007b):

1   In European sport, a professional league is usually integrated into a global hierarchy of governance with an international sports federation at the top, and a national sports federation in each country. Most international federations forbid the creation of more than one major league in a same sport in the same country.
2   Competition results from the league being open each year to the entry of new clubs thanks to a system of promoting the winners and relegating the losers. Club mobility is not geographic but vertical along with the hierarchy (between upper and lower divisions). It depends on a club's sporting performances. A club created in the lowest amateur division can, due to its wins, climb the ladder up to the premier league and then qualify for a European level contest, if there is a local will to finance such a rise. Entry is free without paying for a franchise. Entering clubs must show financial guarantees. The exit of a number of clubs identical to the number of entering clubs keeps a constant number of clubs participating in the league's championship, but the identity of clubs (those promoted and relegated) changes from one season to the other.
3   Relegating the weakest clubs and replacing them with the strongest clubs from the lower league, the open league system operates as an automatic, though limited, rebalancing mechanism of the sporting strengths. It also functions as an incentive mechanism. Clubs engage very strong efforts to avoid the sanction (relegation) or to be rewarded (promotion, European qualification) in games with a high contention regarding the club's future in the next season. There are many fewer games without contention than in the American closed leagues. It only happens when two middle-ranked teams (the championship's 'soft belly') play each other without having promotion or relegation prospects any longer.
4   There is neither territorial exclusivity nor local monopoly of each club on its market within the league.
5   A life-long labour contract, until 1968, then a reservation system with player transfer at expiry date, restricted players' contracting freedom and mobility.

In 1995, the Bosman case phased out any restriction to players' free choice on the labour market in order to comply with the Rome Treaty, which ensures free worker circulation within the European Union. Players/club owners' relationships are now ruled as fixed duration labour contracts that provide a temporary stability to the clubs' manpower over a whole season as a counterpart for players' contracting freedom. In an open league there is no such thing as a rookie draft or roster limits. Moreover, the Bosman case has phased out the quotas of national players (6 out of 11 in 1995 in soccer) that each club had to comply with in fielding its team in official sport contests; it phased out any limitation with regards to the number of recruited players as well. Player transfers are paid cash; barter or player lending are not used very much.

6   Deregulation of the labour market has triggered high player mobility, in particular as regards to superstars. Players are transferred from a major or minor league in a country to any league in another country. Team sports leagues argue that sport is an exception (a very specific industry), and not that much about competitive balance requirement, in view of avoiding the European competition (anti-trust) policy; the outcome of such bargaining is much less successful than the anti-trust exemption obtained by American leagues so far.

7   Player unionization is less developed than in American leagues. Collective bargaining is less elaborate; salary caps are not common practice, with the exception of English soccer in 1900–1961 (Szymanski and Kuypers, 1999).

8   TV rights sales are pooled at the national level in European open leagues with TV rights revenues redistribution across clubs. Since European leagues do not benefit from an anti-trust exemption, they are exposed to pressure from big clubs (and sometimes are sued in court by clubs) willing to obtain the individual property of their TV rights. The latter has been granted to soccer clubs in Greece, Italy, Portugal and Spain. In other European soccer leagues, redistribution criteria applied to TV rights have evolved; the even redistribution across clubs has shrunk to the benefit of a revenue sharing indexed on sporting results and media coverage of each club (Andreff and Bourg, 2006). There is no longer any sharing of gate receipts between home and visitor clubs in European soccer leagues.

9   There is no restriction in initial public offerings of a club's shares. The last European country that phased out a prohibition to float club shares at the stock exchange was France (Aglietta *et al.*, 2008). However, clubs are financially independent and accountable for carrying out their budget.

10 Since clubs are aiming at promotion or avoiding relegation, their objective is (sporting) win maximization under a budget constraint. Compared to a closed league with profit-maximizing clubs, the incentive to invest in sporting talent is stronger and would be infinite without the budget constraint. Resulting over-investment in talent drives European clubs to recruit a larger number of players than needed and more than American teams who have quantitative restrictions (rosters).

11   The promotion/relegation system and win maximization pave the way to a clubs' arms race (Sanderson, 2002) in which each club attempts to recruit the best players on the eve of season in order to improve its relative situation compared with its opponents; in turn, the latter are incited to overbid. Thus, each club's demand for talent is excessive because all clubs aim at winning the same sports contest. However, investing in additional player recruitment is not efficient when a club attempts by all allowed means to have an advantage over its opponents because, consequently, all clubs are then forced to behave the same way in order to remain competitive. Such investment is socially efficient only if absolute quality (and not relative quality as in a game between two teams) considerations prevail (Lazear and Rosen, 1981). There are only a few winners (promoted clubs, those qualifying in a European level contest) in the arms race while cost increases – wage and transfer fee inflation – are all the more generalized across all clubs and so they are not slowed down by profit maximization.

El Hodiri and Quirk (1971) used a two-team Walrasian model of economic equilibrium demonstrating that levelling off sporting strengths is not compatible with teams' profit maximization (in a closed league). The crucial assumption here is that each player 'contains' a given number of talent units, a bigger one for superstars than other players. A quantity of talent units translates into a win percentage that, for each team, also depends on those talents acquired by opponent teams. If one assumes a fixed talent supply (Fort and Quirk, 1995), team owners internalize the following externality: if they recruit one more talent unit, this will make one talent unit less available for the other team in the league and such a competitive imbalance will reduce overall the league's revenues. Under these assumptions, each team recruits talents until the marginal revenue of talent unit is equal to its marginal cost and to an exogenous equilibrium unit wage. In equilibrium, the big (market) team recruits more talent than the small (market) team and competitive balance is unbalanced. *Economic equilibrium generates competitive imbalance* in a closed league. If there is not a sufficient degree of competitive balance, sports fans will have no interest in the league's championship. Thus, team owners' excuse for claiming recruitment restriction in order to reduce competitive imbalance is not entirely without foundation. However, from their monopoly on the labour market comes player exploitation by team owners.

Therefore, in a closed league, a major rationale for introducing regulations is to come closer to competitive balance. Revenue redistribution across teams, whether based on sharing gate receipts or TV rights redistribution, aims at filling the gap between sporting forces and ensuring the financial viability of small teams, but it lowers equilibrium wage and deprives big teams of incentives to invest in talent. A salary cap makes talent distribution less uneven across teams, lowers the wage level and increases owners' profit. Wage losses resulting from a salary cap are bigger than profit increases because the new economic equilibrium diverges from the market equilibrium that maximizes profit (Késenne, 2007). It follows that a salary cap lowers overall league revenues.

Table 5.2 Competitive balance (Noll-Scully index*) in major American leagues and in the five major European soccer leagues, 1966/1967–2005/2006

League	1966/67– 1975/76	1976/77– 1985/86	1986/87– 1995/96	1996/97– 2005/06	Mean 1966/2006
North American leagues					
NFL	1.70	1.51	1.48	1.54	1.56
MLB	1.78	1.81	1.62	1.90	1.78
NBA	2.71	2.43	2.96	2.77	2.72
NHL	2.42	2.32	1.82	1.74	2.08
European soccer leagues					
Premier League (England)	1.44	1.46	1.44	1.61	1.49
Ligue 1 (France)	1.22	1.45	1.30	1.30	1.32
Bundesliga (Germany)	1.26	1.45	1.35	1.46	1.38
Lega Calcio (Italy)	1.46	1.39	1.54	1.67	1.51
Liga de Futbol (Spain)	1.21	1.33	1.47	1.38	1.35

*The Noll-Scully index, $NS = \sigma / (0.5 / \sqrt{N})$, is defined as the ratio between the observed standard deviation of win percentages $\sigma = \sqrt{\Sigma i (v_i - 0.5)2}$ and the standard deviation of a theoretical perfectly balanced league (binomial distribution with an independent win probability of 0.5 in all games), which is $(0.5 / \sqrt{N})$, where N is the number of games played by each team. The closer NS is to 1, the more balanced is the league.
Source: Kringstad and Gerrard, 2007.

Among the gathered empirical evidence, some real facts do not validate this theoretical model of a closed team sports league. The most unbalanced among the four major North American leagues, i.e. NBA, is also the one with the highest attendance growth. Wide revenue sharing maintains, or even improves, competitive balance in the least balanced league, i.e. NFL (Vrooman, 1995). Among the 14 studies devoted to outcome uncertainty as an attendance determinant applied to American closed leagues, only 8 of them confirm the model's assumptions (Borland and Macdonald, 2003). The most paradoxical empirical result is provided by a comparison between North American and European leagues. Being less regulated the latter seem to be closer to idealized economic competition. Thus they should be more unbalanced than American leagues. Table 5.2 shows the contrary. The notion of competitive balance, which is constantly used to justify restrictions to economic competition in the US sports industry when leagues are sued in court (in anti-trust cases), is not necessarily a good tool to study European soccer.

In open leagues, financial deficits lasting over several seasons are proof that European soccer club owners do not maximize profit; club owners could simply stop deficits by leaving this industry but they most often stay in. The previous model has been adapted to open leagues (Késenne, 1996, 2000) with the assumption that clubs maximize their number of wins (or their win percentage) and that they recruit as many talents as possible, given their budget constraint, in a deregulated labour market where entry of new players is entirely free. Under such conditions, a club's demand for talent that maximizes wins is *higher* than the one of a profit maximizing team, its recruitment expenditure is higher – to recruit more talents – equilibrium wage is higher and competitive imbalance is greater. If small clubs have a small budget and are less endowed with talent, then *revenue redistribution improves the competitive balance*. Revenue sharing enhances equilibrium wage as compared to a situation without revenue redistribution. Players benefit from revenue sharing in an open league.

Beyond the theoretical model, now we are going to illustrate the possible effect of changing the sporting, financial and recruitment rules of the game in the four sports contests selected above.

Regulation through changing sporting rules: an example

The tendency to develop defensive tactics in soccer translates into an increasing proportion of low goal scoring, such as 0-0 and 1-0 scores (Alavy *et al.*, 2010; Andreff and Raballand, 2011). The ratio between low scoring games and high scoring ones (four or more goals scored in a game) increases in the five major European soccer leagues, except *Bundesliga*; such evolution is markedly witnessed in French *Ligue* 1, the league with the best index of competitive balance. In this trend, the average number of scored goals in soccer leagues tends to decline. Besides, an increasing share of goals is scored after free kicks, i.e. on a referee decision – 30 per cent in *Ligue* 1 in 2006–2007. The percentage was identical in the final tournament of the 1998 Soccer World Cup. The article by Alavy *et al.* (2010) empirically tests that 0-0 draws attract less TV viewers than 1-0 scores in the English Premier League. Andreff and Raballand (2011) have tested that the percentage of 0-0 and 1-0 scores are two significant variables that explain competitive balance and club standings. Moreover, low scoring also influences the attractiveness of the sport contest to spectators: French *Ligue* 1 has the smallest attendance and the lowest scores while *Bundesliga*, the most attended league, has the least low scores. The number of scored goals is an important component of game quality for attracting fans and spectators, a dimension that Besson (2008) reports about French clubs' competitiveness that has been neglected.

However, such a proportion of low scores are rather astonishing after FIFA has modified, since the 1995–1996 season, the sporting rule that rewards a win with 3 instead of 2 points. The objectives of the new regulation were to augment the number of scored goals per game, obtain less draws and more interesting and attractive games. The observed rise in low scores seems to reveal that the new regulation has not been sufficient. Some empirical testing has shown that the rule change has resulted in an increase in the number of draws (Aylott and Aylott, 2007), a decrease in the number of 0-0 draws, though not significant (Dilger and Geyer, 2009), a fall in the average number of scored goals (Amann *et al.*, 2004) and in the number of attacks on the pitch (Hundsdoerfer, 2004). Garicano and Palacios-Huerta (2006) have tested that the 3 points rule has triggered a decline in the number of games with at least a two goal difference, has pushed up the number of goals scored on free kicks and the number of games won with a one goal difference, as well as the number of yellow cards and the incentive to unfair play, all of which reduce fans' and spectators' interest. A theoretical explanation, based on game theory, of why the 3 points rule has been counter-productive is provided in Brocas and Carrillo (2004).

The debate is still open with regards to other rules that are likely to stimulate scoring and soccer attractiveness. There is the suggestion in Andreff and Raballand (2011) of reducing promotion–relegation to just one club in French *Ligue* 1, giving up the offside rule outside the penalty box, introducing a temporary player exclusion after a foul (as in rugby and ice hockey) and, first of all, changing the reward of sport performances as follows: 3 points for a win, 1 point for a draw, ½ point for a 0-0 draw and 0 point for a loss.

Financial regulation of sport contests

In sport leagues, the majority of regulation comes through revenue redistribution. The Champions League also redistributes financial gains according to equity, sporting results and TV audience criteria. Revenue sharing rules in the Soccer World Cup introduce a financial threshold in favour of those teams that make it to the semi-finals (Coupé, 2007). Each team participating in the final received (in 2006) €3.79 million; qualifying in the last 16 yielded €1.59 million more and the the the quarter-finals an additional €1.90 million. On the other hand, a significant financial jump is associated with getting to the semi-finals, up to an additional €6.33 million, followed with only €6.3 million extra for getting to the finals and €1.27 million for winning it.

Financial regulation raises three issues nowadays with regards to knowing whether: a) revenue sharing in soccer leagues improves competitive balance; b) league regulation encourages a club's financial management to be more balanced; c) the Champions League can be more balanced in order to reduce its unbalancing impact on national leagues.

In European soccer, fan attendance is not highly correlated with club standing in the championship (Table 5.3).[14] Gini coefficients show that attendance distribution across clubs is more uneven in Italian and Spanish leagues. Several studies have found a significant relationship *between the degree of competitive imbalance and disparities in clubs' financial wealth* within each national soccer league as far as overall revenues and payrolls are concerned (Szymanski and Kuypers, 1999; Andreff and Bourg, 2006; Gerrard, 2006). A semi-logarithmic regression of the two latter variables over clubs' standing exhibits a high correlation coefficient in English and French leagues (Table 5.3). The popular belief in the 'glorious sport outcome uncertainty' is moving back in European soccer. Sporting results are increasingly determined by club revenues and payroll expenditures.

Each national league is willing to have its best clubs get to the Champions League and favours a (promotion/relegation) system that selects the best teams. Thus, the league leaves financial and sporting disparities deepening in its national championship. Big clubs soon became aware that competitive imbalance is of interest to them. The winner of a small European soccer league, if it wants to do well in the Champions League, must be 'much too strong' within its national

Table 5.3 Financial disparities and ranking in European soccer
A semi-log regression of clubs' economic variables on   clubs' rankings (value of R², determination coefficient)

| Season | Attendances | | | | |
	Germany	England	Spain	France	Italy
2004/05	0.05	0.38	0.58	0.02	0.25
2005/06	0.21	0.34	0.42	0.24	0.55
2006/07	0.23	0.23	0.25	0.07	0.28
2007/08	0.28	0.35	n.d.	0.10	0.53

| Season | Revenues | | Payrolls | |
	England	France	England	France
2002/03	0.62	0.61	0.60	0.83
2003/04	0.52	0.81	0.47	0.82
2004/05	0.56	0.78	0.39	0.76
2005/06	0.63	0.83	0.56	0.81
2006/07	0.67	0.82	0.57	0.82

B Gini coefficient of the economic variables distribution

| Season | Attendances | | | | |
	Germany	England	Spain	France	Italy
2004/05	0.26	0.18	0.30	0.25	0.31
2005/06	0.21	0.19	0.30	0.27	0.35
2006/07	0.24	0.22	0.31	0.27	0.36
2007/08	0.24	0.21	n.d.	0.27	0.26

| Season | Revenues | | Payrolls | |
	England	France	England	France
2002/03	0.40		0.32	
2003/04	0.38	0.32	0.36	0.31
2004/05	0.39	0.29	0.36	0.29
2005/06	0.36	0.25	0.33	0.26
2006/07	0.35	0.25	0.28	0.30

Source: Andreff, 2009b.

championship. Those well ranked clubs in the most imbalanced leagues in Europe indeed concentrate the majority of wins in European level contests.

On the other hand, one observes that European soccer clubs do not strictly comply with a balanced budget constraint, including French clubs in *Ligue* 1 (Andreff, 2007c). Clubs go on developing their activity despite the fact that they are not able to balance their financial accounts. This means that their budget constraint is not effective due to a continuous bailing out process sustained by financiers who accept losing their money in soccer. With recurrent bail-outs emerges a serious corporate governance issue in soccer clubs. The arms race for recruiting superstars translates into wage and transfer fee inflation while a club will only know at the end of season if its recruitment strategy has been sensible and has accrued enough *ex post* revenues to cover the *ex ante* payroll expenditures. Therefore, good club governance is always a difficult exercise. A lax solution is to endlessly find money providers ready to fill the gap between expenditures and revenues. Such a strategy, which aims at softening clubs' budget constraint, is more easily managed at the league level since the league has a monopoly on the supply side of the market for soccer broadcasting rights. So, a crucial issue for a soccer league is to facilitate or restore the financial balance of those clubs who are incited to develop an excess demand for players on a global, entirely liberalized market for talent.

Ascari and Gagnepain (2006) report, regarding big Spanish soccer clubs, that club owners know that Catalan and Castillan banks are always willing to cover huge financial losses of FC Barcelona and Real Madrid, who they consider genuine national institutions. Bankruptcy of these clubs cannot simply be envisaged and has no chance of occurring. Italian soccer benefits from a central authorities' tolerance towards bad practices in clubs' financial management (Baroncelli and Lago, 2006). Clubs' budget constraints are continuously softened by local authorities and/or patrons, lax bankers and shareholding fans. It is not surprising that most European soccer leagues and a non-negligible number of soccer clubs muddle through a financial crisis.[15] That is the reason why an alternative to a hardly enforced financial discipline in open leagues is often mentioned: introduce the same regulations (salary cap, luxury tax, rookie draft) as in closed leagues ... but this would only be an efficient solution if the open league system is entirely transformed into a closed league system (giving up the promotion–relegation system, introducing a payment to enter the league, etc.).

French *Ligue* 1 and its clubs have overcome the financial crisis of European soccer with second best sporting outcomes and rather honourable financial results (Andreff, 2007d). French *Ligue du Football Professionnel* would like to promote its reputation as the best governed league in Europe and to extend its supervision tools over the clubs to all European soccer. The French league is sometimes considered as an exception to the financial crisis (Gouguet and Primault, 2006) thanks to its *Direction nationale de contrôle de gestion* (DNCG), which, since 1990, is a body that has been auditing French clubs' financial accounts. Despite this auditing, several French clubs remain stuck with repeated current deficits and debts in the long run. Three quarters of French *Ligue* 1's debt are in the form of payment arrears to suppliers, tax arrears and delayed social contribution payments. The very existence of payment arrears is a well-known index of bad corporate governance: *there is no such thing as a French exception* in spite of DNCG supervision. So, outside France and namely in England, financial regulation based on a European equivalent of DNCG is not sufficiently convincing.

We have successfully completed to a successful econometrical testing (Andreff, 2009b) of a *vicious circle* in which the league – in a monopoly situation – negotiates the highest possible TV broadcasting rights in order to finance *ex post* unhandled payroll inflation (and superstars' recruitment) and sustain the finance of those clubs in the red. Despite DNCG supervision, bad governance is found in some French soccer clubs, as in a number of European clubs, because their recruitment strategy does not translate with certainty into a productivity increase in terms of sporting wins in national and European level contests, which would have been necessary to inflate the clubs' revenues. The league then has to renegotiate higher TV broadcasting rights again and again to cover the clubs' deficits, and so on and so forth.

When it comes to the Champions League, it has adopted for the 2004–2005 season a system of licensing of those clubs participating in its contests with the following preconditions. To obtain a licence, a club must provide financial accounts supervised by an auditing body and prove that there are no payment arrears and no wage arrears still to be paid. Since the 2006–2007 season, the regulation has been strengthened: a club must exhibit a business plan showing its capacity to cover its liquidity needs as long as the licence is valid, provide a declaration in case of insufficient liquidity and how it envisages to manage this problem, as well as notification in the case of current discrepancies between actual and foreseen budget and profits/losses account if it happens to occur during the licence validity. So far, such a more demanding scheme has not succeeded in restoring a better Champions League competitive balance. Thus, time is ripe for new 'financial fair play' that UEFA would like to implement: clubs with a current debt in excess of €45 million would be forbidden – and would not qualify for – participation in UEFA organized sports contests. The underlying idea is that financial disparities between participating clubs and the resulting competitive balance deterioration should not be fuelled by too lax financial management of big European clubs, relying on their capacity to endlessly find bail-outs. The question is open as to whether such financial fair play regulation could realistically be enforced if it would deprive the Champions League of the participation of the big four English soccer clubs, Real Madrid, AC Milan and other prestigious clubs.

Deregulation of the global (labour) market for sporting talent

Among the various impacts of post-Bosman deregulation of the global market for sporting talent, one observes a swift increase in the number of migrant players from Eastern Europe, South America, Africa and Asia toward European soccer leagues, in particular the five major European leagues. Frick (2009) has tested that the playing time of 'local players' (those who are not migrants) has diminished but without improving competitive balance in either import-players' or export-players' championships. Indeed, labour market deregulation has accelerated international player mobility but has not – contrary to the expectations of liberal economists (favourable to deregulation) – better balanced sporting forces in different national leagues. This evidence confirms economic analyses (Andreff

2001, 2004, 2010d) that have depicted the Bosman case's impact, for those clubs that cannot afford to pay for European superstars, which consists in buying a less costly substitute to star players, i.e. importing players from developing countries. Less rich clubs prefer to transfer minor players (below 18) who are destined to become the new potential stars after some months or years playing in the team. When they succeed, they are transferred to richer clubs. This phenomenon is well documented in an Italian Senate report for *Lega Calcio* clubs, in the Donzel (1999) report regarding French football and, more generally, in a book by Tshimanga Bakadiababu (2001). An acceleration of the 'muscle drain' (by analogy with the brain drain) of footballers from developing countries toward European soccer championships has ensued.

Most players transferred from developing countries, particularly from Africa, do not sign any labour contract when leaving their home country, family and friends without any revenue source or financial aid. The market for teenage players below 18 has been coined a 'market for slaves', 'children trade' or 'human beings trafficking'. Some young African players have sued professional clubs and/or players' agents in the courts because, after being (unsuccessfully) tested, they have been given up by both the clubs and players' agents. As they were minors, without any labour contract and a prepaid return flight ticket to their home country, they had de facto become illegal migrant workers. Moreover, this muscle drain diverts abroad those most talented sportsmen and women, that is the tiny minority that have been lucky enough to benefit from the few coaches and small amount of sport infrastructure available in their developing home country. It also substantially reduces the home country's capacity to best use its talented footballers in international contests.

After the European Union realized the lasting situation of the muscle drain, a new regulation of soccer players' transfers was adopted by FIFA and started to be enforced as of 1 September 2001. It encompasses a clause protecting teenage players and forbidding their international transfer below the age of 18. The FIFA 2001 regulation is definitely a step in the right direction (Gerrard, 2002). However, though illegal now, teenage player transfers went on after 2001, a sign that FIFA rules are circumvented by some professional clubs, players' agents and players' families. With the FIFA regulation all transfers below the age of 18 are forbidden from all regions in the world except within the EU; this prohibition does not yield even a cent of revenue to the developing home country. On the other hand, FIFA rules entirely block (if strictly enforced and supervised) the functioning of a market mechanism and reduce teenage player mobility, from outside the EU, to exactly zero. As with any absolute prohibition, the FIFA rules have generated a (global) black market for teenage players. The head of FIFA has recently suggested a return to a quota of foreign players required to be fielded by clubs in official soccer contests (the so-called 6 + 5 rule, including 6 national players), which is supposed to resolve competitive imbalance issues and somewhat restrict players' international mobility and its impacts. No doubt, if such restrictive rule were to be adopted, it should be immediately invalidated by Bosman jurisprudence.

Another solution, inspired from the so-called Tobin tax targeted at putting a brake on short-term international capital movements, would consist of the principle of a Coubertobin tax –extensively presented with details in Andreff (2004). The idea is to levy a tax at a 1 per cent rate on all transfer fees and initial wages defined in labour contracts signed by players from developing countries with foreign professional clubs and/or players' agents. Teenage player transfers would be tackled by adding a tax surcharge on transfers of players below the age of 18. The tax rate would increase the further from 18 the players' age is at the transfer date. Of course, it is not a panacea. Such regulation, if adopted at an international level (a political will is still lacking to back it), would not be without its implementation problems, though these hindrances could be overcome. Since the eve of the current global financial crisis, the interest for this sort of tax has increased, in particular in the context of the European soccer financial crisis. UEFA is very much concerned by teenage player transfers and has started to collect information about the principle of the suggested (tax) regulation.

The final outcome of some international athlete transfers sometimes is – though fewer in number in soccer than in athletics – a demand for naturalization by the migrant player. Temporary or permanent sportsmen and women migration generates a demand for changing citizenship in just one direction (with a few exceptions), which is associated with mobility from developing to developed countries. Since those athletes concerned are remunerated and earn their living from their sport performances, athletes' motivation often is to acquire, stabilize and increase their financial gains in demanding their naturalization. Thus, sporting nationality tends to turn into a financial asset.

From the point of view of a naturalized athlete's host country, the advantage is to recruit a highly performing athlete in order to select him/her in the national squad (Qatar), but foreign athletes' recruitment is likely to weaken (or phase out) any local training effort of young domestic players. It is often more expensive to train an athlete than purchase him/her abroad (Husting, 2004), at least when he/she is purchased in a developing country. A host club, in general, is favourable to a migrant athlete's adoption of the host country's nationality. This will avoid counting him/her among foreign players when a rule restricts the number of foreign players on the pitch. For the home country and nursery club of those young sporting talents that migrate, a negative impact is to be mentioned. The financial compensation obtained from abroad rarely covers the education and training costs of the migrant athlete when it comes to home clubs located in developing countries. At the end of the day, the very idea of organizing Olympic Games and World Championships with national squads could be threatened if a number of countries were to adopt a strategy of athletes' recruitment similar to the one of professional clubs, including relying on athlete naturalization.

Aside frome the Coubertobin tax, few regulations are likely to hinder athlete naturalization so far. One can imagine extending to other sports the rules prevailing for nationality change in such sports as soccer, basketball and cycling. FIFA considers that any footballer selected once in a national squad can no longer be selected in another national squad even if he/she has acquired the latter's country nationality. FIBA enforces a similar rule in restricting to one player having acquired (after the age of 16) the nationality of the national squad. The international cycling federation makes it impossible to change sporting nationality. One could also envisage an amount of money to be retained from players' wages and bonuses earned over one year, levied by the national sports federation in the host country and redistributed to the national federation in the home country as soon as a naturalized athlete is selected in the host country's national squad. This scheme could be implemented during the years when a naturalized athlete is selected in his/her host country's national squad (in view of slowing down naturalization of the so-called 'sport mercenaries' who sell their talents to the country offering the most).

Conclusion

Economic globalization of sport operates in such a way that a number of sport contests, namely soccer contests, tend to be unbalanced. Imbalances fuel revenue concentration, which is not favourable to returning to a better competitive balance. Thus, new thoughts about regulation are required, or even urgently needed, in the face of a European soccer financial crisis that results from both insufficiently efficient rules and deregulation of the labour market for sporting talent. Both have been driving sport economic globalization.

Notes

1 Economic analysis distinguishes (Szyamnski, 2001; Forrest *et al.*, 2005; Buraimo and Simmons, 2008) sports fans as those attending to support 'their own team' – with the hope that it will win – and sport spectators as those going to the stadium as they go to any show with the hope of attending a quality show – their preference is more in favour of outcome uncertainty (thus balanced contests) rather than that a specific team wins. The majority of TV viewers belong to the second group.

2 The components of which are, except the so-called 'glorious uncertainty of sporting outcomes', the contest format, the organization of a sports event, its competitive balance, the degree of contention, those athletes (players) that are fielded, scoring, technical aesthetics and the sequencing of fixtures.

3 We concentrate primarily on team sports since presenting contest regulation in individual sports would require us to refer to the mathematical theory of tournaments, which is much too complex to be encapsulated in the present chapter.

4 With three exceptions: intra-EU transfers, players living just across the border, and international mobility of the player's family not linked to football motivations.

5 In which players continuously switch their position on the pitch during the game in a tactic that combines an Italian-style defence (*catenaccio*), German hard work and self-sacrifice and repeated passes à la hollandaise (like the Dutch team in the 1970s).

6 The number of medal wins is counted athlete by athlete in accordance with IOC rules. However, in particular during the Cold War, it used to count them nation by nation and to rank all participating nations according to their medal wins.

7 This commission was created in 1999 after a scandal in the allocation of Winter Games to Salt Lake City (corruption of one IOC member).

8 Other prediction exercises for the 2010 World Cup semi-finalists have been realized by international banks like Goldman Sachs, J.P. Morgan and UBS. They did not

predict more than two semi-finalists either. This is due to 'surprises' created by the early elimination of Brazil, Italy and Uruguay in the qualification for the semi-finals.

9   We have observed a strong correlation between sports ministries' budgets and the number of medal wins at the Beijing Games in a sample of the 27 EU member countries (Andreff, 2010c); it would be interesting to run a similar calculation for the budget of soccer national federations compared to sporting outcomes of national squads at the 2010 World Cup.

10   Athlete naturalizations also affect the selection of national squads participating in the Summer Olympics; they are an issue that concerns the IOC, and they probably will call for regulation in the mid-term (limiting the number of naturalized or foreign players). At the Athens Olympics, France's team included 29 naturalized athletes, Greece 28, Israel 16, the USA and Australia 13 each, Germany 12, etc. (Andreff, 2005).

11   Its TV audience accrues revenues that have enabled UEFA to share €416 million across participating clubs in 2004–2005, €586 million in 2007–2008 and €583 million in 2009–2010.

12   Twenty-five per cent of TV revenues are redistributed evenly across the participants in the interests of fairness, another 25 per cent are redistributed according to a club's sporting results during the sport contest, and 50 per cent are redistributed according to each club's TV audience during the contest. These rules tend to concentrate financial gains derived from the Champions League on those clubs that qualify the furthest in the competition (finalists, semi-finalists) and on those that attract a high media audience whatever their results on the pitch (Manchester United, Real Madrid, AC Milan, etc.).

13   In French *Ligue 1*, revenues derived from the Champions League amount, depending on the year, from 7 to 10 per cent of overall revenues of the league, but are concentrated on five clubs.

14   Szymanski (2001) does not find any clear relationship between win percentage (which is equivalent to club standing) and attendance in English soccer either.

15   The *Journal of Sports Economics* has devoted its issue 7 (1), 2006 and a part of 8 (6), 2007 to this financial crisis.

References

Aglietta, M., W. Andreff and B. Drut (2008), Bourse et Football, *Revue d'Economie Politique*, 118 (2), 255–296.

Alavy, K., A. Gaskell, S. Leach and S. Szymanski (2010), On the Edge of Your Seat: Demand for Soccer on Television and the Uncertainty of Outcome Hypothesis, *International Journal of Sport Finance*, 5 (2), 75–95.

Amann, E., R. Dewenter and J.E. Namini (2004), *The Home-Bias Paradox in Football*, discussion paper, Essen: University of Duisburg-Essen.

Andreff, W. (1999), Les finances du sport et l'éthique sportive, *Revue d'Economie Financière*, 55, 135–175.

Andreff, W. (2001), The Correlation between Economic Underdevelopment and Sport, *European Sport Management Quarterly*, 1 (4), 251–279.

Andreff, W. (2004), The Taxation of Player Moves from Developing Countries, in R. Fort and J. Fizel, eds, *International Sports Economics Comparisons*, Westport, CT: Praeger, 87–103.

Andreff, W. (2005), Pistes de réflexion économique, in D. Oswald, ed., *La nationalité dans le sport : Enjeux et problèmes*, Neuchâtel: Editions CIES, 171–191.

Andreff, W. (2007a), Dérives financières: une remise en cause de l'organisation du sport, *Finance et Bien Commun* (Genève), 26, hiver 2006–2007, 27–35.

Andreff, W. (2007b), Régulation et institutions en économie du sport, *Revue de la Régulation: Capitalisme, Institutions, Pouvoirs*, n°1, varia.

Andreff, W. (2007c), French Football: A Financial Crisis Rooted in Weak Governance, *Journal of Sports Economics*, 8 (6), 652–661.

Andreff, W. (2007d), Governance Issues in French Professional Football, in P. Rodriguez, S. Késenne and J. Garcia, eds, *Governance and Competition in Professional Sports Leagues*, Oviedo: Ediciones de la Universidad de Oviedo, 55–86.

Andreff, W. (2009a), Comparaison entre les prévisions et les médailles gagnées aux Jeux de Pékin, in *Pékin 2008: Regards croisés sur la performance sportive olympique et paralympique*, Paris: INSEP, Secrétariat d'Etat aux Sports, 241–247.

Andreff, W. (2009b), Equilibre compétitif et contrainte budgétaire dans une ligue de sport professionnel, *Revue Economique*, 60 (2), 591–634.

Andreff, W. (2010a), *Economie internationale du sport*, Grenoble: Presses Universitaires de Grenoble.

Andreff, W. (2010b), Les grands clubs de football : des firmes transnationales, *Questions internationales*, 44, 50–57.

Andreff, W. (2010c), *Public and Private Sport Financing in Europe: The Impact of financial Crisis*, 18th European Association of Sport Management Conference, Prague, 15–18 September.

Andreff, W. (2010d), Une taxe contre la misère du football africain?, *Afrique contemporaine*, 233, 89–98.

Andreff, M. and W. Andreff (2009), Global trade in Sports Goods: International Specialisation of Major Trading Countries, *European Sport Management Quarterly*, 9 (3), 259–294.

Andreff, M. and W. Andreff (2010), Economic Prediction of Sport Performances: From Beijing Olympics to the 2010 FIFA World Cup in South Africa, 85th Western Economic Association International Conference, Portland, 29 June – 3 July.

Andreff, W. and J.-F. Bourg (2006), Broadcasting Rights and Competition in European Football, in C. Jeanrenaud and S. Késenne, eds, *The Economics of Sport and the Media*, Cheltenham: Edward Elgar, 37–70.

Andreff, W. and G. Raballand (2011), Is European Football Future to Become a Boring Game?, in W. Andreff, ed., *Contemporary Issues in Sports Economics: Participation and Professional Team Sports*, Cheltenham: Edward Elgar, 176–222.

Andreff, M., W. Andreff and S. Poupaux (2008), Les déterminants économiques de la performance sportive : Prévision des médailles gagnées aux Jeux de Pékin, *Revue d'Economie Politique*, 118 (2), 135–169.

Ascari, G. and P. Gagnepain (2006), Spanish Football, *Journal of Sports Economics*, 7 (1), 76–89.

Aylott, M. and N. Aylott (2007), A Meeting of Social Science and Football: Measuring the Effects of Three Points for a Win, *Sports in Science*, 10, 205–222.

Baroncelli, A. and U. Lago (2006), Italian Football, *Journal of Sports Economics*, 7 (1), 13–28.

Bernard, A.B. and M. R. Busse (2004), Who Wins the Olympic Games: Economic Resources and Medal Totals, *Review of Economics and Statistics*, 86 (1), 413–417.

Besson, E. (2008), *Accroître la compétitivité des clubs de football professionnel français*, Rapport au Premier Ministre, Paris.

Borland, J. and R. Macdonald (2003), Demand for Sport, *Oxford Review of Economic Policy*, 19 (4), 478–502.

Bourg, J.-F. and J.-J. Gouguet (2005), *Economie du sport*, Repères 309, Paris: La Découverte.

Brocas, I. and J.D. Carrillo (2004), Do the 'Three-Point Victory' and 'Golden Goal' Rules Make Soccer More Exciting? A Theoretical Analysis of a Simple Game', *Journal of Sports Economics*, 5, 169–185.

Buraimo, B. and R. Simmons (2008), Do Sports Fans Really Value Uncertainty of Outcome? Evidence from the English Premier League, *International Journal of Sport Finance*, 3, 146–155.

Chappelet, J.-L. and B. Kübler-Mabbott (2008), *The International Olympic Committee and the Olympic System*, Abingdon: Routledge.

Coupé, T. (2007), Incentives and Bonuses – The Case of the 2006 World Cup, *Kyklos*, 60 (3), 349–358.

Dilger, A. and H. Geyer (2009), Are Three Points for a Win Really Better Than Two? A Comparison of German Soccer League and Cup Games, *Journal of Sports Economics*, 10, 305–317.

Donzel, J. (1999), *Rapport sur le recrutement, l'accueil et le suivi des jeunes étrangers (hors Union Européenne) dans les centres de formation de football professionnels en France*, Paris: Ministère de la Jeunesse et des Sports.

El Hodiri, M. and J. Quirk (1971), An Economic Model of a Professional Sports League, *Journal of Political Economy*, 79 (6), 1302–1319.

Forrest, D., R. Simmons and B. Buraimo (2005), Outcome Uncertainty and the Couch Potato Audience, *Scottish Journal of Political Economy*, 52 (4), 641–661.

Fort, R. and J. Quirk (1995), Cross-subsidization, Incentives, and Outcomes in Professional Team Leagues, *Journal of Economic Literature*, 33, 1265–1299.

Frick, B. (2009), Globalization and Factor Mobility: The Impact of Bosman Ruling on Player Migration in Professional Soccer, *Journal of Sports Economics*, 10 (1), 88–106.

Garicano, L. and I. Palacios-Huerta (2006), *Sabotage in Tournaments: Making the Beautiful Game a Bit Less Beautiful*, Research paper, Brown University, Providence.

Gerrard, B. (2002), The Muscle Drain, Coubertobin-Type Taxes and the International Transfer System in Association Football, *European Sport Management Quarterly*, 2 (1).

Gerrard, B. (2006), Analysing the Win–Wage Relationship in Pro Sports Leagues: Evidence from the FA Premier League, 1997/98–2001/02, in P. Rodriguez, S. Késenne and J. Garcia, eds, *Sports Economics after Fifty Years: Essays in Honour of Simon Rottenberg*, Oviedo: Ediciones de la Universidad de Oviedo, 169–190.

Gouguet, J.-J. and D. Primault (2006), The French Exception, *Journal of Sports Economics*, 7 (1), 47–59.

Gouguet, J.-J. and D. Primault (2008), Impact de l'UEFA Champions League sur les championnats nationaux, *Revue Juridique et Economique du Sport*, 88, 141–160.

Hundsdoerfer, J. (2004), Fördert die 3-Punkte-Regel den offensiven Fussball?', in P. Hammann, L. Schmidt and M. Welling, eds, *Ökonomie des Fussballs: Grundlegungen aus volks- und betriebwirtschaftlicher Perspektive*, Wiesbaden: Deutscher Universitäts-Verlag.

Husting, A. (2004), La génération mercenaire, *Sport et Vie*, 1 July.

Késenne, S. (1996), League Management in Professional Team Sports within Win Maximizing Clubs, *European Journal of Sport Management*, 2 (2), 14–22.

Késenne, S. (2000), Revenue Sharing and Competitive Balance in Professional Team Sports, *Journal of Sports Economics*, 1 (1), 56–65.

Késenne, S. (2007), *The Economic Theory of Professional Team Sports: An Analytical Treatment*, Cheltenham: Edward Elgar.

Kringstad, M. and B. Gerrard (2007), Beyond Competitive Balance, in T. Slack, M. Parent, ed., *International Perspectives on the Management of Sport*, Burlington: Elsevier, 149–172.

Kuper, S. and S. Szymanski (2009), *Why England Lose and Other Curious Football Phenomena Explained*, London: HarperCollins.

Lazear, E. and S. Rosen (1981), Rank-order Tournaments as Optimum Labor Contracts, *Journal of Political Economy*, 89, 841–864.

Monk, J. and J. Husch (2009), The Impact of Seeding, Home Continent, and Hosting on FIFA World Cup Results, *Journal of Sports Economics*, 10 (4), 391–408.

Paul, S. and R. Mitra (2008), How Predictable Are the FIFA Worldcup Football Outcomes? An Empirical Analysis, *Applied Economic Letters*, 15, 1171–1176.

Sanderson, A. (2002), The Many Dimensions of Competitive Balance, *Journal of Sports Economics*, 3 (2), 204–228.

Scelles, N. (2009), *L'incertitude du résultat, facteur clé de succès du spectacle sportif professionnel. L'intensité compétitive des ligues : entre impacts mesurés et effets perçus*, Thèse de doctorat, Université de Caen.

Szymanski, S. (2001), Income Inequality, Competitive Balance and the Attractiveness of Team Sports: Some Evidence and a Natural Experiment from English Soccer, *Economic Journal*, 111, F69–F84.

Szymanski, S. (2003), The Economic Design of Sporting Contests, *Journal of Economic Literature*, 41, 1137–1187.

Szymanski, S. and T. Kuypers (1999), *Winners and Losers: The Business Strategy of Football*, London: Viking.

Torgler, B. (2004), The Economics of the FIFA Football Worldcup, *Kyklos*, 57 (2), 287–300.

Tshimanga Bakadiababu, E. (2001), *Le commerce et la traite des footballeurs africains et sud-américians en Europe*, Paris: L'Harmattan.

Vrooman, J. (1995), A General Theory of Professional Sports Leagues, *Southern Economic Journal*, 61 (4), 971–990.

6 Manufacturers of equipment for football clubs

Strategy and internationalization[1]

Michel Desbordes

Introduction: sports marketing versus the marketing of sport

Beginning in the 1990s, the business aspect of European sports has been increasingly emphasized, leading companies to make massive investments in this sector. The profitability of sport, especially when the local team is a winner, can produce a jackpot for the company. This explains the entry of large numbers of companies that might at first sight seem out of place in sport (insurance companies, banks, consumer goods firms, airline companies, etc.), following the lead of more obvious traditional investments by the manufacturers of sporting equipment (Adidas, Nike, Puma, and others), long-time participants in this market.

We thus speak of 'sports marketing' in the case of equipment makers, whereas we say that sponsors (firms that invest in sport without having a 'natural' or semantic connection with it) are engaging in 'marketing via sport'.

Subsequently, in the 2000s, it all became more complicated: the marketers found that the optimization of an investment required a successful '*ménage à trois*', in which each party represented a brand. The team, the equipment maker and the sponsor came together on a jersey. Of course, the FC Barcelona–Nike–UNICEF trio does not send quite the same message as FC Liverpool–Adidas–Carlsberg, Carlsberg being a type of beer whereas UNICEF works to protect children worldwide.

The generic and theoretical principles of sports sponsoring

The 'classic' literature of sports sponsoring

Sponsoring is based on the concept of association or linking. This is a feature of most definitions, and particularly of the three that we have selected. Sahnoun (1986) considers it to be 'a promotional tool which directly connects a brand or a company to an event that attracts a given audience'. According to Piquet (1985), it 'refers to a specific promotional technique implemented by an advertiser,[2] intended to associate its brand, in the mind of the consumer, with a sporting or cultural event'. The UK's Howell Report (1983) sees sponsoring as 'support, by

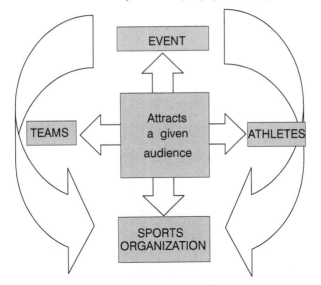

Figure 6.1 The event as the focal point of public attraction

a person or organization unrelated to this action, of a sport, a sporting event, a sporting organization, or a participant in a competition, for the mutual benefit of both parties'.

Sponsoring, then, is a public relations technique employed to convince spectators of a connection between a sporting event represented by a group (sports team, club, factory team, etc.), an institution (professional league or federation), an individual competitor, or the event's venue (facility, stadium, racing circuit, etc.), and the firm doing the promotion (see Figure 6.1).

The objective is to transfer some or all of the values of the sport itself, and the cultural elements associated with it, to the firm as an institution and to its products or brands, in order to render them more efficient in market terms, i.e. to better meet the expectations of consumers.

This gives rise to financial support, in material form or services, designed to make the company, its products, and its brands better known, and thus to reap economic benefits in terms of image.

There are three types of sponsoring:

1 Sponsoring for visibility or power.
2 Sponsoring for image.
3 Relational sponsoring (sporting hospitality).

Broadly speaking, there are two main approaches:

1 A commercial approach (trade sponsoring, product proof).
2 An institutional (corporate) or sports-patronage approach (socially motivated sponsoring).

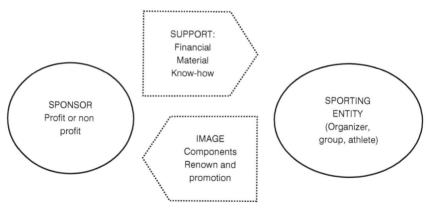

Figure 6.2 The nature of the sports–sponsorship exchange

Source: Tribou, 2007.

Sponsors establish their own priorities. A study by Crowley (1991) identified four types of sponsors, according to their objectives:

- consumer oriented;
- internal-personnel oriented;
- public-opinion oriented;
- commercially oriented.

To target a sponsoring action correctly, it is necessary to have an accurate perception of the event's direct and indirect audience. Such knowledge must be both quantitative and qualitative: socio-demographic characteristics, lifestyles and consumption profiles. This approach leads to a multiplicity of audience-research studies (TNS Sofres, Sports Marketing Surveys, Institut français de démoscopie, Sport Lab, Sport Research International, Eurodata TV, BVA, and others).

If the message has a commercial purpose the sponsorship is naturally designed to increase sales. However, the buying or re-buying act is influenced by a great number of variables connected to the buyer, to the environment and to the marketing activities. More specifically, sponsoring will be used to increase the credibility and renown of a brand, to work on its image, to energize the distribution system or the sales force, to develop business-to-business relationships, and so on (see Figure 6.2).

The 1980s saw a growing integration of sponsorships into public relations strategies. During the 1990s, the concepts and utilization of sponsorships would evolve. Operators would learn to develop synergies between sponsorships and the other variables in the marketing mix.

The study by Patrick Dambron (1991), entitled *Sponsoring et politique de marketing*, testifies to this desire to rationalize 'the relationships that exist between sponsoring and the management of marketing', with particular

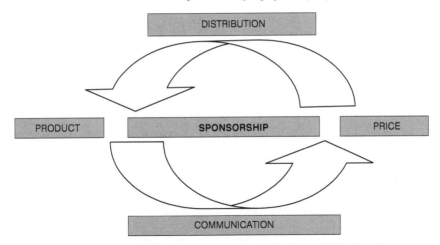

Figure 6.3 The interaction of sponsoring with the variables in the marketing mix

emphasis on 'its overlapping with the variables of the marketing mix: product, price, distribution, and promotion'. This study is based on a qualitative survey of major French firms, some of which are subsidiaries of American or Japanese companies. Its analysis identifies the challenges facing sponsors and sports organizations during the coming decade. Its approach is an integrative one, in which sponsorships are treated in terms of the four variable macros mentioned above (see Figure 6.3). In this regard, Derbaix *et al.* (1994) define sponsoring[3] as a 'technique which, in any organization, consists of creating or directly supporting an event that is socio-culturally independent of it, and using the media to associate the organization with it so as to achieve certain marketing objectives'.

Ambush marketing and the equipment manufacturer

According to Bayless (1988), ambush marketing is the strategy by which an organization associates itself indirectly with an event in order to obtain the same benefits as an official sponsor. The first clear example was Eastman Kodak's strategy during the 1984 Olympic Games, when Fuji was the official sponsor. Kodak notably sponsored the broadcasting of the games on ABC, as well as the official film of the American athletics team. During the 1988 Olympic Games, each official sponsor had at least one competitor that used an ambush marketing strategy. The growth of this phenomenon is linked to its effectiveness. The results of a study carried out by Sandler and Shani (1993) during the Albertville Games in 1992 show that ambushers obtained recognition scores that were higher than their competitors in that product category. Moreover, in product categories where there was no ambusher, official sponsors obtained better results than those for official sponsors who were victims of an ambush marketing operation.

Currently, all the major international sporting events are expressing concern. Meenaghan (1994) compiled a list of the principal methods:

- sponsoring the broadcasting of the event;
- becoming a minor sponsor of the event and massively exploiting this status;
- buying vast amounts of advertising in the event's broadcast time slots;
- engaging in operations that promote its sponsorship actions at the time of the event;
- using photographs of the sites and facilities in its advertising, etc.

This list is far from exhaustive, given the creativity brought to bear in this area. However, following the IOC's example, sponsors and organizations that own rights have learned how to take action against ambush marketing operations. They now:

- exert pressure on organizers to protect the event;
- are beginning to link sponsorship of the venue with sponsorship of the broadcast;
- attempt to foresee their competitors' promotional campaigns;
- must employ sponsorship rights that are protected;
- and may systematically seek legal remedies when a breach is identified.

This debate is far from over, considering the growing numbers of sponsorship contracts: event, team, players, referees, etc. Concerning its campaign for the World Football Cup in 1998, Nike observed:

> We are not engaging in ambush marketing by seeking to pick up the event. We are simply the partners of the teams and players who are going to take part in the World Cup. That makes us legitimate actors in the competition. Nike has set up a promotional program based on football, not on the World Cup.
>
> (Christophe Quiquandon, interview)

Ambush marketing strategies are very common in football because the players are part of a team that has a group contract with an equipment manufacturer, while at the same time they have individual contracts for their shoes, which are often supplied by a competing manufacturer. The message then becomes confused.

This is very ambiguous. Looking at some pictures on the website of the French Football Federation, the consumer might think that the player was sponsored by Adidas, since the 'high framing' of the photo conceals the brand of his shoes; however, the second photo, used by Nike in an advertising campaign, leaves no room for doubt. Since the visibility provided by shoes is low, especially during the anthems (the best time for close-ups), some equipment makers are abandoning individual player contracts and instead refocusing on group contracts. This is the aim of Nike's new contract with the French football team, which will go into effect in 2011 (see Boxes 6.1 and 6.2).

Box 6.1 Nike buys into the French team (22 February 2008)

The American group Nike will become the new equipment manufacturer for the French team during the 2011–2018 period, having won the bidding war with an offer of 42.6 million euros per year, the French Football Federation (FFF) announced on Friday. This change is a bitter blow for the German group Adidas, a loser in the request for proposals along with the 'small' French firm Airness. The Adidas and Nike tenders were 'qualitatively very similar, and it was the financial aspects that made the difference', said the President of the FFF, Jean-Pierre Escalettes. 'I did not have the moral or legal ability to make a different decision.' Mr Escalettes noted that two competitions still remained to be played in Adidas jerseys: Euro 2008 and perhaps the 2010 World Cup, if the French squad qualified. The Federation paid tribute to Adidas for the long journey that it had shared with the German manufacturer, which had been dressing the French team since 1972. Mr Escalettes was pleased to note that the contract, 320 million euros over seven and a half seasons, was 'four and a half times bigger' than the previous one. Mr Escalettes announced that Nike had added to its tender a grant of equipment worth 2.5 million euros per season for all the French teams (A, youth and female teams, etc.), as well as bonuses based on results. This is a long way from the 10 million paid by Adidas in 2004, when the contract was last renewed. And especially far from the 13 million spent by Puma and Nike to acquire the symbols of Italy and Brazil respectively, with nine world-championship stars between them. In the view of the FFF's Vice President in charge of financial matters, Noël Le Graët, the Federation had obtained 'three very fine bids, even the Airness one … We have so many projects that we certainly know what to do with the money', concluded Mr Le Graët.

Source: www.france24.com/fr/20080222-nike-equipe-france-football-equipement-vetement-Adidas (last accessed 29 May 2010)

'Traditional' sponsoring versus the equipment makers' strategy: what are its goals?

Table 6.1 refers to France. If we look at the broader European picture, there are considerable disparities between countries: in Italy sponsors spend about five times more than in Spain, and about twice as much as in France, Germany and Great Britain.

There is a traditional alternation of investments: reduced in slack years (odd-numbered years) and then we see a catching up during prosperous years (even-numbered years with Olympic and football events).

Experts regularly call for a 'stop blow' for sponsoring, for example when a national team has a setback.[4] However, the sponsorship market is not yet mature:

Box 6.2 Comments on ambush marketing by Alain Pourcelot, Adidas's marketing director for France

How do you handle the conflicts between individual and group contracts? For example, Ribéry is now more closely associated with the Nike brand, which sponsors him, than with the Adidas brand which sponsors his team...'

Alain Pourcelot: 'That's a bit complicated. You have to be an expert in the business to sort all that out, and it's not necessarily very easy for the consumer. This is why you have to work at using the players, as we do with Benzema, that's essential. In addition, we're in a market where the clubs have contracts, and until 1998, for example, when you played football for France you were obliged to wear the brand of the federation's partner, so everyone saw you in Adidas from head to toe.

For fairly simple reasons, connected to the fact that in certain sports it had been officially decided that brands of equipment specific to that sport should be selected by the athletes themselves, for example in fencing or swimming. So right away, beginning in the 1990s and to stimulate business, it was decided that shoes were an essential item for the player, like a swimsuit or a foil, and that they ought to be able to choose their own manufacturers. So before, everyone who played for Olympique de Marseille wore Adidas, and all the Paris-Saint-Germain players wore Nike, and so on.

Now there are individual contracts and club contracts, which lead to confusion. In this situation where anything goes, the ones who succeed are those who are able to most effectively associate their brand with these players, so that people directly associate them with these players. You can also have a different strategy, called ambush or disruption marketing, which consists of using players who are with Nike but who play for an Adidas team, and photograph them wearing Adidas, and that causes a disruption. But that's not a big thing, what's important is to sign the players you want to have, and who will be yours. It's no longer a settled market, and you can't do much about that, each brand has to manage as best it can.'

Source: qualitative interview, 23 November 2008

it grew by a factor of four between 1990 and 2007, and increases about 10 per cent each year. Moreover there are new openings for this promotional instrument, such as the ramping up of sponsoring in simulation (virtual) games and the development of online betting in Europe.

The figures for sponsorship vary, depending on the definition adopted: from 4 per cent of promotional expenditures if patronage operations include only the acquisition of rights, to about 10 per cent if we add the support and activity-related operations carried out for an event (public relations, posters and direct

Table 6.1 Sponsorships in France: average entry costs in 2009 (in millions of euros)

Sport	Type of sponsorship	Price
Formula 1	Partner major stable	50.0
	Partner mid-range stable	15.0
	Partner average driver	0.4
WRC	Partner major stable	8.0
(rally)	Partner average driver	0.2
Cycling	Featured partner winning French team	8.0
	Major partner Tour de France	5.0
Football	Jersey partner major League-1 club	6.0
	Major partner French Cup	4,0
	Major partner French team	2.5
Rugby	Official partner French team	3.5
	Top partner of the League	2.0
	Jersey partner major Top-14 club	1.6
Tennis	Top partner Roland-Garros	3.0
Sailing	Major partner big multihull*	3.2
	Major partner single hull*	1.9
Athletics	Major federation partner	1.0
Handball	Official federation partner	0.8
Basketball	Jersey partner of a Pro A team	0.3
Golf	Official partner, French Open	0.5
Skiing	Federation partner	0.2
Horse-riding	Major partner of a French CSIO	0.3
Swimming	Federation partner	0.3
Climbing	Federation partner	0.1

*(including depreciation)
Source: TNS Sport, 2009.

marketing). There is a rule of thumb for optimizing a partnership: for every €1 of purchased rights, the sponsor spends €2–3 on downstream developments.

The role of sports management agencies is becoming ever more important. They are involved in the negotiation of marketing and TV rights, carry out consulting assignments, and sell public relations programmes. In France Havas Sports and Sportfive, the two leading firms, are in competition with the French subsidiaries of IMG McCormack and Octagon (Interpublic Group). There is also a swarm of small and medium-sized firms that operate in the same environment, and have the status of sports marketing agencies.

As regards sponsorship *stricto sensu*, sports marketing agencies have four main functions:

1   Marketing brokers: selling marketing rights to support advertisers in exchange for a commission (10 to 20 per cent of sales).
2   Consulting: helping advertisers to make strategic choices for promoting themselves via sport, and in negotiating.
3   Studies for measuring the return on investment (media visibility, gross rating point (GRP), etc.).
4   Field operations: organizing events, and public relations.

Traditionally, there may be an ethical problem because the agency provides advice both to the buyer and to the seller.

Managerial aspects: how equipment manufacturers are internationalizing sporting brands

Football clubs, national teams, the American professional leagues and the major sporting events have now become brands in their own right. They find themselves in a competitive situation where the financial stakes are substantial: they do everything in their power to increase their visibility on the international level and, ultimately, to obtain new income through merchandising. In this context the tennis championship at Roland-Garros is competing with the one at Wimbledon, Manchester United arranges tours in Asia to sell more jerseys than Real Madrid, and the NBA moves into China to get ahead of the NFL. This competition is especially fierce now that in Europe and in the United States certain brands seem to have reached a development plateau in markets that are virtually saturated.

Under the life cycle concept (showing the sales of sporting products versus time), shown in Figure 6.4, we find that firms try to export their products during the decline phase, thereby attempting to offset this phase through internationalization. The attempts to penetrate the Asian markets (promotional tours, sales of TV

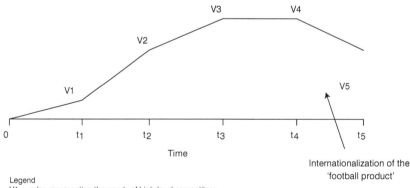

Legend
V1 = sales representing the needs of high-level competitors
V2 = sales covering the entire practice of the sport
V3 = sales covering the whole national market (including non-sporting purchases and replacement needs)
V4 = sales representing the start of the declining phase

Figure 6.4 The life cycle of a sports product (sales versus time)
Source: Andreff, 1989.

rights, development of online stores and websites) seem to fit this theoretical explanation. Given a partially saturated European football market, Asia appears to offer a credible escape route for clubs looking for new sources of financing and seeking to internationalize their brand (Desbordes, 2006).

Professional European sport versus professional American sport: the institutional differences that affect the brands

European professional sport is structured in a very different fashion from American sport. In the United States, universities train players (generally between 18 and 22 years of age) for team sports, and then the best players turn professional. In Europe, in both rugby and soccer, the clubs themselves fill this role, using training centres.

The American system is also more strictly regulated. For several decades the governing authorities have tried to maintain a level of uncertainty in the leagues, in order to preserve the value of the competitions. When the same team wins all the time the TV audiences fall, which in turn reduces the advertising revenues and the prices of television rights that the channels are willing to pay. At the same time, ticket receipts decline. For this reason American sports have decided to regulate their competitions more or less vigorously, rather than allow the market alone to decide.

An American professional league is a self-contained organization which has two objectives:

- To organize a balanced sporting competition (maintaining an uncertainty of result by matches between teams of equal level) so as to increase revenues.
- To establish a fair economic competition, where each team receives an equitable return on its contribution, to the equal profit of the league.

In the NBA, putting it simply and without going into the details, the three cornerstones of the regulations are:

1 The draft: this is a system for sharing the college players who are entering the NBA. Broadly speaking, the poorest-performing teams during the previous season will have first choice during recruitment, so the best players from the previous year will go to the worst teams.
2 Equitable distribution of television rights: the TV rights, both for the networks and for cable, are shared by the NBA almost dollar for dollar between the teams, no matter how many broadcasts take place during the year. Thus the champion receives the same amount as a team whose matches were never broadcast that year.
3 The salary cap: to avoid a bidding war over salaries that could be financially risky for the teams, the total payroll cost has been capped every year since the 1980s.

Overall, this system of regulation has made the championship more attractive as regards uncertainty than the championships in European team sports,[5] where

Box 6.3 UEFA adopts a financial fair-play policy (*Le Monde*, 28 May 2010)

This project, supported by Michel Platini since he took over at UEFA, has finally borne fruit: on Thursday the European football authority adopted the principle of financial fair play, aimed at putting a brake on cost inflation in the clubs. It will come into force progressively, and the first penalties may be applied beginning in 2014–2015. *'It's a thorough-going change in European football'* declared the UEFA president.

The objective is to ensure the financial health of European football by forcing the clubs to stop living beyond their means. Eventually, says UEFA, 'the clubs should not have to spend more than they are able to generate over a given period'. In order to acquire new players, they will therefore have to use the money obtained from TV rights, ticket sales, merchandise, sponsorships, and bonuses paid back by the organizers of competitions. Injections of capital from rich benefactors will be capped.

'If clubs want to spend 50, 60, or 70 million euros, why shouldn't they, but on the condition that they have enough income to ensure their future', explains Gianni Infantino, UEFA's Secretary General. He told the press that these new regulations had been adopted unanimously by the European authority's executive committee.

Failure to obey these rules could be punishable, beginning in the 2014–2015 season, by becoming ineligible to participate in a European competition organized by UEFA, starting with the Champions League. In the meantime, financial fair play will be progressively implemented over a period of three years (2010–2012). *'Its cornerstone ..., the principle of financial stability, will become effective for financial reports issued at the end of 2010, to be evaluated by UEFA during the 2013–2014 season'*, the European authority explained. It has appointed Jean-Luc Dehaene, the former Prime Minister of Belgium, to head a group charged with examining the clubs' accounts.

On Thursday Michel Platini explained that it was not a matter of punishing the clubs: *'We worked on the concept of financial fair play in close cooperation with the clubs. Our purpose is not to punish them, but to protect them. We have an agreement with them'*, he said. He then stated that this agreement marked 'a new start for the finances' of football clubs, and that it would enable 'the re-establishment of stability and economic commonsense.'

According to a recent UEFA study, nearly half of Europe's clubs are in the red, and the financial situation of one out of every five clubs is a cause for concern. The European Club Association welcomed this decision: 'This is a big success' said its President, the German former international player Karl Heinz Rummenigge. *'These measures will lead football clubs in Europe towards a more responsible and ultimately more sustainable economic system.'*

Source: www.lemonde.fr/sport/article/2010/05/28/l-uefa-adopte-le-fair-play-financier_1364225_3242.htm (last accessed 31 May 2010)

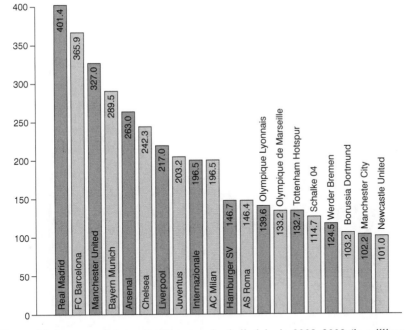

Figure 6.5 Incomes of the major European football clubs in 2008–2009 (in millions of euros)

Source: Deloitte Football Money League, 2010.

great disparities between the clubs lead to disparities in their sporting results. For this reason the European authorities have attempted to establish a kind of financial fair play in recent years (see Box 6.3).

We note very great disparities between the incomes of the major clubs (Figure 6.5). Real Madrid's resources are twice the size of those of Juventus, number 8 in Europe by this measure, and four times bigger than Newcastle's, which ranks 20th. Within its own championship, the *Liga*, Real sometimes plays against clubs whose budget is 1/20 of theirs. In this situation, competitive balance, the mainstay of the economic analysis of the sport and the guarantor of the result's uncertainty, is seriously threatened.

Overall, a modern football club is financed by ticket sales (often now a minority item, even though it was historically the clubs' primary resource), television rights and commercial resources (these include sponsorships and sales of public relations spaces, VIP boxes and business seats; see Figure 6.6).

Sponsorships are still a growing source of income in European football, but we are seeing marked disparities in the amounts of the contracts for jersey sponsorships (see Figures 6.7 and 6.8).

This income disparity became even greater during 2010 (Figure 6.9). This sponsorship trend is growing ever more widespread: the brands are making bigger bets, but on fewer targets. This means that financial efficiency is now a serious concern, and this applies to events, to athletes and to teams.

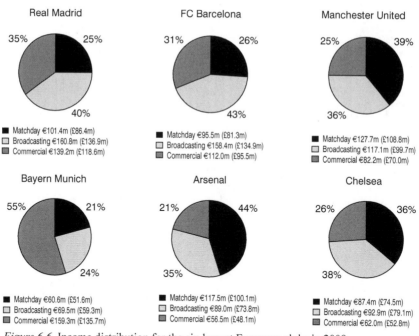

Figure 6.6 Income distribution for the six largest European clubs in 2009

Source: Deloitte Football Money League, 2010.

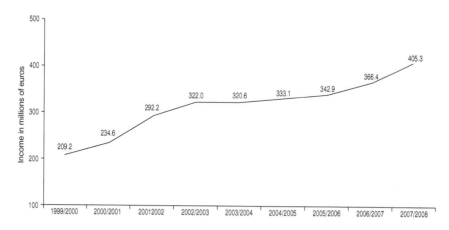

Figure 6.7 Income generated by the sponsoring of jerseys in the six European football championships. These include the clubs that play in the 'big five' championships (England, Germany, Italy, Spain, and France), to which we have added The Netherlands.

Source: Sport + Markt AG, 2007.

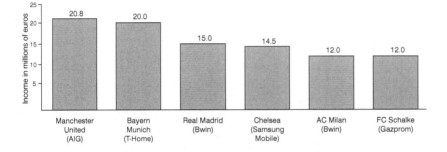

Figure 6.8 The six largest jersey sponsorships in European football

Source: Sport + Markt AG, 2007.

Real Madrid	Bwin	€15m–20m	up to 33%
Manchester United	Aon Corporation	€23m	42%
Bayern Munich	Deutsche Telecomm	€24m	10–20%
Liverpool	Standard Chartered Bank	€23m	167%
AC Milan	Emirates	€12m	–
Hamburger SV	Emirates	€7m	27%

Figure 6.9 Increase in sponsorship contracts during 2010 for the major clubs in European football

Source: Deloitte Football Money League, 2010.

Sanctification of the venue and the jersey: the NBA

Although for several years all of the 29 NBA arenas have taken the name of a private sponsor – the well known 'naming' phenomenon – the league takes the protection of its brand very seriously, whether in the venue or on the players' jerseys.

At an NBA game there are almost no electronic advertising billboards: only announcements by loudspeaker or on the giant screen (with no advertising) are used. This is a long way from what one sees in European football, particularly in the Champions League. On the other hand televised retransmissions are heavily sponsored, using what is called the sponsor billboard or 'broadcast patronage'.

The NBA regards the venue as absolutely sacred, and protects the players' jerseys even more fiercely.

At the same time there is no commercial sponsor on an NBA team jersey, not even that of the equipment manufacturer Adidas, which signed an 11-year contract in 2006 for 400 million dollars. Moreover, that was the main reason why Adidas acquired Reebok in the same year, the NBA being the quickest way for the three-stripe brand to internationalize itself on the American market.

Only the players' warm-up uniforms carry the Adidas logo, also the replica jerseys sold in the store, but the brand is absolutely invisible on the players' jerseys.

The NHL occupies an intermediate position between the NBA and European football as regards the visibility of sponsors and equipment makers, both on the players' jerseys and in the arenas.

An intermediate case: the NHL

If we have a look at some pictures used in the NHL, we see that the players' jersey has the Reebok logo on the back, and that the gloves and sticks also show the brand.

In the same way, the arena displays an abundance of advertising signs, which vary depending on the venue, with national or local brands according to the location.

Lastly, as in the NBA, the equipment maker's visibility is assured by the sale of replica jerseys, the traditional merchandising product.

Relative individual freedom: European football

The context of European football is different. The clubs individually negotiate contracts for jersey sponsorships, also the contract with their equipment manufacturer. Similarly, they are responsible for the electronic billboards in the stadiums. They thus have much greater freedom as regards marketing than do teams in the NBA. In the American system the power is held by the league, whereas in Europe the clubs are the more powerful, especially under the influence of the G14.[6]

The generic strategies of the equipment manufacturers

Overall, Nike, Umbro and Adidas are the brands responsible for most of the contracts in Europe (Figure 6.10). We note three major trends:

- The passage of time: Adidas, which held a quasi-monopoly into the 1990s, has been progressively erased. Firstly, the increasing cost of the contracts meant that the firm was unable to hold on to as many as before (30 million euros per year for Real Madrid beginning in 2007, 7 to 10 million euros per year depending on their sporting results for Olympique Lyonnais from 2010 to 2020). In addition, the equipment firm's marketing positioning made it more logical to concentrate its sponsorships on a few contracts with leading teams (Real Madrid in Spain, Marseille in France, Liverpool and Chelsea in England, AC Milan in Italy and Bayern Munich in Germany).
- During the 1990s, Nike took the title of world number one sporting equipment manufacturer away from Adidas. The brand could no longer ignore soccer, the world's most popular sport. It made its move with an unconventional image: Eric Cantona, the capricious and provocative French player, became its standard-bearer. Today, Nike holds some of the biggest and best contracts in Europe (30 million euros per year with FC Barcelona, 18 million euros per year with Inter Milan, and 12 million euros per year with Juventus from 2009 to 2016).

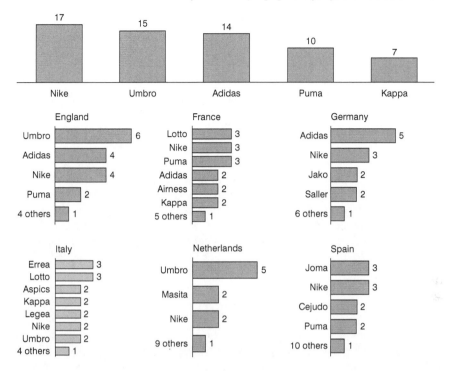

Figure 6.10 Number of club contracts held by equipment makers involved in European football and their distribution by country

Source: Sport + Markt AG, 2007.

• Lastly the outsider Puma, which resurfaced in the 2000s with a lifestyle positioning after the brand had almost disappeared, gave itself an off-beat aspect in Africa by becoming the equipment maker for Cameroon and Côte d'Ivoire among others.

Case studies: Adidas, Nike and Puma

We have made a broad evaluation of the outlook for the internationalization of sporting brands by examining their co-branding relationships with the clubs, the national teams, and the sporting events that they sponsor. For this purpose we employed the case study method, and 22 experts were interviewed in order to compile qualitative information. A list of these 22 experts is presented in the Appendix. For reasons of confidentiality it was not possible to disclose all the information gathered or to cite individuals on all of the points raised in our conversations.[7]

In this study, we begin with the following generic definition: '*co-branding is the association of two or more brands for the development, marketing, and promotion of a product (or a service) or a range of products (or range of services) that they will jointly offer*'.

Adidas

In this section we will see how the Adidas brand carried out its internationalization process by means of sports sponsorships with clubs, federations, national teams, events and athletes.

> Co-branding is a rather specific term that we employ for the association of two true brands, whereas we speak of partnerships or sponsorships when the association is with a club or an event.
>
> (Definition by Alain Pourcelot)

> Among its strong points there's the aspect of fame, and the brand image which is obviously going to help us wherever we go. That's the case in France, and it's probably the same worldwide: Adidas is the favourite brand (Danone is second), according to a recent study. So it's easier to move into other countries if you call yourself Adidas than if you call yourself Umbro.
>
> (Christophe Gante)

Traditionally strong in Europe but weak in North America, the Adidas brand was seeking to make up for lost ground by means of partnerships.

> North America is the priority, because in terms of market volume it's enormous, and Adidas's market share over there is very small (around 6 per cent). So potentially, out of a much bigger cake, where they currently have a pretty small slice, you have to say that it's a huge opportunity.
>
> (Christophe Gante)

This lost ground that the brand is trying to make up is explained by the brand's proximity, which, although it is strong in Europe for historical reasons, is weaker in America.

> In proximity it's a brand which is quite strong, a brand which has a significant relationship of proximity with consumers. This proximity is a real factor in Europe, because it's a European brand. The same is no doubt true in Asia, in view of its development over there. In South America, definitely, and in the United States a bit less because it's not one of the leading brands, far from it.
>
> (Alain Pourcelot)

> Africa is a special continent: the level of development varies a lot from one country to another. For the time being this continent is being handled by our European team. The FIFA World Cup allowed us to focus on that continent and to put resources in place to develop a strategy.
>
> (Isabelle Madec)

Since World War II Adidas has associated itself with various sporting institutions (FIFA, IOC and UEFA), to ensure the global expansion of its brand. This was a very visionary policy, since at the time it was primarily a matter of providing free equipment to the federations, even though their events were receiving little media attention.[8]

> When you form a partnership with the World Cup or the Olympic Games, you become something close to a popular brand, since the event reaches a television audience of three or four billion people. So by definition you're reaching the whole world, in the true meaning of the term.
>
> (Alain Pourcelot)

The equipment maker paid more than 70 million euros to become the IOC's official partner in Beijing. This event was the occasion for the brand's most important promotional campaign. The German company was counting on the Games to overtake its competitor Nike in the Chinese market: a battle involving expenditures of hundreds of millions of euros (2008 Olympic Games, 28 February 2008, www.strategies.fr , last accessed 10 June 2010).

Even in 'minor' sports, Adidas asserts its presence on the world level through partnerships. But in this case only the biggest teams interest it.

> As regards the All Blacks, for example, of course it's rugby, and rugby is a sport that's not much played around the world, certainly in the world as a whole, a sport with a rather limited audience. Why did we choose the All Blacks, well exactly because in this rather limited sport there is one team that stands out from the pack, and it's the All Blacks. So if we're talking about co-branding, it was the only team that might have an international impact. For example, Nike chose the French rugby team, that's big news here, but outside France it doesn't mean anything. On the other hand the black of the All Blacks, their history, a jersey that's easy to wear, it was obvious that we should go after them. But after all, it's still a fairly limited business, with a restricted influence.
>
> (Christophe Gante)

When a brand forms partnerships, it is important not to 'cover' a country too closely, while neglecting others. There should be a presence in each country, with flagship partners.

> They've invested in clubs with a national influence, even an international one: that's why the brand's decision makers wanted to be represented in each country by a stand-out club. If I'm in Spain I need either Real or Barca, if I'm in Italy I need either Milan or Juve, in France OM or PSG, and so on. And other things being equal, if I lay out the map of Europe, the coverage has to be uniform.
>
> (Christophe Gante)

Besides offering worldwide visibility, these partnerships assert the Adidas values, and in particular confirm its deep commitment to sport. These clubs are legends, and confer real credibility on the brand in the world of football.

THE FRENCH FOOTBALL TEAM

It is interesting here to consider the case of France. Because although one of the great successes in the area of sponsorship was its partnership with the French team for the 1998 World Cup, Adidas has just lost the national team to its arch rival, Nike. Since the new contract goes into effect in 2011, or one year after the World Cup in South Africa, it will be interesting to observe the attitude of Adidas in the coming months. It must strike an acceptable balance between promoting the team too vigorously (which could ultimately benefit Nike), and a desire – even a necessity – to secure a return on its partnership.

> Nike purchased the contract for 45 million euros per year from 2011 to 2018, which is a considerable sum as regards income, but it clearly shows that there is a strong interest in terms of image and business in an association.
>
> (Christophe Gante)

Partnerships with athletes are more risky than ones with a club or an institution, owing to the risks of injury and of player performance.

> As concerns athletes it's more complicated because there are more risks: they can get injured and never be heard from again. Beyond that, there's the fact that an athlete is harder to control, and there are more unforeseeable complications. You can break his contract: he was in Germany and then he turns up in Spain: control is more difficult.
>
> (Christophe Gante)

> Signing with the NBA two or three years ago looks to be a pretty decisive event, because Adidas is rather weak in North America, and basketball is one of the big three sports over there.
>
> (Christophe Gante)

There was still one problem, however, since the Champion brand was still the holder of the official licence until 2010. Thus Adidas cannot fully exploit the jerseys to gain visibility. For the time being the logo is seen only at the top of the shorts. Adidas is therefore working with various appearances during the matches, being shown for example on the substitutes' bench (often seen on the screen), on the display panel (seen by the spectators), or by using billboarding,[9] during television broadcasts of matches.

The brand has, however, developed a variety of merchandise, such as shoes for all the teams, and clothing.

Adidas intends to strengthen its position in the basketball category, on the one hand, and in North America generally on the other hand. The brand is emphasizing its positioning as a unique brand. In this regard the NBA partnership contract is an essential asset.

This exclusive-licensing agreement includes rights for textiles but additionally ensures that Adidas will have visibility during all NBA games. It also allows Adidas to promote and exploit players such as Kevin Garnett, Dwight Howard, Tim Duncan, Chauncey Billups, Tracy McGrady and Gilbert Arenas. More than 20 per cent of NBA players currently wear Adidas shoes.

Because of the growing visibility and popularity of basketball worldwide, the partnership constitutes a significant vehicle for carrying this sport and Adidas to other continents, such as Asia and Europe. The brand will be able to make sales outside North America.

Thirty-two nationalities are already represented in the NBA, including major foreign players such as Ginobili, Parker, Gasol, Ming and Kirilenko, who have a considerable impact in Argentina, France, Spain, China and Russia respectively.

The NBA and Adidas are also exporting themselves by means of tours to other continents: the NBA 5ive Tour, NBA Europe Live Tour, Basketball without Borders (India, Turkey and South Africa), and the China Games.

> Typically, the NBA is a nearly global partnership. Even though it's extremely powerful in the United States, Adidas remains a brand that has worldwide range. Our objective is obviously to be the brand for every sport.
>
> (Christophe Gante)

Nike[10]

In this section we will see how the Nike brand carried out its internationalization process by means of sports sponsorships with clubs, federations, national teams, events and athletes. This need to be seen with the biggest champions was essential for this young brand, created in 1972, because its arch rival Adidas had been in existence since the beginning of the century. The need for renown and visibility is in fact one of the primary motives of brands that engage in sponsoring.

'We are there to be a source of inspiration and to bring product innovations to every football player.' Nike's vision of football is as follows: 'In 2010, we will be the most exciting brand in football, and the world leader.' In this sentence the word 'leader' means, in business terms, a desire to achieve an income of 2.5 billion dollars by 2015.

Nike is positioning itself in football by playing on the spectacle and the longings of adolescent fans. Overall, the brand is targeting a footballer in the 12–20 age range who wants his team to win and who wants to win a place on a fantasy team. He wants to be the best player on the field, and he's a huge fan of football and everything about it (the fan club is his community, amateur football, the media, video games...).

Nike's football sponsorships are organized in traditional fashion around three concepts: an association with the biggest clubs, sponsoring of national teams and sponsoring of great players. Among the major clubs, we know that Manchester United is under contract (440 million euros for 15 seasons), just like Arsenal, Boca Juniors, FC Barcelona (30 million euros per season), Inter in Milan, and Juventus in Turin. Among the national teams there is of course France (42.6 million euros per season for seven years, beginning in 2011) and also Brazil, The Netherlands, Portugal and Belgium.

The great players who represent the brand are usually both great on the field and also off it: they are often athletes 'who look good', or who express themselves convincingly. The brand is not looking for consensus. We should mention in particular Cristiano Ronaldo, Paolo Maldini, Andrea Pirlo, Kaka, Franck Ribéry, Wayne Rooney, Zlatan Ibrahimovic, Ronaldo, Florent Malouda, Lilian Thuram and Ronaldinho.

To supplement the sponsorship operations it has established, there is a whole promotional system that specifically involves major advertising campaigns. The most recent of these was the one for Euro 2008, entitled 'Take It To The Next Level', which was judged advertisement of the year. For each major football event Nike has launched a very striking product campaign. For Euro 96 in England, for example, it featured the launching of Air Zoom, with a high-profile advertising campaign that pitted God (symbolized by Eric Cantona) against a devil; in the end, God wins out because of the superiority of his new shoes.

Nike is considered to be a dominant brand in the United States. It also occupies a leading position in South America, but is seen more as a challenger in Europe.

It is associated with a young, subversive image, 'more subversive than its main competitor Adidas' (Isabelle Madec).

As regards the Asian market, Adidas and Nike are neck and neck. 'Nike is competing with an institution' (Vincent Duluc).

This means that Adidas has always been the favoured brand in France, and that Nike has made its way onto the French scene as a result of a few big contracts, like the one with PSG.

Duluc says that Nike 'has come to play on Adidas' home turf in both European and French football.' It should also be added that the brand got there more in an individual fashion, through individual shoe contracts, than through group contracts.

According to Isabelle Madec and Christophe Gante, Nike is developing a very definite strategy aimed at strengthening its position in the markets for football, athletics and lifestyle textiles. Its modus operandi is as follows: to put in place strategies that are quite straightforward and attack-oriented, consisting of selecting extremely striking symbols, paying them well, and using them as soon as a need makes itself felt.

Christophe Gante describes the mix applied by Nike as follows:

- the product is the key element and it is usually perfect;
- the strategy generally aims to position the products towards the high end of the range, but pragmatism is the order of the day if there is a need to reposition the campaign in response to aggressive competition;
- advertising campaigns are innovative and subversive;
- events are rare but massive;
- distribution is controlled by a relationship based on the force ratio.

'The slogan "Just do it", from the 1980s, which is still associated with the brand, has developed into a veritable state of mind, in the American fashion, corresponding to the precepts of a self-made man' (Nomen).

One could certainly say that the launching of one of their latest football shoes, the Vapor, is an example of a successful launch, one that has an impact on the market. This is indeed a 360° campaign, i.e. it is not just the good promotional campaign or the athlete who wears the product, but something about it that touches the consumer at the moment of the buying act at the point of sale, and acts in such a way that the product takes off. It is a strategy that is designed to be multichannel in its actions regarding the consumer.

Every commentator is in agreement on the following point: Nike set up a real brand strategy from the very beginning of its operation.

'Each item of merchandise is an ambassador for the association between the club and the brand' (Isabelle Madec). The fundamental issue when a brand signs a contract with a top team or an athlete is to draw attention to the association between the brand and the symbol. To do this we can engage in promotion and advertising around this action, or promote the merchandise that contributes to this recognition and at the same time earn money – whereas promotions are expensive.

'In Europe the markets are more or less frozen' (Vincent Duluc). The markets that can be won over and invested in are mainly to be found overseas. This is another reason why sporting brands and the clubs that they supply with equipment are travelling to Asia. Such actions enable the promotion of the club and the sports equipment manufacturer, and at the same time increase sales of merchandise. There is a convergence of interests between the professional club and the jersey's sponsor.

According to Isabelle Madec,

> there is a slight problem when we seek to internationalize a product, in the sense that there is always a little chauvinism behind a club or a federation. Both in Europe and abroad the goal is to put these products together in an attempt to have more impact on the targets of the marketing. Beyond that there are countries that are naturally more interested in France than others, so there are elements and trends that one can cash in on, but it's not easy to create those trends.

Puma

In this section we will see how the Puma brand carried out its internationalization process by means of sports sponsorships with clubs, federations, national teams, events and athletes. This process was especially necessary because the Puma brand was moribund and had almost disappeared in the late 1990s, before initiating a change in strategy (see Box 6.4).

Today, Puma is an unconventional and original brand. This is clearly displayed in its positioning and in its favourite motto: 'To be the most wanted sports and lifestyle brand.'

Box 6.4 History of the Puma brand[11]

Phase 1 (1993–1996) was devoted to restructuring the group and establishing a sound financial situation, with the goal of consolidating the brand and its image. For this purpose Puma capitalized on the image of football and its stars, knowing that the game has always been the most popular sport in the world (example: sponsoring Pelé, Cruyff and Maradona).

Phase 2 (1997–2001) was devoted to substantial investments in the areas of product marketing, research and development (R&D). This targeted the conduct of and investment in R&D. Significant actions during this phase were the development of the concept of Puma stores, the forming of partnerships with leading designers, e.g., Nuala and Icana, and the creation of the brand's website.

These various initiatives involved an exclusive distribution system for Puma products, aimed at positioning Puma in the sports lifestyle and making up for a lack of visibility on the international market.

Phase 3 (2002–2005) was designed to exploit the brand's potential. The idea was to make it 'appealing and sexy'.

To do this Puma obtained new collections from designers such as Miyara Yasuhiro and Alexander McQueen.

The sponsorship policy was centred on athletes such as Serena Williams, and particularly on African football teams. Puma also began to equip a number of European personalities, for example Paolo Nutini, Yann Barthès and Sinclair. These actions capitalized on the lifestyle image while still retaining a sports style aspect.

Phase 4 (2006–2010) addressed the development of new categories (golf and sailing) while also investing in marketing actions, with the goal of accelerating the brand's international expansion.

Puma's intention is to surprise the public by using a 'policy of differentiation'.

The brand is therefore developing a whole range of merchandise for its different partnerships, such as golf, motor sports, and sailing (the Volvo Ocean Race). Its sponsorships are also carefully targeted, choosing athletes and teams that act as symbols for their sport (S. Chabal for rugby and the world champion *Squadra Azzura* – Italy's national team – for football). Lastly, Puma is maintaining its policy of selective distribution, especially since the brand has become a member of the PPR Group.[12]

Key statistics

Puma: number three sporting brand behind Nike and Adidas.
2007 French sales: 223 million euros.
2010 (Puma International): sales of 4 billion euros.

Its sponsorship and co-branding policy obviously follows this plan. The selection of teams, athletes and co-branding partners is primarily made on the basis of their being both unconventional and high profile. The brand is featured in three types of sport:

- team sports (soccer and rugby football);
- motor sports (Formula 1);
- athletics.

Concerning football, for example, having a high-profile team or sport in each country is the primary rule. To comply with the above criterion, they must be easily noticed, have a novel image, be impertinent, nonconformist, and so on. The examples of Monaco and Bordeaux for League 1 are representative for France. On the international level, Italy is their flagship team. The 2006 Football World Cup strongly emphasized the team's image, its legendary cheekiness making it a team that Puma vigorously highlighted. Another decisive theme for the future: African teams. The African continent has many teams that are winners and also nonconformist. This provides a powerful theme for promotional purposes, based on novelty. Cameroon, Senegal, Ghana and Côte d'Ivoire are its principal representatives.

Athletics is another sport in which Puma is prominent. The Jamaican team is the best example. As David Dinis says 'In 2001, when they were signed, people said: what is the point of signing Jamaica? Now, in 2010, we look almost like visionaries.' In this team, Usain Bolt is the one who most represents the brand and its values. These were on display in the flesh during his victory in the 100 metres at the Beijing Olympic Games, when he showed off his winning pair of shoes. According to a study by TNS Sport, this 'free' promotion for the brand was the equivalent of 80,000 30-second advertising spots in one week, or about €250 million in advertising investment. And it didn't cost a penny...

The final sporting theme is Formula 1, where Puma provides equipment for several racing stables. Here it mainly produces shoes for the drivers and the teams, and also merchandise for the general public and lifestyle purposes. Its models then become bestsellers, such as Speed Cat and Sparco.

Away from sports, Puma is endeavouring to develop partnerships with designers such as Sergio Rossi, Alexander McQueen and Mihara Yasuhiro. The objectives are to associate the images of the two brands to obtain a high-range look combining luxury and sport. As David Dinis says: 'No sport without lifestyle, and no lifestyle without sport.'

PUMA: 'IMPERTINENT-DESIRABLE-DIFFERENT-NONCONFORMIST'

Puma's objective is to hold on to its number three position, while attempting to chip away at the market shares of the two giants: Nike and Adidas.

Puma's strategy of international expansion via sponsorship actions has long been established. In future, Puma wants to invest in a new sport every two years, always with the same aim: to discover an atypical sport expressing the brand's values in an unexpected area, so as to quickly achieve legitimacy and a return on investment. Puma has therefore made the choice to become involved in sports such as sailing, golf and motor sports, with a parallel development of ranges of dedicated clothing products.

> Why try to go and invest, for example, in tennis, where it will be necessary to put substantial sums into product research and development and in sponsorships to have any legitimacy: that would be beyond huge ... and it wouldn't be worth it, because the return on investment would be too slow. In sailing you can have a return on investment more quickly than in tennis.
>
> (J.R. Sainflou)

According to Mr Sainflou, it is no use goading the two giants, Nike and Adidas, in an area that they already control.

AFRICAN FOOTBALL

Puma wants to preserve its legitimacy in the football sector, and maintain its investments in teams that express the values looked for by the brand: the African football venture is a long-term commitment.

Puma impatiently awaited the FIFA 2010 World Cup in South Africa: 'That's going to be our World Cup!' (J.R. Sainflou, 2008). A dozen African teams were sponsored by the equipment manufacturer. 'African football represents all the values that we've been trying to convey for years' (J.R. Sainflou). This World Cup was launched very early on by Puma (in October–November 2009), and the brand endeavoured to capitalize on all of its merchandise (replicas and textiles).

THE VOLVO OCEAN RACE

Puma recently initiated the development of new categories in sport. Puma was looking for a long-term investment, but always with the objective of positioning the brand. With this in mind it selected an investment in sailing, with the 'Volvo Ocean Race' (conveying strong values such as ecology, freedom, solitude, immensity, etc.).

Three ranges of products were developed around this competition, which lasts for almost a year.

Puma's Sailing collection comprises:

- a technical range for people who sail;
- a lifestyle range (distributed to department stores);
- an intermediate restricted range (time of the event, year), or 'event-related merchandise'.

THE 'JACKPOT': USAIN BOLT

The equipment maker's other objective is to capitalize on the fame and image of Usain Bolt, and to put in place actions such as the marketing of a 'Special Gold-Medal' range and a promotional campaign bearing the effigy of 'the Lightning' (posters, press and film), so as to ever more concretely express Puma's strategy of differentiation, to optimize the return on investment, and also to surprise, by developing a new range of products.

OTHER TYPES OF CO-BRANDING

The brand has attempted to develop very specialized, very 'niche' and basically 'fashion' segments, intended to be accessible only to a certain elite section of the population. These products must on no account be made commonplace and become accessible to 'Mr and Mrs Nobody'.

Puma has therefore attempted to develop a collaboration between the creative world and the world of sport, in order to reach those at the top of the pyramid and to maintain the close connection that exists between the fashion segment and the world of lifestyle sport, but without the two ever becoming merged.

Actions:

* To propose to a worldwide selection of designers – such as Sergio Rossi, Alexander McQueen, Mihara Yasuhiro, Nuala and Hussein Chalayan – the creation of a new lifestyle sporting line.
* To find designers who are already working in high-end segments (McQueen with the PPR Group and the Gucci brand, for example).
* To develop sporting lifestyle product ranges, e.g. official balls for League 1 and League football.

THE ASIAN MARKET

Another objective for Puma is to establish itself in the Asian market. For this purpose Puma is equipping 15 Chinese national teams, creating and developing ranges of products suitable for the Asian market, establishing an online sales policy (with a Chinese website), and developing partnerships with professional athletes. The potential of the Chinese market is enormous, and the PPR Group is currently evaluating it. The group is expanding rapidly on Chinese soil.

Conclusion: from co-branding to tri-branding (a textbook case: FC Barcelona-Nike-UNICEF[13])

As we conclude this chapter, we believe that it is important to identify the best practices among our case studies. We have chosen to illustrate them by citing the example of FC Barcelona, whose sporting success and originality have become a byword. The FC Barcelona club enables Nike to develop its merchandise sales in the international market because it is a club of great international renown. Its championship and Champions League matches are re-broadcast by a number of media outlets worldwide. We should also add that the fact that the club is now more than a century old (it was founded in 1899) lends credibility to the brand and promotes its influence throughout the world.

We also know that for many years 'Barça' refused to have a sponsor for its jersey. This was to render the product both rare and exclusive. But since 2006 the UNICEF logo has been displayed on the front of the home and away jerseys. We should add that FC Barcelona pays 1.5 million euros per year for UNICEF to put its logo on the textiles associated with the club.

Nike is also innovating in its relationship with the club, because they are jointly designing and developing a line of textiles called '*Mes*', which echoes Barça's famous motto, written on the collar of each jersey: '*Mes que un club*', which means 'more than a club'. This refers to a relationship between the United Nations High Commissioner for Refugees (UNHCR) and the club. UNHCR establishes programmes devoted to education and sport, intended for child refugees worldwide. The goal of this partnership is to portray the image of a citizen of the world, for the club and for the Nike brand. The products will be distributed via the FC Barcelona Foundation, on the UNHCR website, and in Nike Stores.

Why has FC Barcelona never had a jersey sponsor before 2006? 'Because its President, Josep Lluis Nuñez, practiced an excellent economic management' according to J. Gil-Lafuente. 'FC Barcelona has become the richest club in the world without being a public limited company!' The president protected the 'virginity' of the jersey for two reasons:

- Differentiation: being the only club in the world to have a 'clean' jersey.
- Protection of the future: the president at the time explained to everyone that the jersey should be a resource in the event that, 'hypothetically', Barça should run into serious financial difficulties in the future.

Was the partnership with UNICEF a surprise? Yes. The '*socios*'[14] were expecting some kind of '*mana*' that would help the club to pay its debts, and a 'sponsor' to increase its financial resources.

Officially, this patronage operation is recorded as an investment by the FC Barcelona brand. Has the relationship with UNICEF changed the way that supporters and sponsors look at the club? According to Jaime Gil-Lafuente, the answer is no. The club has only become more popular, while continuing to win titles (in 2009, Barça won all of the six championships it entered).

This three-way relationship is evidently controversial. Nevertheless, it prefigures the future of sponsorship. Three logos or brands co-exist on one football jersey: the club's, the equipment maker's and the sponsor's. The innovation in the area of promotion that FC Barcelona introduced in 2008 may not yet be widely applied, but it remains an avenue to be explored by other clubs, as part of the 'socially motivated sponsorship' increasingly employed by brands.

Appendix

List of the 22 people interviewed for the compilation of this chapter

1 Thierry Batteux, Lifestyle Manager, Le Coq Sportif
2 Sébastien Bellencontre, Manager, Sports Marketing, Reebok France
3 Johann Bondu, Marketing Manager, Puma France
4 Nathalie Caron, Marketing Director, Reebok France
5 Philippe Dardelet, Former Marketing Director, Reebok Europe
6 David Dinis, Product Manager, Puma France
7 Marta Espejo Fiaz, Marketing Director, Le Coq Sportif
8 Vincent Duluc, Sports journalist and manager of the football section, *l'Équipe*
9 Alain Ferrand, Professor of Marketing at the University of Poitiers (France)
10 Gilles Gabillet, Former International Director, Reebok France
11 Christophe Gante, Key Account Manager, Adidas France
12 Jaime Gil-Lafuente, Professor of Sports Economics at the University of Barcelona (Spain)
13 Amandine Girny, Junior Footwear Developer, Le Coq Sportif
14 Sophia Huynh-Quan-Chieu, Manager, International Strategy, Nomen (specializing in the consulting on and creating of brand strategies)
15 Thomas Lanis, Brand Manager, Football, Nike France
16 Isabelle Madec, Business Development Manager, Adidas France
17 Julien Pierre, Journalist, *Sport Stratégies*
18 Alain Pourcelot, Marketing Director, Adidas France
19 Christophe Quiquandon, Brand Manager for Rugby, Tennis, and Basketball, Nike France
20 Jean Roger Sainflou, Director, Major Accounts, Puma France
21 Gary Tribou, Professor of Sports Marketing at the University of Strasbourg (France)
22 Hubert Weiss, Hardwear Manager (1982 to 1989), Le Coq Sportif

Notes

1 This chapter was compiled from secondary data but also reflects qualitative interviews with experts. A list of the 22 experts interviewed is presented in the Appendix.
2 Advertiser (*annonceur*) is the term used in the French advertising business. In the area of sponsorship, it may be likened to that of sponsor.
3 It should be noted that these authors used the term '*parrainage*' (patronage) instead of '*sponsoring*' (sponsoring or sponsorship). This expresses the desire of francophone countries to separate themselves from the Anglo-Saxon connotations of the word '*sponsoring*'.
4 In 2002, during the World Football Cup, the early elimination of the world championship French team was prematurely described as 'the beginning of a decline for the sports business and for sponsorships', but that did not happen. Today's advertisers know that investing in sponsorships carries a risk and that there are alternative promotional strategies that will allow them to recover from a setback.

5 For further details on this matter, see for example the work of Stefan Késenne, Bill Gerrard and Stefan Szymanski.

6 The G14 was a lobbying organization established by Europe's most powerful, biggest, most influential and richest professional football clubs. It was created in 2000 with 14 members and was disbanded in 2008 under pressure from UEFA and FIFA. Its purpose was to protect the interests of clubs affiliated with UEFA, FIFA, sponsors and broadcasters. Its slogan was 'The voice of the clubs'. Its headquarters was in Brussels. Since its February 2008 dissolution the G14 has been replaced by 'The European Club Association'.

7 We wish to express our grateful thanks to the 2008–2009 class of master's students in 'Marketing and sports management' at the University of Strasbourg, who provided much valuable assistance in carrying out these interviews.

8 In 1936 Adidas had been the sponsor of Jesse Owens, the winner of four gold medals at the Berlin Olympic Games.

9 Sponsorship of a broadcast by a brand.

10 Source: conversation with Thomas Lanis, Brand Manager, Football for Nike France.

11 Source: Puma France, 2010.

12 PPR (formerly Pinault-Printemps-Redoute) is a group of French commercial firms created by the billionaire François Pinault. The PPR Group is assembling a portfolio of global brands (both popular and luxury brands), and operates in 59 countries. In 2009, the principal companies in the Group were:

- Gucci Group: world-class luxury firms (Gucci, Yves Saint-Laurent, Sergio Rossi, Boucheron, Bottega Veneta, Alexander McQueen, Stella McCartney and Balenciaga).
- Puma: sporting equipment and fashion clothing (69.4 per cent).
- Redcats Group: one of the foremost international groups in the online distribution of fashion and decoration (Redoute, Ellos, Brylane, Cyrillus, Vertbaudet, Somewhere, Daxon, La Maison de Valérie, The Sportsman's Guide, The Golf Warehouse, Jessica London, Chadwick's, Roaman's and King Size).
- Fnac: leading distributor of cultural and leisure products in France and seven other countries (Belgium, Spain,= and Portugal in particular).
- Conforama: major European player in domestic furnishings.

13 We wish to thank Professor Jaime Gil-Lafuente, sports economist and professor at the University of Barcelona, for the invaluable assistance he provided in compiling information on the relationship between FC Barcelona and Nike.

14 One of the special features of FC Barcelona is its very large number of *socios* (the Catalan for season ticket holders) and worldwide supporters (*aficionats* in Catalan). The club passed the 170,000 socio mark in 2009 (173,194 on 1 January 2009), making it the football club with the most season ticket holders in the world, even more than Benfica and Bayern Munich. In addition, there are more than 1800 clubs for Barça supporters (*les penyes* in Catalan) around the world. FC Barcelona is one of only four professional clubs in Spain (the others are Real Madrid, Athletic Bilbao and Osasuna) that is not a public limited company, and is therefore owned by its season ticket holders.

References

Andreff, W. (1989), *Économie du sport*, PUF, Paris.

Bayless, A. (1988), 'Ambush marketing is becoming a popular event at Olympic Games', *The Wall Street Journal*, February, p. 8.

Crowley, M. (1991), 'Prioritising the sponsorship audience', *European Journal of Marketing*, 25, 11, 11–21.

Dambron, P. (1991), *Sponsoring et politique de marketing*, Éditions d'Organisation, Paris.

Deloitte Football Money League, 2010.

Derbaix, C., Gérard, P. and Lardinoit, T. (1994), 'Essai de conceptualisation d'une activité éminemment pratique: le parrainage', *Recherches et applications en marketing*, 9 (2), 43–67.

Desbordes, M. (ed.) (2006), *Marketing and football: an international perspective*, London, Elsevier, 544 p.

Howell, D. (1983), *Committee of inquiry into sport sponsorship*, London, Report prepared for the Central Council of Physical Recreation.

Meenaghan, T. (1994), 'Point of view: ambush marketing, immoral or imaginative practice?', *Journal of Advertising Research*, September–October, 24–32.

Piquet, S. (1985), *Sponsoring*, Éditions Vuibert, Paris.

Puma France (2010), http://fr.puma.com

Quiquandon, C. (1998), interview with Christophe Quiquandon, Brand Manager for Rugby, Tennis, & Basketball, Nike France.

Sahnoun, P. (1986), *Le sponsoring : mode d'emploi*, Éditions Chotard et Associés, Paris.

Sandler, D.M. and Shani, D. (1993), 'Sponsorship and the Olympic Games: the consumer perspective', *Sport Marketing Quarterly*, 2 (3), 38–43.

Sport + Markt AG (2007), European Jersey Report 2007–2008, October.

TNS (Taylor Nelson Sofres) (2009), 'Sponsorship in France.' Results presented at the Sport Marketing Awards, Paris, France, November 23rd 2009.

Tribou, G. (2007), *Sponsoring sportif*, Éditions Economica, Paris, 3rd edition.

7 Be ready to be excited

The World Wrestling Entertainment's
marketing strategy and economic model

Boris Helleu

Introduction

'Be ready to be excited, be ready to be entertained, and be ready for anything!'
boasts John Cena, the star wrestler of World Wrestling Entertainment (WWE),
in a promotional video for the federation. The WWE is a sports entertainment
firm based in Stamford, Connecticut. Its principal business is the organization
of professional wrestling events, for which it also provides management of the
media rights and merchandise. It has been listed on the New York Stock Exchange
since 1999, and is currently ranked 182nd among *Forbes* Magazine's Top 200
small companies[1] (122nd in 2008); it has 585 employees (excluding wrestlers). In
contrast to a professional sports league its role is not to regulate the athletic and
economic aspects of its sport, but to create original content designed to draw the
public into the arenas or towards their television sets. The federation's corporate
development strategy is described in this quote from Linda McMahon, its former
CEO: 'the company has come a long way from being a northeastern [US] events
group. We've made it a global brand. We are a content company. We produce it,
we create it, we own it and we distribute it.'[2] Starting as a local firm, the WWE
has become a global lifestyle brand, distributing original content on a number of
platforms, which operate synergistically. Adopting a 'Made at Home' strategy
to control its product from creation to distribution, the WWE is a true integrated
media and entertainment company.

Nevertheless, wrestling has rarely been the subject of an academic study. A
number of reasons have been advanced to account for this. In the first place,
wrestling is not a 'respectable' or legitimate subject for study. It is a scripted
entertainment, not a sport. Moreover, academics working in the sports field,
whatever their discipline, do not see these events as appropriate topics for research.
At best, wrestling is cited as the antithesis of 'real' sport, when it is a matter of
defining the latter. It is true that in spite of the trappings of a physical confrontation
overseen by a referee, the result of a wrestling match is decided in advance. This
implies that it has little interest for sports economists and marketers. In fact, it is
the attraction of uncertainty that needs to be preserved in event sports: by arousing
the interest of fans it generates income in the form of ticketing and television
rights (Fort and Maxcy, 2003; Sanderson and Siegfried, 2003). Consequently, by

focusing on ways of maintaining a competitive balance in a sporting competition by establishing regulatory tools, sports economists inevitably neglect wrestling. In spite of this, the WWE remains an interesting topic, for at least two reasons:

•   While its glory days may seem to be behind it, the federation has steadily developed its brand equity and its product, increasing its sales year after year. This aspect will be addressed by repositioning the firm's development in an historical perspective, and then by describing its business model.
•   The WWE takes it as a given that its product is a masquerade. By doing so it turns a weakness that could be crippling (scripted combats) into a strength, through a calculated marketing strategy. After a review of the theoretical foundations of experiential marketing, we will examine the ways in which the WWE's product is favourably placed for a consumption experience.

From a local WWF to a global WWE

The WWE is really only a small family company, and in more than one way. First of all, it was the grandfather of Vince K. McMahon, the current owner, who embarked on the organization of these events in the early 20th century, after being a boxing promoter. The McMahon family still holds the key posts in the firm. Vince McMahon is the Chief Executive Officer (CEO), while his daughter Stephanie manages the Creative Development and Operations Department. His wife, Linda, has left the WWE, where she was the Managing Director, to devote herself to politics.[3] Lastly, his son Shane left the federation in 2010. He had been in charge of the Global Media Division and of developing the company in the international market. It may be a family firm, but the WWE is nevertheless an internationally recognized brand. Without listing all the steps in the company's upward progress, we can identify the decisive strategic choices that enabled it to move from the regional to the international stage.

In 1948 six wrestling promoters join together to found the National Wrestling Alliance (NWA). Its members pledge not to compete on each other's territories. They also agree to share the most talented wrestlers and to blacklist those who are liable to cause problems. Lastly, the six organizations recognize a single world champion who will defend his title in the other federations (Greenberg, 2000). In this regard the promoters organize themselves like a professional sporting league that protects its franchises by means of the exclusive-territory system[4] and limits the power of the players by using the reserve-clause system.[5] Under this format the NWA extends its operations to some 40 territories, including foreign countries. In 1953, the Capitol Wrestling Corporation (CWC), founded by Jess McMahon and Toots Mondt, joins the NWA. After a disagreement with NWA over the procedure for awarding the title, in 1963 the CWC takes the name of World Wide Wrestling Federation (WWWF), which in 1979 would become the World Wrestling Federation (WWF). Managed at this time by Vince McMahon Senior, the federation is restricted to the northeastern United States, presenting shows in New York City, Washington DC, Baltimore, Philadelphia, Pittsburgh and Boston. In 1982 Vincent K. McMahon, the grandson of the founder, together with his wife Linda purchases the WWF from his father by making four $250,000 payments. His goal is to make the WWF brand familiar at the international level. He intends to do this by distributing its programmes on cable, putting the biggest events on pay-per-view,[6] by hiring away emerging stars from the competition, and by ignoring the gentleman's agreement that protected promoters from competition within their own territory.

While the WWF is able to achieve national exposure, the media magnate Ted Turner creates World Championship Wrestling (WCW) in 1988. The real competition begins in 1995. The WCW launches its programme, *Monday Nitro*, on the TNT channel on the same day and at the same time as *Monday Night Raw*, the WWE's flagship broadcast. As a direct, credible competitor the WCW attracts some of the WWF's best wrestlers. As it becomes more daring in constructing its storylines,[7] the WCW soon overtakes the WWF in the ratings. Since the WWF had lost much of its fame and tarnished its brand image during the early 1990s,[8] the emergence of this competition provides an opportunity for Vince K. McMahon to reposition his product. During this period, known as the Attitude Era, the storylines become more complex, the content more risqué and bloody, and the wrestlers' costumes more flimsy. Although the programmes are more eye-catching (it is the beginning of trash TV), they bring together a young-adult public[9] and in 2001 enable the WWF to emerge victorious in the Monday Night War.[10]

Having put an end to the competition, the WWE reacquires some of its wrestlers from the now-defunct WCW. The strategic choice then consists of establishing two separate shows. Vince K. McMahon explains it as follows: 'With the acquisition of WCW, and the talent development work we have been doing, we now have the depth of talent necessary to provide the star power to drive two compelling, distinct, prime-time television programs.'[11] In 2002, the wrestlers are assigned exclusively to one of the two shows, each of which develops its own storylines: *Raw* (the red brand) and *Smackdown* (the blue brand). This choice, described by the WWE as Brand Extension, is in fact more of a range extension. *Raw* and *Smackdown* are actually two programmes located under the same 'WWE' umbrella trademark. There is little to distinguish them: both the product offered and the public targeted are very similar. This is above all a recipe for increasing the number of events and television contracts, and thereby covering a larger market, including the international one. In addition, following the example of the major leagues, a draft lottery is held each year so as to rebuild the rosters[12] for each broadcast.

In April 2000 the World Wide Fund brings proceedings against the World Wrestling Federation over the terms for using the acronym 'WWF'. The non-governmental organization, founded in 1961 for the protection of nature and the environment, is recognized throughout the world by its logo and the initials WWF. The wrestling federation had built its fame during the 1980s, and a portion of its business depends on the sale of merchandise marked with the 'WWF' logo. In 1989, and again in 1994, an agreement between the two parties settles the terms for using the acronym. The wrestling federation is closely restricted in its use of the abbreviation, especially overseas. This is a huge constraint, and because the Stamford federation is so well known in the United States and internationally under this trademark it ignores the agreement. In 2001 the High Court in England rules in favour of the nature protection organization (a decision confirmed on appeal in 2002). From November 2002 the Stamford federation is under an injunction prohibiting it from using its acronym or logo in any of its areas of business (events, merchandise, websites, etc.) and finds itself forced to change its name. It opts for 'WWE', and relentlessly comments on the name change in a humorous and ironic manner by using the slogan 'Get the "F" out.'

The WWE repositions itself in a consensual, domestic marketing niche, reducing its violent content so as to avoid competing with free-style fighting programmes. Since 2008, according to the parental-guidance system for TV programmes employed in the United States, the WWE's more civilized and toned-down content has moved its programmes from a TV-14 to a TV-PG classification.[13] Although this new cycle, described as the PG Era or Kid'z Era, has caused some of its disappointed fans to switch to the competition, making over its image in this way has enabled the WWE to sign new sponsorship contracts. This move to embrace a younger audience represents a true strategic choice. The WWE has developed a magazine for its youngest fans (*WWE Kids Magazine*) as well as a special website (WWEKids.com). According to Linda McMahon, this 'from the cradle to the grave strategy' is designed so that the WWE becomes an early favourite and remains the preferred brand over the long term.[14] The WWE nevertheless retains a diversified public (Ashley *et al.*, 2000).

The WWE's economic model

In the past, the classic business model for wrestling relied exclusively on the income generated by ticket sales. In future the WWE will operate under a more complex model (Table 7.1). The product's ability to attract customers is based on Star Power (Rein *et al.*, 2006, pp. 155–156), i.e. the Superstars' charisma and their skills in the ring and at the microphone.[15] As with any traditional sporting event, the WWE must entice its consumers to enter its arenas and watch their TV sets. A number of television programmes (*Monday Night Raw*, *Friday Night SmackDown*, *WWE NXT* and *WWE Superstars*) are broadcast in the United States and throughout the world. Although these programmes are relatively accessible, about 15 major events per year are available on pay-per-view only. The star power of WWE wrestlers is also expressed in a range of physical products. A fan who subscribes to the brand's values can thus not only watch wrestling events, but also purchase action figures, video games, DVDs, biographies, magazines, clothes, music and even movies in which the principal roles are played by Superstars. The experience also continues into the digital realm, since fans can access its content via the Internet and on their cell phones.

In 2009[16] the WWE had sales of US$475.2 million, mainly consisting of television rights (24 per cent), attendance at arenas (23 per cent), sales of

Table 7.1 The WWE's economic model: original content distributed on multiple platforms

Content	Talent: 100 Superstars and Divas (Intellectual property)		
Show	342 shows in 2009	4 TV programmes: • Raw • Smackdown • NXT • Superstars	14 pay-per-view shows in 2009
Merchandise	160 licensees worldwide: Videogames, toys, action figures, clothing, books, magazines, music, DVDs, etc.		
Electronic media	e-commerce, internet content and cell phones		

merchandise (21 per cent) and pay-per-view revenues[17] (17 per cent). Every week, 16 million American television viewers watch all or some of the seven hours of programming produced by the WWE. In 2009, the WWE presented 268 shows in North America to an average of 6500 spectators (average ticket price US$37.64). The WWE produced 14 pay-per-view shows, which brought in US$80 million. The 25th WrestleMania show, the biggest event of the wrestling year, generated more than a million purchases worldwide and brought in US$22.5 million.

Finally, with income of less than US$500 million, the WWE lags far behind its indirect competitors in the sports sector. By way of comparison, in the same year the NFL's 32 teams generated US$7.6 billion and Real Madrid all by itself earned income of US$576 million.[18] Nevertheless, the WWE has certain strengths. Although its business is cyclic, because it depends on the quality of the event offered, it still manages to prosper: in 2006 the WWE was generating income of less than US$300 million, and less than US$100 million in 1996 (see Figure 7.1). Secondly, the WWE is a brand of great renown, which has assumed the position of a 'global lifestyle brand', recognized throughout the world. According to the *Forbes* website: 'Now WWE is global and has a market cap of $1.2 billion, which we calculate to be 30 per cent attributable to the value of its name alone.'[19]

Globalization of its brand is one of the WWE's priority objectives. From 2000 to 2009, income generated outside North America rose from $9 million to $127.1 million, and now represents more than a quarter of all sales. Its television programmes are broadcast in 145 countries and 30 languages, and the federation maintains offices in Toronto, London, Sydney, Tokyo, Shanghai and Singapore. Last year, 74 shows were presented outside North America, with a total audience of 8500 and an average ticket price of US$66.08.

Shuart and Maresco (2006) report that Kurt Schneider, then responsible for the WWE's marketing, saw the product's simplicity as a factor favouring globalization: there are no rules to understand, and the dramatic impulse is mainly based on an opposition between good and evil. Note, moreover, that the WWE's globalization strategy is not a recent development. In the early 2000s, the Manchester United soccer team and the WWE had signed an agreement to distribute each other's merchandise. At about the same time the Manchester club was considering an

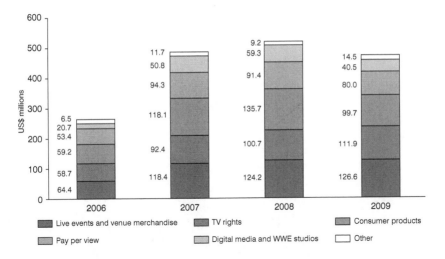

Figure 7.1 The WWE economic model: variation and distribution of income (2006–2009)

investment in the North American market through a similar agreement with the New York Yankees. For the WWE the strategy was a winning one, because apart from North America the United Kingdom is the WWE's biggest market, at US$36.5 million

In this way the WWE was able to develop from a traditional local carnival spectacle into a diversified business on the world scene. Although Vince K. McMahon's sometimes controversial strategic choices (Assael and Mooneyham, 2002), have proven decisive, the 'Right Man' theory is not enough by itself to account for this success. We will attempt to show that, by its very nature, wrestling is a spectacle that favours a consumption experience that can be promoted by innovative marketing tools.

Experiential marketing

Drinking beer, chewing gum, brushing one's teeth, shaving, watching television: these are the relatively commonplace behaviours that punctuate our daily life. However, they share the property of having been upgraded to the level of an 'experience'. We must immediately acknowledge that this term can be confusing, because it has so many meanings (Carù and Cova, 2002). We are not referring here to the learning accumulated over a lifetime (experience that is acquired or received) but rather to the act of feeling and trying something out. One might say that there is an experience of the mind, and another of the heart. The first, formal or scientific in nature, leads to knowledge, while the second, based on real life and the emotions, causes sensations and feelings. It is the second meaning that interests us here, since the emotions seem to play a fundamental role in the buying act. It follows that it is no longer a matter of quenching one's thirst, taking a bath, or relaxing, but of experiencing the freshness and the softness, and awakening

Table 7.2 Traditional and experiential approaches to the product and the consumer

	Traditional marketing	Experiential marketing
Product	Understood in terms of its functionality (advantages and characteristics), it is consumed to meet an objective or to respond to a problem	The product is consumed for its own sake
Consumers	Rational choices: they acquire information, assess the competition, make the best choice and make repeat purchases if satisfied	Affective and emotional factors guide the purchase

Source: After Schmitt (1999).

one's senses. There are now countless numbers of brands that invite us to enjoy or sample the experience of their product or service. Ultimately, it becomes as if the utilitarian value of the products were consigned to the background, and the consumer – no longer driven by reason alone but also by the passions – must seek out both the useful and the pleasant.

In future, positioning a product or a brand properly, targeting the appropriate consumers and opening a dialogue with them are of course still necessities, but they are no longer enough. Consumer marketing analyses have long been constructed around the transactional/relational duality. Transactional marketing more specifically addresses the buying act, whereas relational marketing involves customer satisfaction and loyalty. However, between these two extremes consumers have the experience of what they buy. This in-between area is the domain of experiential marketing (Hetzel, 2002). It was as a result of the pioneering article by Holbrook and Hirschman (1982) that the idea of experience became a key element in understanding the behaviour of the consumer. The authors developed a theory according to which consumers' filling a need or a wish by satisfying themselves through the utilitarian or material advantage obtained from a good is an outmoded concept, or at least an incomplete one. In fact, hedonistic consumers also seek comfort, well-being, the involvement of their five senses and emotion (Table 7.2).

Schmitt (1999) observed that traditional marketing, in focusing on a product's properties and advantages, no longer answered the new expectations of consumers. He suggested a number of tools for addressing experience through its five facets (sense, feel, think, act and relate: its sensorial affective, cognitive, actional and relational aspects). Pine and Gilmore (1999) broadened the concept of experience to include economics, and found that it was not enough in a competitive environment to offer a good service or product: importance also had to be attached to the experience itself. This latter element fundamentally altered the manner of consumption, to the point that it became a new way to segment the market and enabled a new pricing policy. To illustrate, the following ways of enjoying a coffee have nothing in common in terms of product, service and experience (other than the raw material): drinking it in a 'traditional' café, making it at home in a traditional coffee pot or espresso machine and drinking it in a Starbucks. This said, the consumption experience is not limited to the consumption of the product, but is constructed around a number of stages (Arnould *et al.*, 2002). There is a before (we budget, imagine and dream about the experience), a during (the purchase, the environment of the place of sale, the use of the service or product), and an afterwards (the memory, the narrative and the sharing of the experience with others).

A live event is by its nature an experiential product, such that there have been many research studies on artistic and cultural subjects (Bourgeon-Renault *et al.*, 2003). However, studies with a sporting subject are fewer in number. As regards participatory sport, Ladwein (2005) views trekking as a consumer experience and shows that its participants are not seeking danger but rather opportunities to put themselves into a narrative. As regards spectator sport, Kao *et al.* (2007) examine the parts played by certain elements of the experience (surprise, participation and immersion) in satisfying the audience and winning its loyalty to Taiwan's professional basketball league. They show that although surprise and interaction with the audience are significant components, immersion is a much greater one. According to these authors, encouraging the experience means improving the arrangements for receiving the public and the tools that play on their senses (sounds and lights). Lastly, concerning the experiential aspect, Allan Stenhouse, the marketing director of the Fox Kids channel, describes a practical example: the Fox Kids Cup. He shows how the 2002 match in this international football tournament acts as a vector of experience and enables the channel to develop its brand image (Stenhouse, 2003).

Since then, many sporting clubs have revived the concept and promise their fans a big match-day experience, multiplied even further by the fact that the match will be watched from comfortable box seats. In the same way that the consumer/ actor is a co-producer of the experience, the spectator/actor increasingly becomes a stakeholder in the sporting event. As Rein *et al.* emphasize: 'As Entertainment values have escalated and fan expectations have risen, programmed anticipation, architectural venue integration, and an overall Entertainment experience are now expected' (2006, p. 221).

The WWE's experiential power: mundus vult decipi, ergo decipiatur[20]

According to Pons and Richelieu (2004), a sporting event is intangible, ephemeral, unpredictable and subjective, thus bringing about significant involvement on the part of the consumer. The authors emphasize that 'attitude towards a sports event is based on the satisfaction of an emotional need (excitement or joy), a need for communion (exchange and socialization), and a need for knowledge about the sport adopted' (2004, p. 163). A sports event, which is consumed while it is being produced, has the properties of an experiential good: it is co-produced, dramatized, a vector for emotions and is shared. It may not be a sport, but we would like to show how the WWE's entertainment offers much the same characteristics.

In the episode entitled 'W.T.F.' the kids of 'South Park' decide to set up the Wrestling Takedown Federation after attending a WWE event.[21] Trey Parker, the creator of the series, parodies wrestling and specifically the WWE by stressing the outrageous dramatization of these events, which overshadow the capacities of the Superstars. By doing so the series highlights a basic feature of this entertainment: 'Wrestling is drama' (De Garis, 2005, p. 193), even a melodrama, specifically aimed at working-class men (Jenkins III, 2005). It is true that the dramatic impulse and attraction of the WWE's productions borrow from the scripts of a *telenovela* series. Thus when the WWE seeks to recruit a creative writer, we can read into the advertisement that WWE is borrowing from the sitcom, the talk show, the soap opera, the action-adventure, and from drama.

This raises the following question: are these events real or rigged (Mazer, 1998, 2005)? In his autobiography, the wrestler Mike Foley leaves no doubt: 'I'll answer your question, or at least confirm your thoughts for you. Yes, wrestling is Entertainment, and no, I didn't actually "win" the belt in the way that World Series or Super Bowls are won' (Foley, 2001). But in fact, the issue of veracity is unimportant. As Roland Barthes (1957) has shown, it matters little to the spectators that the fight is scripted: it is a spectacle of excess which takes its dramatic impulse from Greek tragedy. By adopting the basic categories of play proposed by Roger Caillois (1958), we can say of wrestling that it occupies a theoretical space at the intersection of competition (agon) and imitation (mimicry), giving rise to a combination of sport and theatre.

It is a matter of make-believe. Barnabé Mons (2008) notes that the art of wrestling consists of giving the illusion of blows, of convincingly pretending to give them and of receiving them with pain. Brett Hart, one of the best wrestlers of all time, explained that his art resided in his way of striking blows in a convincing manner.[22] Believability is an essential element in a wrestling match. Because although they never doubt that the fight is fixed, the fans subscribe to the feigned, overdone emotions of the wrestlers and the reversals of situation, just as they would for a real sport.

The fights are thus scripted within the strict framework of a story. Finally, the absence of uncertainty, so long concealed by the promoters, is what makes wrestling strong. In daily life, a human being lives in a society replete with uncertainty, risks and fears of the future. In the context of event sport, uncertainty may cause eustress (positive stress), but it also involves its quota of disappointments (relegation, early elimination and unfairness). In wrestling, the result of the fight is unimportant. Just as the narrative surrounding a product has a role in the consumption experience (Filser, 2002), what counts in wrestling is the story being told. In fact, in the agon/mimicry pair, the second item is the more important of the two. The story and its narration being the determining factors in the success of this entertainment, we should then regard the storytelling as the fuel for the WWE's experiential motor. Indeed, according to Christian Salmon (2007, pp. 16–17), storytelling tacks artificial narratives onto reality, blocks exchanges, and saturates the symbolic space with series and stories. It says nothing about past experiences; it traces the paths and guides the flows of the emotions. ... storytelling establishes the narrative mechanisms by which people are led to identify models and follow instructions.

The WWE's events follow emotional vectors that vary with the roles assigned to each participant (audience, wrestlers, announcers and commentators). The WWE creates an experience by the unremitting dramatization of its events, immersing its spectators in a fake reality. Far from arousing mistrust or resistance, a wrestling event requires the loyalty of is audience, which pretends to be deceived. To all appearances the audience prefers the pretence to the reality (Cova and Cova, 2004). To adopt the words of Christian Salmon (2007), we can say of the WWE that, following the example of Disney, it is an industry that manufactures emotions and sells collective fables. This remarkable positioning is what makes the WWE a show and not a sport.[23] Moreover, by its very nature the WWE is offering an experiential show. Carù and Cova (2006) summarize the production of experiences under three headings:

- The consumer is placed in a setting that promotes the show's staging, especially by multi-sensory stimulation: the arenas hosting WWE shows are arranged to optimize the audience's reactions (giant screen, dramatic entry of the Superstars, lightshows, and pyrotechnic effects).
- Active audience participation: as Laurence De Garis emphasizes: 'matches must be constructed in a dialogue (or maybe colloquy) between or among the wrestlers and the crowd' (2005, p. 206). More broadly, it is a matter of arousing a response from the audience by skill in the ring or at the microphone. The audience can then participate actively by holding up signs with messages of encouragement for its favourites, and by chanting to show its (dis)approval of certain matches. It can also react to the taunts of wrestlers playing the roles of bad guys, or on the other hand show its sympathy for the 'nice' ones.[24]
- The story that is told to the consumer who wants to keep a souvenir (memorabilia mix): during its shows the WWE sells its merchandise (T-shirts, caps, goodies of all kinds) with images of its Superstars and/or carrying its logo. The WWE says: 'the WWE Fan experience does not end when the fan leaves the arena or turns off the television'. In 2009 these sales yielded US$19.8 million. In addition to the ticket (US$37.60 in North America, US$66 overseas), a WWE fan spends an average of US$9.58 on merchandise.

In this way '... the WWE has established credibility by not only letting the fans know up front that their sport is theatrical, but by setting high entertainment benchmarks for the experience' (Rein *et al.*, 2006, p. 113). The federation's objective thus consists of transforming this experience into a sustained dialogue. The WWE's website is used 'to promote our brands, to create a community experience among our fans, to market and distribute both our offline, online and mobile products, and sell online advertising'.[25] Each month, 14 million unique visitors log on to wwe.com to see its 423 million pages and 22 million videos. In 2008, the WWE launched its own online social network, called WWE Universe. This platform allows fans to register in a community, creating their own blogs or taking part in discussion forums. Finally, the WWE provides opportunities for interaction and dialogue with its fans in two separate spaces: an institutional space devoted to what it supplies (wwe.com) and a space devoted to the fans, representing the corresponding demand (WWE Universe). Anxious to expand its net marketing, the WWE uses the full arsenal of social networks. Both wwe.com and WWE Universe have a presence on Facebook and Twitter.[26] This is where the WWE displays its business-to-fan (B2F) marketing expertise. In contrast to the traditional CRM strategy, the WWE uses these tools to target a very specific portion of its customer base: fans who are already enthusiastic about the product, loyal to the brand and are also used to multitasking. Moreover, the WWE encourages its athletes to open their own Twitter accounts. By enabling fans to forge direct links with their favourite athletes, Twitter acts as a simple tool for conducting grass roots electronic marketing, promoting its coming shows, and remaining active and visible on days without events.

The fans' appropriation of the WWE brand goes as far as the design of the product. This approach is not new: a number of other firms invite their customers to personalize their own product, or to become spokespersons for it via advertising campaigns.[27] However, the WWE's approach is particularly interesting, since the federation is generally reluctant to authorize its fans to become involved in the product. On its website, the WWE makes its policy clear: 'Please do not send or e-mail any materials (including scripts, screenplays, story-lines, ideas, music, business proposals, marketing concepts, etc.) having to do with character development, story-lines or in-ring activities. WWE does not consider or examine these materials.'[28] Now there is not just co-production of an event but also co-development. The pay-per-view show 'Cyber Sunday' allowed fans to vote on the WWE website to select the matches, the wrestlers and the title to be won.[29] Jonathan Zerden, then the VP for Interactive Technology, stated:

> We use customer feedback to impact our story lines and for marketing. It enables us to surround the customer with 360 degrees of marketing. We get to see how they interact with mobile platforms, how they interact with us, how they interact with their arena, and how they interact with their cable company.[30]

Although fans may have very few opportunities to become involved in WWE productions, the 'SmackDown vs. Raw' videogame published by THQ allows them to appropriate their favourite shows by telling their own stories. Available on the most commonly purchased consoles (Sony PlayStation 3, PlayStation 2, PSP, Nintendo Wii and DS, Xbox 360, and even the iPhone), it reaches a broad public. In 2008 and 2009, sales of games yielded nearly US$45 million for the WWE. Since the launch of the 'SmackDown vs. Raw' series in 1999, 51 million copies have generated more than US$1.5 billion in earnings. The game follows

Table 7.3 The various ways of appropriating the WWE brand

Recognize it (brand awareness)	Identify the WWE among its direct and indirect competitors
Know its values (brand knowledge)	A Global Lifestyle Brand producing a family event. A brand its audience relates to, attentive to its employees and fans, and involved in the community
Know its advantages (brand utility)	A show acting as a vector for the emotions; a show co-produced and sometimes co-scripted with its audience
Remain loyal (brand preference)	Overcome the artificial aspect of the event, watch the free TV programmes
Buy it (brand purchase)	Acquire merchandise and buy pay-per-view shows
Live it (brand experience)	See the event live, join the electronic community (forum, blog, WWE Universe), maintain a dialogue with the brand (Twitter and Facebook), live the experience via videogames

the narrative codes of wrestling (Costantino and Gordon, 2009). In its 2010 version the game has two cornerstones: identification and customization. Players can thus either pick a Superstar and become part of the match, just as in the TV programmes, or take over the story by creating a character of their own and their own storylines. In the promotional campaign for the show the slogan was 'It's Your World Now', so as to encourage the fans to extend the experience according to their own ideas.

These strategies are really only ways to have the fans adopt the WWE brand, as we show in Table 7.3. At an initial level the potential consumer must be able to recognize the WWE and distinguish it from other wrestling federations. This promotional work is primarily achieved via the visibility afforded by television programmes, but also, in the United States, by having the Superstars take part in advertising spots and variety shows.[31] Secondly, the consumer must be able to identify with the positioning of the brand and its values. In order to stay away from items liable to harm its image (the accidental, violent or overdose-related death of its wrestlers, or the use of drugs), the WWE emphasizes its philanthropic activities (encouraging young people to vote, involvement in the Make a Wish Foundation, relocating an event for the troops fighting in Iraq and Afghanistan, etc.). In a third stage, the consumer must be capable of recognizing the product's benefits. In the short video that introduces the WWE's television broadcasts, we hear the words: 'Yes Sir, we promised you a great main event here tonight'. That represents the WWE's product benefit. Because it makes no difference that the fights are scripted, it is this very dramatization that feeds the fans' experience. Once these three stages are completed, brand loyalty can be achieved. This step is not so easy, because becoming or claiming to be a fan of wrestling sometimes means having to face the scorn of people who refuse to see the element of play in the show. Consumers can become fans of the brand. To show their commitment, they have at their disposal a whole range of merchandise. Lastly, fans can have the WWE experience outside the television programmes. They can attend a

WWE event, share their passion with their peers, interact with the brand and its representatives, and finally identify with their favourite Superstars or transport themselves into the world of wrestling through videogames.

Conclusion

Although the WWE has succeeded in becoming a global brand, it should not be forgotten that its first attempts to diversify, undertaken in the early 2000s, ended in defeat. The World, a theme restaurant it opened in New York's Times Square in 1999, closed its doors in 2003 on the grounds that the federation was 'reallocating resources to the continued growth of our global business, rather than focusing on a single, site-specific and local project'.[32] Founded in 2000 as a joint venture between NBC and the WWE, the XFL was a professional football league that operated after the end of the NFL season, with the aim of attracting both football and wrestling fans. Although attendance averaged 23,000 spectators per match, their numbers quickly dwindled. Because it was launched by a wrestling promoter, the product lacked credibility, and the XFL went out of business after only one season. The setback was such that ESPN rated the XFL as the second-greatest flop in the history of sport.[33]

Nevertheless, the WWE dominates the wrestling market, having managed a transformation 'From margin to mainstream'. By becoming a show calculated to attract a family audience the WWE increased its base of potential customers, but at the same time gave up a base of older male fans, who turned to events of more limited general appeal that catered to their expectations. For example, the Ring of Honor (ROH) is an independent federation based in Philadelphia that targets an audience of purists who are more drawn to long fights that emphasize skill over entertainment. Only Total Nonstop Action Wrestling (TNA) has serious plans to compete with the WWE.[34] This includes the recruiting of stars who more often appear with the WWE. It even attempted, unsuccessfully, to reopen the Monday Night War by programming its broadcast in the same time slot as the WWE's broadcast of *RAW*.

Paradoxically, it may be the absence of serious competition that constitutes the real danger for the WWE. As we have seen, the aggressiveness of the WCW forced the WWE to innovate. That period of competition produced unprecedented attendance figures. In an ultra-competitive and fragmented entertainment market, it needs to ensure that its product does not become stale. Thus although the Stamford-based federation has succeeded in recruiting a new class of younger fans overseas, it must now take care to develop effective marketing strategies to retain their loyalty, or risk seeing them join the competition.

Notes

1 *America's 200 Best Small Companies of 2009*, by Brett Nelson, Kurt Badenhausen and Christina Settimi, *Forbes*, 14 October 2009 (www.forbes.com).
2 Wrestling's bottom line is no soap opera, by Brooke Masters, in the *Financial Times*, 25 August 2008.

3 See *The Smackdown Candidate*, by Andrew Rice, 3 June 2010, on businessweek.com

4 An exclusive territory is a privilege granted to a franchise that preserves it from competition by another team in the league, within the market assigned to it. In economic terms, potential consumers in a specific geographic area have no substitute product in the sport concerned. This protective measure confers on such franchises a true monopoly in their sport. With the competition destroyed, the owners are in a strong bargaining position for optimizing their profits.

5 Created at the end of the 19th century, the reserve clause was an understanding among the owners of baseball teams in the National League to make a limited number of players untransferable and thereby limit their power to negotiate increases in their salaries.

6 The first WrestleMania took place in Madison Square Garden on 31 May 1985 before 19,121 spectators.

7 A storyline is the fictional narrative that creates the rivalries between wrestlers.

8 The WWF was then prosecuted for having encouraged the use of steroids, and Vince K. McMahon was accused of sexual harassment.

9 In 2001, broadcasts of *Raw* attracted an average of 6.2 million viewers, including 1.4 million young men between 18 and 34.

10 The WWE has produced a documentary about this period: *The Monday Night War – WWE Raw vs. WCW Nitro* (2004).

11 *WWE to Make Raw and Smackdown! distinct TV Brands*, 27 March 2002, http:// corporate.wwe.com

12 A federation's staff of wrestlers.

13 TV-14: the programme is not recommended for children under 14; TV-PG: the programme may be viewed by young children, although adult guidance is suggested.

14 *UBS 36th Annual Global Media Conference*, 8–10 December 2008.

15 This is what the WWE calls its wrestlers.

16 All economic data for 2009 and preceding years were taken from the WWE's annual reports for 2006, 2007, 2008 and 2009, available at corporate.wwe.com

17 Pay-per-view: access to a WWE programme is billed at US$39.95 except for *WrestleMania*, which is sold for US$54.95.

18 *Forbes* lists of *Most valuable soccer team* and *football team 2009*, available at www.forbes.com

19 *Vince McMahon: Heavyweight Champion of Branding*, by Peter Schwartz, 8 February 2010 at http://blogs.forbes.com

20 The world wants to be deceived, so let it be deceived.

21 Episode 13 of the 10th season, broadcast on 21 October 2009 on Comedy Central.

22 *Hitman Hart: Wrestling with Shadows*, documentary by Paul Jay, released in 1998.

23 The WWE always endeavours to make the boundary between sport and show a permeable one. On several occasions, top athletes from other disciplines have taken part in WWE events (Dennis Rodman, Karl Malone, Shaquille O'Neal, Mike Tyson, Floyd Mayweather, and others). Moreover, it is not without significance that Eddie Hill, the WWE's new Senior Vice President for Marketing, has worked for Disney and for the ESPN sports channel.

24 The nice wrestlers (face) arouse cheers (pop) while the bad guys (heel) try to attract jeers (heat), for example by running down the sports team of the town that is hosting the show.

25 *Strength in Numbers, World Wrestling Entertainment 2009 Annual Report*, p.6, available at corporate.wwe.com

26 WWEUniverse has more than 600,000 fans on Facebook and its Twitter account is followed by more than 56,000 people.

27 NIKEiD (Nike), mi Adidas (Adidas) and Mongolian Shoe BBQ (Puma) are services that allow fans to design their own pair of sneakers. In 2006, for Super Bowl 41, Doritos launched its "Crash the Super Bowl" competition, allowing consumers to make their own advertising spot.

28 corporate.wwe.com, accessed January 27 2011.
29 Cyber Sunday was presented from 2004 (when it was known as 'Taboo Tuesday') to 2008. In 2010 the WWE established a similar concept, 'Viewer's Choice', for its *Raw* broadcasts.
30 *WWE Wrestles with Customer Feedback Marketing*, by John Gaffney, 3 May 2007 on SearchCRM.com
31 Following the example of Thierry Henry, Roger Federer and Tiger Woods, John Cena has taken part in advertising spots for the Gillette brand in the United States.
32 *World Wrestling Entertainment, Inc. to Close Restaurant*, 25 February 2003: 2003 news on corporate.wwe.com
33 ESPN25: The 25 Biggest Sports Flops, ESPN.com
34 *TNA Turns Violent in Fight for Wrestling Fans*, by Bruce Goldberg, 14 June 2010, on sportsbusinessjournal.com

References

Arnould, E. J., Price, L. and Zinkhan, G. M. (2002). *Consumers*. New York: McGraw-Hill.
Ashley, F. B., Dollar, J., Wigley, B., Gillentine, J. A. and Daughtrey, C. (2000). Professional wrestling fans: your next-door neighbors? *Sport Marketing Quarterly*, 9(3), 140–148.
Assael, S. and Mooneyham, M. (2002). *Sex, Lies and Headlocks. The Real Story of Vince McMahon and the World Wrestling Entertainment*. New York: Three Rivers Press.
Barthes, R. (1957). *Mythologies*. Paris: Editions du Seuil.
Bourgeon-Renault, D., Filser, M. and Pulh, M. (2003). Le marketing du spectacle vivant. *Revue française de gestion* (142), 113–127.
Caillois, R. (1958). *Les jeux et les hommes*. Paris: Gallimard.
Carù, A. and Cova, B. (2002). Retour sur le concept d'expérience: pour une vue plus modeste et plus complète du concept. *7èmes Journées de Recherche en Marketing de Bourgogne*, Dijon, France.
Carù, A. and Cova, B. (2006). Expériences de consommation et marketing expérientiel. *Revue française de gestion* (162), 99–113.
Costantino, O. and Gordon, C. (2009). *Fake Rules, Real Fiction: Professional Wrestling and Videogames*. digra.org (Digital Games Research Association).
Cova, B. and Cova, V. (2004). L'expérience de consommation: de la manipulation à la compromission? *Les troisièmes Journées Normandes de la Consommation. Colloque 'Société et Consommation'*, Rouen, France.
De Garis, L. (2005). The 'Logic' of Professional Wrestling. In N. Sammond (ed.), *Steel Chair to the Head: The Pleasure and Pain of Professional Wrestling* (pp. 192–212). Durham and London: Duke University Press.
Filser, M. (2002). Le marketing de la production d'expériences: statut théorique et implications managériales. *Décisions marketing* (28), 13–22.
Foley, M. (2001). *Foley is Good: And the Real World is Faker Than Wrestling*. New York: Harper.
Fort, R. and Maxcy, J. (2003). Competitive balance in sports leagues: an introduction. *Journal of Sports Economics*, 4(2), 154–160.
Greenberg, K. E. (2000). *Pro Wrestling: From Carnivals to Cable TV*. Minneapolis, MN: Learner Publishing.
Hetzel, P. (2002). *Planète conso: Marketing expérientiel et nouveaux univers de consommation*. Paris: Editions d'Organisation.
Holbrook, M. B. and Hirschman, E. C. (1982). The experiential aspects of consumption: consumer fantasies, feelings, and fun. *Journal of Consumer Research*, 9 (2), 132–140.

Jenkins III, H. (2005). 'Never Trust a snake': WWF Wrestling as Masculine Melodrama. In N. Sammond (ed.), *Steel Chair to the Head: The Pleasure and Pain of Professional Wrestling* (pp. 33–66). Durham and London: Duke University Press.

Kao, Y.-F., Huang, L.-S. and Yang, M.-H. (2007). Effects of experiential elements on experiential satisfaction and loyalty intentions: a case study of the super basketball league in Taiwan. *International Journal of Revenue Management*, 1 (1), 76–96.

Ladwein, R. (2005). L'expérience de consommation, la mise en récit de soi et la construction identitaire: le cas du trekking. *Revue management et avenir* (5), 105–118.

Mazer, S. (1998). *Professional Wrestling. Sport and Spectacle.* Jackson, MS: University Press of Mississippi.

Mazer, S. (2005). 'Real' Wrestling/'Real' Life. In N. Sammond (ed.), *Steel Chair to the Head: The Pleasure and Pain of Professional Wrestling* (pp. 67–87). Durham and London: Duke University Press.

Mons, B. (2008). Les corps à corps du catch. *Vacarme* (48).

Pine, B. J. and Gilmore, J. (1999). *The Experience Economy: Work is Theatre and Every Business a Stage.* Boston, MA: HBS Press.

Pons, F. and Richelieu, A. (2004). Marketing stratégique du sport. Le cas d'une franchise de la Ligue nationale de hockey. *Revue française de gestion* (150), 161–175.

Rein, I., Kotler, P. and Shields, B. (2006). *The Elusive Fan: Reinventing Sports in a Crowded Marketplace.* New York: McGraw-Hill.

Salmon, C. (2007). *Storytelling, la machine à fabriquer des histoires et à formater les esprits.* Paris: La Découverte.

Sanderson, A. R. and Siegfried, J. J. (2003). Thinking about competitive balance. *Journal of Sports Economics*, 4(4), 255–279.

Schmitt, B. H. (1999). *Experience Marketing: How to Get Customers to Sense, Feel, Think, Act and Relate to Your Company and Brands.* New York: Simon and Schuster Inc.

Shuart, J. A. and Maresco, P. A. (2006). World Wrestling Entertainment: achieving continued growth and market penetration through international expansion. *The Sport Journal*, 9 (4).

Stenhouse, A. (2003). 'Experience' marketing in action: the Fox Kids Cup. *Young Consumers: Insight and Ideas for Responsible Marketers*, 4(4), 11–16.

8 The establishment and management of sports arenas

A neo-marketing approach

Michel Desbordes

For many years, ticket sales were the sole component of sports financing. At the beginning of the century, football matches in Europe and baseball in the United States were exclusively financed by their spectators. The event was produced for them, according to a commercial model: the players, if they were professionals, were more or less directly paid by the spectators. Cycling was the only exception: it was free, so at an early stage it had to develop alternative methods of financing, such as sponsorship (Desbordes, 2006). During the 1960s, the merchandizing of sport contributed to a change in the situation, leading in due course to a hierarchy of sports financing based on four sources of income: ticket sales, television rights, sponsorships and other income (mainly merchandizing) (Table 8.1).

Table 8.1 The financing structure of major sporting events

Sporting event	TV rights (%)	Sponsor- ship (%)	Public authorities (%)	Ticket sales (%)	Other (%)	Budget (€ million)
World Cup football (1998)	38	24	0	38	0	370
ASO (2001)	43	40	5	0	12	90
Salt Lake Olympics (2002)	41	47	0	10	2	2,100
Paris–Dakar (1988)	39	60	0	0	1	76
Roland-Garros (2001)	38	24	0	29	11	82
Athens Olympics (2004)	37	28	12	9	14	1,960
Tour de France (1998)	28	65.5	6.5	0	0	42
World Cup rugby (1987)	20	50	0	30	0	9
The Race (2004)	15	65	15	0	5	23
World Cup Athletics (2003)	0	22	50	21	9	57

Sources: Bourg and Gouguet (2004), Halba (1997), organizers' data (excluding investment costs).

Table 8.2 Ticket receipts for the main European football championships in 2007

Match-day receipts: average for clubs	
England	€40.1 m
Germany	€17.2 m
Spain	€17.2 m
Scotland	€10.8 m
Italy	€8.7 m
France	€6.9 m
Netherlands	€6.6 m
Portugal	€4.9 m

Source: Ineum Consulting (2008).

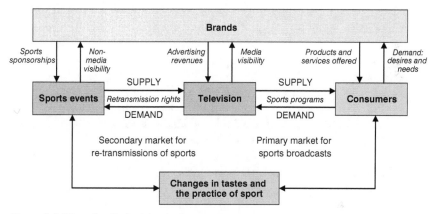

Figure 8.1 The role of television in the sports system

Source: Desbordes (2008).

We note that for recent events ticketing never exceeds 40 per cent of the total financing. The same situation prevails in football: the central role of television in the system and the great number of indirect (television) spectators compared to the number of direct (stadium) spectators has reduced ticket sales to a minor share in the clubs' financing (Table 8.2).

The globalization of major sporting events has further underscored the pre-eminence of television, which has become the true link or driving force between the consumer and brands investing in sport through sponsorships. The players are now paid by television, since the internet model has not yet found a way to replace it (Figure 8.1).

In this situation, we may legitimately ask the following question: is it worth paying attention to the spectators, when their financial contribution is only a marginal item in today's sports business?

In spite of the facts presented above, saying no would make no sense at all, and would overlook some of the special features of the sports services marketing

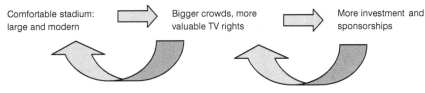

| Comfortable stadium: large and modern | Bigger crowds, more valuable TV rights | More investment and sponsorships |

Figure 8.2 The 'virtuous circle' of professional sports financing

that now surround a supporting event. Television companies pay amounts for TV rights that are out of proportion to the size of the crowd at the match, but they also want to broadcast quality programmes. And a quality sporting event is a contest in which the stadium is full and the atmosphere festive. This atmosphere is produced by the spectators themselves, something that is very specific to the marketing of sport: the person who pays also produces the service (Eiglier and Langeard, 1987; Tribou, 2007). But these spectators need help: they will be more inclined to blow off steam if they enjoy being in the stadium and if the service provider gives them the means to create this atmosphere. A comfortable, high-capacity stadium, with top-class security so that families will come and feel at ease there, is therefore favourable to a good ambiance, which makes the sports event that much more profitable to broadcast, and thus automatically increases the market value of the television product for the broadcasters. In the same way, a widely seen sports event automatically causes a rise in sponsorship contracts, because the brand has a better opportunity to increase its fame and to capitalize on the value of the event if there are more people in the stadium and more watching the small screen (Tribou, 2007) (Figure 8.2).

Thus the issue of sporting arenas is a crucial one, and goes far beyond that of the '4th P' in the marketing mix.[1] The stadium cannot be seen only as a distribution site that fits in with the three 'other Ps': as a recreation centre and a real-life showcase that enhances the product, it affects all the components of the mix. But to appreciate its full scope and complexity this variable must be viewed in a 'neo-marketing' context (Badot and Cova, 1992). This is the approach taken in the present chapter: after providing details of the main theoretical models that address the concepts of the consumer, the fan and the spectator, we examine how this work may be incorporated in the process of optimizing the management of sporting arenas.[2]

Theoretical aspects of the stadium/arena: a neo-marketing approach to the production of sporting events

Consumer behaviour and what fans want

Traditionally, a creditworthy consumer (the only kind that interests a marketer) is defined as an individual who has a need to be satisfied and the financial ability to do so by purchasing a good or service. A sports consumer can be either a spectator or an athlete.

There have been few studies of 'traditional' spectators. Attention has instead focused on supporters, referred to as fans in the Anglo-Saxon literature; they have the following characteristics:

- they identify with a team or a player – and follow the team both on and off the field;
- they own team merchandise;
- they regularly buy tickets;
- They pass a significant amount of their social time discussing the life of the club with people who share their enthusiasm.

According to Pooley (1978), this difference between fan and spectator can be expressed as follows:

> Whereas a spectator of sport will observe a spectacle and forget it quickly, the fan continues his interest until the intensity of feeling toward the team becomes so great that parts of every day are devoted to either his team or in some instances, to the broad realm of sport itself.

But a sports spectator does not attend a sports arena in the same way as a 'traditional' consumer. The seminal work of Holt (1995) on baseball spectators at Wrigley Field in Chicago (the Chicago Cubs' ballpark), whom he studied for two years, identified four manners of consumption:

1. Consumption as experience: this is consumption as a personal psychological state; everyone refers to a certain number of rules to interpret what they are consuming, then they assess the object or the service consumed, and enjoy it or not. In an event, the emotional reaction is one of the main signs of the valuation.
2. Consumption as incorporation: in this approach the consumer considers that the object or the service consumed is an integral part of his or her identity.
3. Consumption as play: a framework that enables interactions with others, based on common rules. Holt distinguishes two kinds of play: communion and socialization. In communion, consumers share a consumption experience. This experience, lived as a group, may be centred on a totem. In this approach 'the spectators influence each other in a spiral interaction which raises the level of emotional intensity'. In its other aspect, socialization, the consumption experience generates communication between the consumers, who thereby assert their tastes and values.
4. Consumption as classification: in this last approach consumers make use of objects to classify themselves in comparison with others. We see here the affiliation–distinction duality. Supporters who wear the jerseys of the team they support affiliate themselves to their team by distinguishing themselves from their opponents.

In parallel with the work of Holt, other authors have studied fans in attempts to measure the level and the intensity of their attachment to the team. It is no longer just a matter of differentiating consumers, but of classifying them on the basis of their beliefs and behaviours. Wann and Branscombe (1993) developed the Sport Spectator Identification Scale (SSIS) by applying four variables (reading about sport, talking about sport, sports knowledge, and attachment to the players and the team); other writers (Kahle *et al.*, 1996) have highlighted the influence of identification with the team, self-investment, the search for emotion, loyalty tied to the sports results and the search for social interactions.

These models show that consumers of sport may have various relationships with a team. Consumption is not simply guided by attachment to the team but also by 'entertainment', or a search for social interaction.

In conclusion, the factors that affect the consumption of sporting events are:

1   The appeal of the match: the players, the teams, the ranking, the rivalry, the league, etc.
2   Economic factors: income from spectators, ticket sales, the club's commercial strategy, etc.
3   Environmental factors: the schedule, the weather, the infrastructure, etc.
4   Demographic factors: gender, age, etc.
5   Emotional factors: identification with the team and motivation.

The consumption of a sports event, then, is a complex phenomenon: not all of the spectators are enthusiasts or total fans, not all of them use their team as a vector for asserting their identity, and not all of them are faithful to their team: there is a wide variety of behaviours, and thus of consumptions.

From a marketing viewpoint, compiling a typology of spectators can help to identify products that are likely to please, to redefine promotional campaigns, to adjust prices (for tickets and products), or just generally to adapt 'the sports experience' to the requirements of each segment.

This consumption experience is what will become central to motivating possible customers.

A study carried out on 2215 NBA fans led to a three-category classification (Mullin *et al.*, 2007; Figure 8.3).

1   Level 1. Light users: those who are coming for the first time, received a free ticket and are taking advantage of an opportunity. They are influenced by the following factors: the opponent, the weather, the day of the week, the team's performance and the fact of meeting other people.
2   Level 2. Medium users: they attend 10 to 30 per cent of the matches. They have to be persuaded to come by offering various options involving the schedule and the price.
3   Level 3. Heavy users: those who attend all the games (or half of them). They sometimes have box seats.

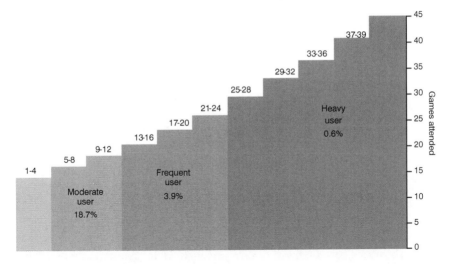

Figure 8.3 The sport consumer escalator
'The escalator is a graphic representation of consumer movement to higher levels of involvement in a sport, as a player or a fan. The escalator suggests that sport organizations should invest more in nurturing existing consumers than they should in trying to create new ones.' (Mullin *et al.*, 2007: 42).

Country	2003/2004	2006/2007	Variation
England	588	802	36.4%
Germany	207	310	49.8%
Spain	275	344	25.1%
Italy	186	156	−16.1%
France	120	139	15.8%

Figure 8.4 Variation of ticket receipts in the major European championships

Source: Ineum Consulting (2008).

There needs to be an attractive strategy for rewarding loyalty: comfort, service, interaction and promotion. Ultimately, the stadium is the critical variable that can lead the consumer up the steps of this escalator. For example, the construction and renovation of stadiums for the 2006 World Cup enabled Germany to stimulate attendance and increase the number of season ticket holders, all other factors being equal (see Figure 8.4).

This increase was due to the fact that Germany built five new facilities and renovated seven, at a total investment cost of 1.411 billion euros (see Box 8.1); by way of comparison, for the 1998 World Cup, France built only one new stadium and renovated nine, at a total budget of 612 million euros (Ineum Consulting, 2008).

Box 8.1 Attendance: The Bundesliga pats itself on the back

According to the *Bundesliga's* official website, for the first half of the 2009–2010 season Germany had the *highest average attendance in its stadiums out of the five major championship leagues* (England, Spain, Italy, France, and Germany).

The 162 matches in the German first division attracted an average of *42,630 spectators,* considerably more than the Premier League (33,934 spectators), Spain (28,706 spectators), Italy (25,169 spectators) and France (19,965 spectators).

Of the 20 European clubs with the highest average number of spectators per match, eight are German: Borussia Dortmund, Bayern Munich, Schalke 04, Hamburg SV, Borussia Munchengladbach, FC Cologne, Eintracht Frankfurt, and Hertha Berlin.

The prize goes to *Borussia Dortmund,* with *75,311 spectators,* followed by *Bayern Munich (68,896 spectators)* and *Schalke 04 (61,050 spectators).*

To take a somewhat wider view, the *Bundesliga's* average attendance is really third in the world for a sports championship, *behind American* (NFL) football and the Indian Premier League (cricket).

Even the *Bundesliga 2* (the second division) attracts an average that would make our western championships green with envy, at 14,944 spectators per match, i.e., only 5,000 fewer than the French League 1…

It goes without saying that these 'scores' are not only due to the sporting spirit of the Germans, who travel to the stadiums in droves, but also to the infrastructure constructed for the 2006 World Cup, and finally to the quality of the play presented.

This is the third consecutive year that the *Bundesliga* has drawn the highest average crowds in Europe. As a reminder, the 2008–2009 season saw an average of 42,521 spectators in German stadiums, and the 2007–2008 season 39,444 spectators.

Source: http://mad-marcus.over-blog.com/article-affluences-quand-la-bundesliga-s-auto-congratule-42069726.html (30 December 2009, last accessed 16 March 2010).

An experiential recreational centre for the community[3]

The live experience in a stadium or a sports arena has become one of the priorities of the promoters and producers of sports events (Van Uden, 2004; Apostolopoulou *et al.*, 2006). Under this new approach, the media and trade journalists now speak of 'entertainment' when describing the content of a sporting event. According to Robert Johnson, the owner of the Charlotte Bobcats, a new NBA franchise, 'There is no separation between sports and entertainment … merge them together and create something unique' (Maltese, 2010).

This unique quality renders certain sports organizations, clubs and events extremely attractive and especially meaningful in the eyes of the fans, the media and the public at large. The first people to introduce this fashion of experiential production of events were the operators of the North American NFL, NBA, NHL and MLB franchises, and even, in an exaggerated manner, the promoters of wrestling matches for the notorious WWE. This way of producing, even scripting, a sporting event has become professionalized, to the point of taking on numerous similarities with the production of live events such as concerts, or popular entertainment in general. Indeed, certain suppliers such as stage managers and firms specializing in the renting or setting up of audio, video and pyrotechnical equipment are now in high demand, and may work both in the production of a Madonna concert, for example, and also a basketball or tennis match.

Consumers of sports events have thus become very demanding: they are no longer drawn by the sporting event alone, but also by whatever is going to make the experience surrounding the match or competition a special one. According to Van Uden (2004), who studied the Dutch football club Vitesse Arnhem, there has been a radical change in the terms of management: the organization has now redefined itself as a 'multi-entertainment football company'.

The experience of sports consumption has thus acquired a number of new aspects that revolve around the athletic performance offered on the field. This performance, comprising a match between two teams or two individuals, is obviously the core of the offer, and represents the major portion of the cost of production for the organizer or manager of a professional sports organization. However, this offer is now noticeably 'magnified' by means of a great variety of event production techniques, which act to strengthen and broaden the sports consumption experience.

The most striking and best-known examples of sports event productions that link sporting performance and entertainment are the inescapable North American sporting encounters represented by All-Star Games (especially basketball) and championship finals (particularly the Super Bowl). The All-Star Game consists of a weekend organized in mid-season and designed as an exhibition between, for example, the best basketball players from the eastern and western United States, chosen by the public and the coaches of the NBA franchises. Here the entertainment aspect becomes the core attraction of the event, and the sporting performance becomes secondary, since the competitive pressure is relatively weak. These All-Star weekends offer spectators the possibility of taking part in the event through numerous activities and displays. This type of production is primarily designed as a very powerful advertising tool, which originated in the encounters organized by the celebrated Harlem Globetrotters team, who emphasized the show and display aspects of their sport in numerous world tours. A number of exhibitions have been devised, with no great sporting interest in terms of competition: they favour spectacle over pure sporting performance. This is the case, for example, with the matches organized in Asia and New York between the two tennis legends Pete Sampras and Roger Federer, or the tenth anniversary celebration of the French football team's victory in the World Cup, held in the Stade de France on 12 July 2008. In these cases, the consumption experience finds its climax in the nostalgia associated with the event presented.

Infinitely more competitive as a sporting contest, and offering a production that combines high quality and great sporting interest with a scripting that makes the consumption experience even more singular and entertaining, the Super Bowl (the North American football championship final) remains the indisputable gold standard. Apostolopoulou *et al.* (2006) examine the Super Bowl from the standpoint of experiential marketing, particularly as discussed in the relevant works of Holbrook and Hirschman (1982), Pine and Gilmore (1999), and Keller (2003). In the course of a study aimed at identifying and classifying the various supporting elements of the entertainment offered during the Super Bowl, these same authors show that in spite of the competitive nature of the match and the identities of the teams playing for the championship title – which are of course the overwhelming aspects for those involved – the commercial advertising specially created for this event, such as the concerts and displays presented, especially at half-time, are the most attractive and entertaining for the consumers. For events like these, a group of experiential supporting features is deployed, of two kinds:

•   Intensification of the sporting spectacle: the introduction and entrance of the teams, presentation of the Most Valuable Player (MVP) award at the end of the game, statistics, expert commentaries, audio feeds from the referees and coaches, slow-motion replays, live interviews, etc.
•   Expansion of the sporting spectacle: pre-match show (jugglers, performers, tightrope-walkers, mascots, etc.), concert and introduction of sports celebrities at half-time, special advertising spots, post-match fireworks, cheerleaders during any dead time, and so on.

The stadium or arena should therefore be designed to encourage this quest for the experience of consumption. The era of transactional marketing is over: individuals now view the sports event as a competitor of Disneyland, which is why the show presented must promote this unforgettable consumption experience. A stage manager is essential: the business has changed, and we are now in the world of entertainment (Desbordes and Falgoux, 2007). In Europe, however, where – unlike North America – sporting performance is still the primary motivation for spectators and organizers alike, this transformation of 'traditional' sport into sport as event has not gone so smoothly. Max Guazzini, the chairman of the Stade Français rugby club in Paris, and organizer of the famous 'shows' at Stade de France, is often criticized by the 'purists' of traditional rugby.

'From the economic and media viewpoints, this makes sense. But it is by no means certain that Stade Français's glitzy Parisian show-biz side will not alter the identity of rugby over the long term.'[4]

Nevertheless, this transformation seems an inevitable one for European sport.

Geomarketing and geolocalization strategy, or how to establish a sports arena

Although the spectators' motivations and the event organizers' marketing strategies have been discussed earlier in this chapter, a crucial question remains: where should the stadium be built?

Geomarketing is a branch of marketing: it consists of analysing the behaviour of economic individuals, while taking into account the concept of space (Cliquet, 1992). It involves a combination of the skills of marketers and geographers.

Geomarketing has various applications, such as studies of customer catchment areas (a point of sale's area of attraction), studies of business localization, studies of potentials, sectorization, the optimization of direct marketing methods (direct mail, phone campaigns, etc.), network optimization, etc. Geomarketing often makes use of geographic information systems (GIS) to process geographic data using computer tools.

Anglo-Saxons use the term location business intelligence, which is more appropriate when the approach concerns marketing, but the discipline also embraces land-use planning, in the context of socio-economic studies.

Geomarketing employs several kinds of software, although its application is in no way dependent on any of them, but rather on mastering its specific expertise and applicable models (Baray, 2003):

1   geolocalization and geocoding software;
2   geographic information and spatial-analysis systems;
3   data processing and statistical software;
4   integrated operating systems.

However, few commercial programs are capable of dealing with the complexity of the discipline, too often reducing it to a simple operational tool.

In professional sport, the North American leagues have been using geomarketing for some years. The establishment or transfer of a franchise is decided on the basis of market criteria: the size of the customer catchment area, its business potential and its possible competitors in the local market will guide the decisions. In NHL ice hockey we can point to the story of the Quebec Nordiques, who after experiencing financial difficulties were sold to Denver, becoming the Colorado Avalanche, even though Denver is located 2800 km from Quebec! It traumatized their fans in Quebec, who saw the sale as yet another takeover by 'the damn Americans' of a traditional Canadian sport.[5] Nowadays the development of hockey franchises in the southern USA is a matter of market demand: the population there is increasing, and it is reasonable to establish teams in areas where there are growing numbers of people, for commercial reasons. This also makes sense on the sociological level: the creation of the Florida Panthers in Miami targets a clientele of retirees who spend the winter in Florida, and who come for the most part from the north-eastern United States and Canada, traditional hockey territory. San José, Tampa and Atlanta similarly obtained their own teams during the 1990s. In 2010, 24 teams are located in the United States (versus 6 in Canada), and 10 of the 24 are in southern states (California, Florida, Texas, Georgia, North Carolina, Tennessee and Arizona). Nevertheless, the commercial success of these southern teams is not always up to expectations, because it is sometimes difficult to establish a traditional northern winter sport in tropical regions, and only a redistribution of income by the NHL is enabling some of the teams to stay afloat.

Following the same line of thought, geomarketing can suggest changes in European sport when imbalances are found: in France, in 2010, only two of the teams in rugby's Top 14[6] are in the northern part of the country, whereas nine of them are in the south-west.

Conversely, in women's basketball, only 4 of the 14 teams are located in the south of the country.[7] Both leagues are aware of this imbalance, which creates problems because, for example, it is difficult to involve the rest of the country in these championships, and so it becomes hard to sell the TV rights. The leagues are therefore trying to encourage the development of clubs in major cities that are not represented in the league, while also encouraging mergers in areas where there are too many teams. But in spite of all this, nothing can be imposed by fiat, and an all-powerful league cannot decide the matter on a financial basis: it is sporting performance that ultimately determines whether they are part of the league or not.

Theoretical studies in geomarketing

In France, Loic Ravenel, a geographer who first became involved in sport and then in sports marketing, carried out pioneering work in this area beginning in 1996. His association with colleagues such as Boris Helleu, Emmanuel Bayle and Christophe Durand enabled him to take up all of the issues in geomarketing, from sport as leisure to sport as event, as demonstrated by the experiences of European football players (see the summary in *Habilitation à diriger des recherche'*, Ravenel (2009)).

Professional sport in general offers fewer impediments to geomarketing, because its commercial nature predisposes it to the use of such business tools. Its first aspect, which appears simple, is the demographic criterion: although for example a connection exists between sporting success and demography in European football (Durand *et al.*, 2005), things are not in fact so simple, because the definition of an urban area is so complicated.[8] Similarly, the traditional application of time contours to indicate the time of access to new facilities has to be changed, because various forms of transport have been introduced. There is also a problem with the scale of reference (local/national/global): the work on long-distance supporterism (Lestrelin, 2006) might lead one to believe that, since fans are scattered throughout the world and the internet or television can replace direct contacts, the concept of a customer catchment area no longer apples. This is not so: as we emphasized earlier, a full stadium is always a necessary condition for the generation of other income (TV, sponsorship and merchandizing). The question of access to the stadium must therefore be considered.

More generally, in the European system geomarketing is positioning itself at the point where demand from the cities (elected representatives and inhabitants) meets supply from the professional leagues (Figure 8.5). The leagues are considering spatial policies designed to ensure their viability by investigating the potential along with the competition.

As we mentioned earlier, the application of geomarketing *stricto sensu* (merger, moving to a new location, league reorganization, as suggested by Helleu (2007)),

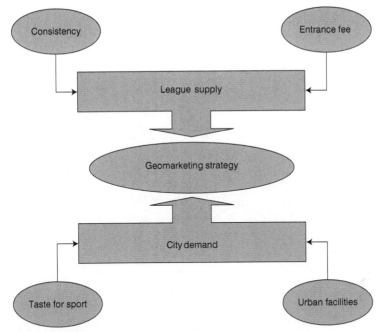

Figure 8.5 Geomarketing strategies of cities and professional leagues

Source: Ravenel (2009).

runs up against numerous institutional, sociological and historical obstacles. Nevertheless, spatial marketing actions can be implemented at the club level, especially as part of a process of sustainable development, now that considerations of transport and distance are assuming ever-greater importance for ecological reasons. All the items listed in Table 8.3 now need to be taken into consideration in the construction of a stadium.

Having laid the theoretical foundation for the creation and management of stadiums, we will now address the more directly managerial aspects of these sports arenas, in the second section of this chapter.

Managerial aspects: the implementation of consistent policies concerning fans, to optimize the sporting venue

CRM policies as applied to fans: from knowing the customer to the provision of increasingly customized services

CRM consists of knowing how to target, attract and retain good customers, and constitutes a decisive factor for the success of the firm. Building and developing relationships with customers is a challenge, particularly when the firm has thousands (even millions) of customers, who communicate with it in many ways. To achieve a satisfactory result, systems for CRM must enable the firm's managers

Table 8.3 Spatial marketing actions for a club

Actions	Benefits	Difficulty of execution	Sport
1 . Minimize transport cost.			
Highway partnership	Flexibility	System management Match timetables Compatibility of timetables	All
Train partnership	Transport cost, comfort	Location of stadium/arena with respect to the station	All
Car sharing	Flexibility, social interaction, ecologically correct		All
2. Parking supply			
Park-and-ride	No traffic jams, speed	Logistics	Football
Onsite parking	Flexibility		
3. Points of sale			
Internet	Easy	Internet access	All
Local kiosks	Existing system	Computing equipment; cost and location of services	

Source: Ravenel (2009).

to better understand their customers, so that they can adapt and personalize their products or services.

The four basic components of CRM are as follows:

1 knowledge of the customer;
2 relational strategy;
3 communication;
4 customized value propositions.

Knowledge of the customer

An individual knowledge of each customer is essential for developing a lasting relationship, and for being able to make appropriate offers. His or her buying history, preferred manner of communication, preferred payment methods, and preferences and interests in terms of services, etc., are all information that is absolutely necessary for the development of long-term relationships. The information mentioned above is generally scattered among various information systems, and firms must collect them in a customer data 'warehouse'.

Although it is important to have the data required for developing customer relationships, it should not unnecessarily burden the firm's information systems. Any information that does not contribute to CRM objectives should therefore be excluded.

Relational strategy

Companies that concentrate on the success of their short-term business transactions display only a limited interest in their customers. Their success is measured in the number of transactions completed and sales made. For them, their market share is the primary indicator of success.

Companies that develop a relational strategy are interested in developing long-term relationships with their customers. They engage in communication with the customer more often than they sell. Among the mass of customers, the company unabashedly favours those who are the most interesting and the most profitable. The commercial transaction does not mark the end of the relationship. This relationship, beginning with the purchase, leads to a deepening association based on confidence and a growing mutual commitment.

Communication

The relational strategy established by the firm must be strongly demonstrated in its communications with the customer. It should show its ability to create a personalized dialogue during which real content will be provided, including concrete items that are relevant to the customer. To achieve this it must be conveyed through a system of integrated communication channels that allow for communication anywhere and at any time. This ability to communicate through multiple channels is essential. For example, a bank may use a number of channels: a branch, regular mail, its website, the ATM, a voice server, Short Message Service (SMS), Multimedia Messaging Service (MMS), and so on.

According to a 2009 study by Markess International,[9] the telephone is still the preferred channel when firms interact with their customers, with nearly 36 per cent of such interactions taking place in this way, versus 21 per cent via email and 16 per cent via the internet. According to the same study, the forecast for 2010 shows that the telephone is marking time, falling to only 28 per cent of customer interactions, in favour of email and the internet, which now each account for 24 per cent of the volume of customer interactions. Interactions employing mobile applications are also expected to register a significant breakthrough.

Multichannel communications are becoming increasingly dominant in CRM. The goal is to promote interactions with the customer. In addition to telephonic media, the use of tools such as web callback or virtual agents is becoming inescapable.[10]

Customized value propositions

The development of a close relationship and a real dialogue with the customer should result, for the firm, in the creation of customized offers in terms of both product and price. In this way the firm can design – sometimes in cooperation with the customer – a service that perfectly responds to the customer's needs. This can be achieved, for example, by means of 'service modules' that can be linked to one another to create an overall service that meets the customer's expectations. The firm must take special care to maintain full control of its costs and avoid sacrificing the economies of scale. Similarly, the creation of customized offers may involve a greater risk for the firm, and an excessive complexity in its production processes. It must work to combine a relatively standardized production with the flexibility demanded by any customization of service.

In the world of sport, equipment manufacturers have long since incorporated CRM into their strategies, especially in running.[11] They endeavour to create communities of runners by setting up meeting places that generate traffic on the brand's website. The strategy generally employed by these brands consists of offering customized training plans for reaching a running objective, but this training plan is not sent until information has been provided that is of value to the manufacturer regarding segmentation (gender, age, height, weight, occupation, number of workouts per week, etc.) and the CRM relationship (email address and mobile phone number). Once this information is supplied the database will be 'worked' in a Web 2.0-type relationship.

A good CRM policy thus requires, first of all, a good database. This is why the manufacturers of sporting products, and also sports clubs, compete for ingenious new ways of obtaining reliable information to compile into so-called 'qualified' databases. The basic element is still of course the gift that will be sent if the consumer returns a little information sheet, but this can take forms that are much more subtle and sophisticated.

In the world of European football, marketing policies and especially CRM have not developed naturally. Security, which became a major issue during the 1990s after the dramatic events that took place in the stadiums, has dictated the development of these venues. All the stands have progressively been equipped with seats, and for major events tickets have become non-transferable at the time of their reservation. The development of season ticket policies has also changed the situation. This means that for certain clubs with a high percentage of season ticket holders, 'each seat is occupied by a well-identified person', which is a complete change in terms of marketing. For example, in the Arsenal stadium 99.8 per cent of the spectators hold season tickets! Thus on the pretext of security everything is known about each person entering the stadium (times of arrival and departure, bar tab, stadium attendance, number of children, marital status, mobile phone number, etc.), which multiplies the possibilities when approaching the consumer. This aspect of information systems is often forgotten when we praise 'the effectiveness of merchandizing policies in England': the English clubs are simply not competing with their European counterparts (see Figure 8.6 for example) on a level playing field, because they have more season ticket holders, and therefore more qualified and comprehensive databases, which greatly facilitates the work of the downstream marketer.

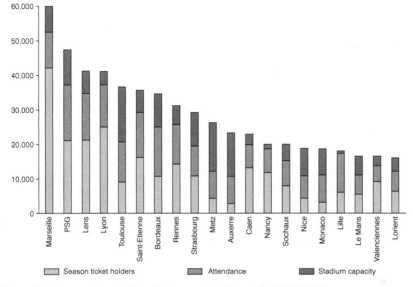

Figure 8.6 Season ticket holders in League 1 in France in 2007–2008
Source: Helleu (2010).

76 per cent of the tickets sold in France are sold before the event, versus 98 per cent in England. Three clubs say that they make 50 per cent of their ticket sales on the night of the match. With only one exception, all the clubs that limit the number of season-ticket holders have an occupancy rate of more than 80 per cent. The 'cap' is variable, but is generally located around 65 to 70 per cent of the total capacity. In England, this cap, if one exists, is more usually located at 80 or 85 per cent. This practice makes sense only in a situation where demand exceeds supply.[12]

Although the clubs unquestionably want to increase the numbers of their season ticket holders, seeking both cash flow and knowledge of their audience, having ticket holders is not without drawbacks (Table 8.4).

In 2010 in France, CRM policies are employed by only about half of all clubs. Paradoxically, it was a 'small' club, AJ Auxerre, with one of the smallest budgets in League I that was one of the first to implement such a policy with its AJA card, in 2008.[13]

In the United States, CRM practices became the norm some time ago, among certain pioneer teams in the 2000s (Miami Heat in the NBA, Seattle Mariners in MLB, Arizona State Devils in the National College Athletic Association (NCAA)), and even in 1995 with the San Diego Padres of MLB, which enabled the creation of huge databases (185,000 fans in the United States for the Padres and 68,1000 in Mexico!) and an increase in the number of spectators (two million per year for the Padres since establishing CRM), and in average spending per match, which has grown exponentially (US$280 per match in the NBA for a family outing, see Box 8.2).

Table 8.4 Benefits and drawbacks of season ticket holders

Benefits	Drawbacks
• Assured ticket receipts, not dependent on sporting results • Guarantee of full seats, promoting the club's image and the atmosphere in the stadium • Captive audience likely to be more inclined to consume merchandise • Compilation and exploitation of a marketing database • Security	• Little turnover of the audience, limiting the club's ability to attract greater numbers of spectators/consumers • Tendency for some season-ticket holders to consider themselves to be the symbolic owners of the club (OM/PSG) • Possibility of weak segmentation (type profile: male, convinced fan) • Saturation of the venue: harder to capitalize on good results by means of commercial initiatives

Source: Helleu (2010).

Box 8.2 CRM scores points with the fans

If you recently attended a sporting event you paid $7 for a beer and $5 for a hot dog. You probably groused on the way back to your $40 seat, where you waved a $12 flag, wearing the $26 T-shirt you bought in the store. But who cares? It's a holiday. The average cost of taking a family to an NBA match reached $280 this year, which makes it the most expensive sport. But when you spend that much for a sports event, it's not just the sport, you're getting the fan experience.

In 1995 the San Diego Padres were the first to establish a CRM program and a loyalty system for their customers. Since then they have been pulling in two million fans every year, according to Brook Govan, the manager in charge of these programs.

The Padres have increased the loyalty of the fans since that time (+6.7% in stadium occupancy in 1995, +10.7% in 2002).

Under this program their supporters can use a loyalty card in the stadium's stores, which allows them to pay lower prices for their future tickets, food, drinks, and merchandise. The reductions depend on the points accumulated, according to the match and the purchases made. In return, this enables the Padres to compile valuable socio-demographic information and to track the habits of their fans. The club's management says that it also enables it to provide them with better service during the matches.

The Padres' database comprises about 185,000 members. By collecting these data the Padres have also discovered that a large portion of their 681,000 loyal fans come from Mexico, on the other side of the border. Accordingly, they now offer a special loyalty card for Mexico, and specifically target Hispanic fans in advertising campaigns on television and radio, both in the United States and in Mexico.

'Before we started this CRM policy we had no information about them', says Govan, adding that the Padres obtain a return rate of 6% in e-mail campaigns, which is double what they obtained previously from a traditional mail campaign.

Source: article from August 2003, www.destinationcrm.com/Articles/Editorial/Magazine-Features/CRM-Scores-With-Sports-Fans-48324.aspx (last accessed 16 March 2010).

Yield management

For the last few years, the marketing of sporting venues has also incorporated yield management (Box 8.3), designed to optimize the occupancy rate by adjusting the price and the last minute promotional offers.

For stadiums, the problem is the same as in the hotel business or in airline companies: sports arenas must be filled, because empty seats represent an opportunity lost. We must therefore apply the techniques that have been proven elsewhere (one seat purchased = one free seat; one seat purchased for a man = one free seat for a woman; children are free, and so on). But in the case of sport, yield management encompasses a much more important issue. Half-full aircraft and hotels are not shown on television! In contrast, as we have seen in Figure 8.2, having a full stadium is an essential requirement for a quality televised event (a half-filled stadium is a tragedy for the team hosting the event[14]), and for the atmosphere to live up to expectations. For this reason, in the last resort it may almost be necessary to pay people to fill the seats!

Yield management companies specializing in sport began to appear in the United States during the 2000s. These companies generally developed sophisticated computing techniques based on optimization programs applied to the filling of stadiums. The data are continuously updated, and the control panels are monitored hour by hour, so as to make any necessary changes in the pricing policy. The object is always to follow a line representing the 'perfect' forecast, by making the necessary adjustments.

However, all these tools would ultimately be worthless if the clubs were not able to persuade the consumer. Knowing consumers better, having accurate socio-demographic data on them and on their family circle, having the most sophisticated databases possible, and being able to implement CRM and yield management policies with efficient software – all of this is necessary, but it is not sufficient: the consumer has to be convinced that the product is a good one, and that it will be delivered in a worthy setting. It is also essential that the promise made to the consumer be kept.

For this reason, programmes offering virtual tours of stadiums, which allow a future spectator to visualize the nature of the event, provide a guarantee of quality that can reassure the consumer because, typically, everyone believes that they are going to be closer to the field than they are, and are disappointed when they enter the stadium.

Box 8.3 The history of yield management

Yield management is a system for managing available capacities (hotel rooms, aircraft seats, etc.) with the goal of optimizing sales: it is also known as revenue management, or in a more limited sense, real-time pricing. Many other definitions have been proposed, depending on the approach being considered. According to the former Chairman of Delta Airlines, the company where the revenue management technique was created in the early 1980s, when airline traffic was deregulated, 'revenue management is a technique that enables a specific service to be offered at the right time, in the right quantity, and at the right price', or, when applied to an airline company: ten seats at 100 euros, ten days before departure. In this case one can imagine that the previous day there were 15 available seats, or that the unit price was 90 euros, or perhaps both.

In 1984, following the deregulation of the US airline sector, Robert Cross of Delta Airlines (Charles Lindbergh, the famous aviator, was a former employee) was already using the revenue management technique as we know it today. With a budget of less than three million US dollars and about 50 employees (who at that time were working for a company department called 'space control') he was able in less than a year to achieve additional returns of more than $300,000,000 by segmenting the supply, the demand, the quantity, the price and the time.

Source: http://fr.wikipedia.org/wiki/Yield_management (last accessed 16 March 2010).

Case studies: European versus North-American arenas

The various generations of stadiums[15]

Although the Greeks invented sports sponsorships, since the Greek cities financed the athletes who went to the Olympic Games (establishing the model for today's skiers, usually sponsored by ski resorts), the concept of the 'modern stadium' is also historically dated. In the time of the Romans, the Coliseum was already a multi-functional facility and had present day architectural features (50,000 seats, with a roof, a hydraulic system, unimpeded sight lines, a central location, spectacles and special seats for senators). However, these features were not to be copied immediately. At the start of the 20th century, the so-called 'first-generation' stadiums were dilapidated, with low stands and limited sight lines. The 1930–1940 period saw a rebirth of interest in the Olympic spirit, expressed in what were called 'second-generation' stadiums. The antiquated buildings were rehabilitated and, in the opinion of some, were restored to their original purpose. A number of venues were constructed throughout the world to host the games (Berlin in 1936, London in 1948).

The primary features of these stadiums are:

- a bowl shape;
- accommodation for the greatest possible number of spectators;
- athletics and cycle tracks are central to the design.

However, the distancing of the crowd and the mixture of disciplines were inconsistent with the highest quality. This led to the construction, during the 1970s and 1980s, of so-called 'third-generation' stadiums (the Westfalen Stadion in Dortmund and the Olympiastadion in Munich). At that time, attending a sporting event was considered to be an experience comparable to seeing the same event on television, which is why the comfort and functional aspects of stadiums were improved, to persuade TV viewers to become spectators rather than staying at home:

- these were the beginnings of an interest in design;
- providing more comfort for spectators;
- moving to improve the facilities.

But the tragedies (Table 8.5) that played out in stadiums during the 1980s and 1990s led the authorities to improve stadium safety. This improvement was expressed in stricter legislation, which radically transformed these arenas.

In Europe, unlike North America where hooliganism and safety problems are unknown, the progressive development of fourth-generation venues (Stade de France in Paris, Reebok Stadium in Bolton) would not initially be dictated by business and marketing considerations, but simply by endeavours to provide greater safety for the spectators.

These places have the following features:

- a more sophisticated design;
- an optimal organization of the facilities to emphasize safety;
- the first signs of multi-functionality;
- the introduction of luxury seating (VIP boxes, business seats), which earn more money for the organizer.

See also Table 8.6.

Reports published in France (the Besson, Séguin and Arena 2015 reports)

In France, the need for modernization of sporting arenas, together with France's bid to host the Euro 2016 football championship, has led government bodies to sound the alarm and establish commissions, so that public authorities will be provided with reports offering a better understanding of the issues affecting the facilities for professional sports, and thus, if possible, take action to assist sport in general. The successive setbacks for France's

Table 8.5 Stadium disasters

Date	Stadium	Type	Victims
April 5 1902	Ibrox Park, Glasgow, Scotland	Collapse of a stand	26 dead, 587 injured
March 9 1946	Burnden Park, Bolton, England	Crowd surge (85,000 spectators for a capacity of 65,500)	33 dead, 400 injured
May 24 1964	Estadio Nacional, Lima, Peru	Panic	320 dead, 800 injured (some sources report 400 dead)
September 18 1967	Kayseri, Turkey	Panic	40 dead, 600 injured
June 1968	Estadio River Plate, Buenos Aires, Argentina	Panic	80 dead, 150 injured
January 2 1971	Ibrox Park, Glasgow, Scotland	Collapse of a stand following a crowd surge	66 dead, >200 injured
February 17 1974	Cairo, Egypt	Panic following the collapse of a wall	49 dead, 47 injured
February 8 1981	Karaiskaki Stadium, Piraeus, Greece	Crowd surge	21 dead
October 2 1982	Loujniki Stadium, Moscow, USSR	Panic	Various figures: 61 dead (official, 1982) 99 dead (unidentified source) 340 dead (figure revealed in 1989)
May 11 1985	Valley Parade Stadium, Bradford, England	Fire	56 dead
May 29 1985	Stade du Heysel, Brussels, Belgium	Fights, panic	39 dead, 600 injured
April 15 1989	Hillsborough (stadium), Sheffield, England	Panic	96 dead, 766 injured
May 5 1992	Stade Armand-Cesari, Furiani, France	Collapse of a temporary stand	18 dead, 2,857 injured
October 16 1996	Estadio Mateo Flores, Guatemala	Panic	84 dead
June 2 2007	Chililabombwe Stadium, Chililabombwe, Zambia	Collapse of a stairway and panic	12 dead, 46 injured
November 25 2007	Fonte Nova Stadium, Salvador, Brazil	Collapse of a stand	7 dead, 10 injured
September 14 2008	Stade Municipal de Butembo, Butembo, DR Congo	Rush following intervention by police	13 dead, 54 injured
March 29 2009	Stade Félix Houphouët-Boigny, Abidjan, Côte d'Ivoire	Rush of supporters	19 dead, 135 injured

Source: *Ligue de Football Professionnel* (2010), www.lfp.fr (accessed 16 March 2010).

Table 8.6 Current trends in European stadiums

Trend	Example of stadium
Urban development tool: nowadays, stadiums must support the development or redevelopment of a neighbourhood or a town, and contribute to its influence and reputation.	Amsterdam Arena (The Netherlands)
Design: as a means of expressing a brand, the stadium must be communicative, convey strong positive values and arouse the emotions	Allianz Arena, Munich (Germany)
Sustainable and eco-compatible: as a major issue, sustainable development must necessarily apply to stadium projects, from their design to their operation	Stade des Alpes, Grenoble (France)

Source: adapted from http://losangelesfootballstadium.com/stadium (last accessed 15 March 2010).

Olympic candidacies (1992, 2008 and 2012) have also drawn attention to France's backwardness in this area. The 1998 World Cup did not succeed in closing this gap, since the majority of the budget was devoted to building the Stade de France: other stadiums received only superficial renovations, which made them obsolete before their time.

Frédéric Thiriez, the President of the Professional Football League (LFP), describes the situation as follows: 'The future of soccer depends on renovating our stadiums. ... As regards stadiums, we are 15 years behind, and need to catch up. ... Our stadiums are now dilapidated. There is not a single club stadium in France presently capable of hosting a Champions League final: it's a disgrace to French football. ... France should also be a candidate for the Euro 2016 Championship. This would be the way to speed up our stadium-construction programs.[16]

The Besson (2008) report on the competitiveness of French football, submitted to the Prime Minister on 5 November 2008, suggests several approaches for improving this competitiveness on the sporting and economic fronts:

- Increase efforts to modernize stadiums by encouraging the use of private investments, especially in the context of public/private partnerships.
- Initiate discussions on reducing the number of training centres, so that they become 'centres of excellence'.
- Amend the legal status of sports companies to align it with general company law.
- Increase the financial strength of clubs in the first division, in particular by paying them a share of the receipts from sports wagering, or by reducing their contributions to the lower divisions.
- Reform the LFP's board of directors, to provide a majority of seats for the club chairmen.
- Promote a European authority for the management and control of professional football.

The Séguin (Séguin and Valentin, 2008) report, devoted entirely to stadiums and submitted to the Prime Minister on 25 November 2008, made a number of radical proposals:

- Take action to have stadiums declared to be public-interest facilities, whether they have private or public financing.
- Encourage the development of other models for the ownership and management of stadiums, which are now exclusively run by their communities.
- Encourage private initiatives for the construction and management of stadiums.
- In this regard, naming rights are one method for obtaining financing, and this approach should be encouraged whenever possible. A reduction of the tax burden is recommended.
- Similarly, the value added tax (VAT) on sporting events could be reduced, so as to encourage stadium initiatives.
- In conclusion, if a single theme emerges from the commission's results, it is the necessity of finding a new method for financing stadiums.

The Arena 2015 report (Constantini and Besnier, 2010) submitted to the Prime Minister on 10 March 2010, addressed the issue of the major facilities and their suitability for the organization of high-level sporting competitions, both national and international. It found that France lags behind in this area. It emphasized that future facilities should be multi-functional (for sports and spectacles), in line with the model provided by the arenas that have appeared throughout Europe over the last two decades. Calling for action by the State and the use of private investments, the report presented 18 recommendations, for example the construction or renovation of a facility with more than 20,000 seats, a 15,000-seat facility and two facilities with 10,000 seats (when configured for sports). The findings are indeed overwhelming: France is totally deficient in this class of facility (6000 to 20,000 seats). In 2010 the country had only one facility with more than 10,000 seats, the Palais Omnisports de Paris-Bercy (POPB), out of 90 such sites listed in Europe.

Institutional differences and naming

There are a number of institutional differences between the European and North American sports systems. Even in Europe, uniformity is not the rule. The ways of owning stadiums are highly variable (100 per cent public, 100 per cent private, mixed), which makes the financing and operation of the facilities very different. In France, for example, sporting venues are at present the property of local governments, which makes it almost impossible to sell naming rights. However, the progressive transfer of ownership and the construction of new facilities should alter this situation.[17]

Naming is one of the many English terms used in the advertising world; it describes a sponsorship technique consisting of giving a sports facility (usually a stadium) the name of the sponsoring brand or company. Naming agreements are generally of long duration, typically between 15 and 30 years. This practice of course affects local nomenclature if it seeks to replace an old name with a new one, for commercial reasons and for advertising's sake. In Europe, naming is still in an early phase of development. Since the beginning of this decade, we have observed a breakthrough of the tactic in Germany, England and The Netherlands. In Germany 12 of the 18 clubs in the *Bundesliga* play in stadiums bearing the name of a brand.

According to the Sportfive agency (www.sportfive.com) naming is a very effective advertising tool, which reaches a great number of people via all media. It can be regarded as a comprehensive communications platform.

- Naming quickly and significantly increases the renown of the sponsor, especially during the construction phase.
- Naming generates billions of media contacts every year, divided among every kind of publication, television channels, radio stations and the internet.
- To achieve this level of media presence through traditional advertising would require a far greater investment.
- The perception of the sponsor is independent of the club's sporting success. Having acquired the naming rights, the brand benefits in the eyes of the public from a permanent positive association with an exceptional piece of architecture, a place conveying emotion and enthusiasm.
- The holder of the naming rights also benefits from all the events organized in the stadium.

In the United States in 2006, according to www.bonham.com.[18]

- 78 naming contracts have been signed in the five major leagues;
- for a total amount of four billion US dollars;
- in 26 different categories of sponsorship (see also Tables 8.7 and 8.8).

There is a strong correlation between the organization of major competitions and the use of naming (2006 World Cup in Germany, 2002 World Hockey Championship in Sweden, 2003 in Finland, 2004 in the Czech Republic) (See also Figure 8.7.).

In England, and especially in the United States, the agreements are of long duration, sometimes lasting 25 or 30 years. Such contract durations are an American specialty, owing to the absence of risk for the investor, since there is no divisional promotion or relegation in the NFL, MLB, NBA or NHL, in contrast to the European system (Table 8.9).

Germany has a shorter average contract term, although the 2006 World Cup stadiums mostly have contracts lasting at least nine years.

Contrary to conventional wisdom, naming is becoming accepted, although there are still some signs of opposition here and there (Table 8.10). But it is hard to see why a practice that has been accepted for several decades in other sports (cycling, sailing and Formula 1 motor racing) should present a problem for a stadium (Table 8.11; but see also Table 8.12).[19]

Table 8.7 Top ten biggest naming contracts

Name of stadium	Team	Rights	Duration	Date signed	Amount per year
Reliant Stadium	Houston Texans	300	32	2002	9.4
FedEx Field	Washington Redskins	205	27	1999	7.6
American Airlines Center	Dallas Mavericks and Stars	195	28	2000	7.0
Philips Arena	Atlanta Thrashers and Hawks	182	20		
Minute Maid Park	Houston Astros	178	20	2004	8.9
Univeristy of Phoenix Stadium	Arizona Cardinals	154	20	2008	7.7
Bank of America Stadium	Carolina Panthers	140	21	2003	6.7
Lincoln Financial Field	Philadelphia Eagles	140	21	205	6.6
Lucas Oil Stadium	Indianapolis Colts	122	20	206	6.1
TD Banknorth Garden	Boston Celtics	120	20	2005	6.0

Source: www.bonham.com

Table 8.8 Number of naming contracts by country

Country	Stadiums	Arenas	Total
Germany	21	14	35
England	14	3	17
Sweden	4	13	17
Netherlands	11	1	12
Czech Republic	1	8	9
Finland	4	4	8
Denmark	4	2	6
Switzerland	1	4	5
Italy	0	4	4
Spain	2	1	3
Russia	1	2	3
Austria	2	0	2
Wales	2	0	2
France	1	0	1
Belgium, Norway, Greece	1	0	1
Lithuania, Israel, Ireland, Estonia, Ukraine, Slovakia	0	1	1
Total	71	62	133

Source: www.bonham.com

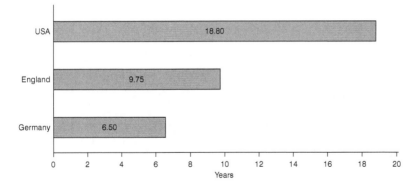

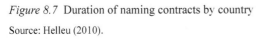

Figure 8.7 Duration of naming contracts by country

Source: Helleu (2010).

Table 8.9 Number of people in favour of naming

Italy	47%
France	48%
Spain	48%
Germany	60%
England	70%

Source: Helleu (2010).

Table 8.10 Acceptance of naming in France

	France	*European average*
I would not be upset if a football league sold its name to a company to generate additional income	38%	47%
I would not be upset if, for its own good, a club changed its name to that of its sponsor	44%	42%
I think it's a good thing that the name of a stadium can be sold	48%	55%

Source: Helleu (2010).

Table 8.11 The benefits of naming

For the host club, the operator and the owner	For the partner
• Long-term contract, often for big sums, which may be combined with financing for a sports arena • Ensures resources for a long period, allowing for securitization (a critical benefit in a sector characterized by risk) • Good management of public finances for the community owners	• Entry costs relatively low in France: €1m per year for ten years for the MMA Arena, or one third of the average cost of sponsoring a jersey in League 1, for a clearly better exposure • Major exposure in France, because process little used (only one example, the MMA Arena, opening in 2009) with huge press spin-offs • Improves legitimacy and local ties • Possibility of incorporating hospitality suites in the partnership and use of the stadium as a showcase for the brand • Improvement of image by this 'public-interest sponsorship'

Table 8.12 The limits of naming

For the host club, the operator and the owner	For the partner
• Difficult to change partner to target a growing sector of activity • Repercussions on host club and city if partner suffers economic setbacks. Houston Astros successfully broke the naming contract they had signed with Enron, after its market failure • Some communities reluctant to be associated with commercial brands	• Sporting risks: host club may be relegated to a lower division, even if it is a major club (Olympique Marseille, Juventus Turin). • Need to provide for this in the contract • Seeing the brand associated with host-club violence or safety problems (should links with club be strengthened, or keep a safe distance?) • Difficulty of being remembered by the public at large during early years due to 'force of habit' (for pre-existing stadiums) • Habitual mentions by journalists (certainly less true for new stadiums) • 'Clean stadium' policy of many international federations (FIFA, UEFA, International Rugby Board (IRB)). Seven out of twelve 2006 World Cup stadiums were de-baptized during the competition • Competition with sponsor of team jersey (hence decision of Emirates to do both with Arsenal)

Conclusion: stadium profitability via non-match-day income

We have seen in this chapter that the stadium has become an essential development tool in the marketing of a sports team. However, the financial viability of a sporting facility also assumes a diversification of its income, made possible by the multi-functionality of the arena. The Amsterdam Arena hosted 81 events in 2005–2006 (including 41 non-sporting events). By way of comparison, the Stade de France, handicapped by not having a roof, hosted about 30 in 2010. In this situation, how can an organization that 'works' less than once a week be made profitable?

The time has come for integrated, multi-functional facilities that are less dependent on sport. The City of Pittsburgh, for example, extensively revised the urban development of its old Three Rivers Stadium, and replaced it in 2001 with Heinz Field (American football) and PNC Park (baseball) on the same site, thereby creating a major centre for sports and other events. Along the same lines, the Globe in Stockholm, incorporating the Söderstadion (football), the Ericsson Globe (hockey and concerts), the Hovet (mult-functional hall) and the Annexet (concerts) is an interesting concept, hosting 1.4 million spectators at 287 events during 2007.

However, the ultimate model of profitability seems to be the Staples Center in Los Angeles (Box 8.4), which benefits from an exceptional sporting situation with a unique concentration of professional teams, combined with a uniquely fertile area for non-sporting events.

With its new stadium, Arsenal has become one of the five richest football clubs in Europe: by switching from 'Highbury' to 'Emirates' Stadium, the club increased its sales by 37 per cent from 2006 to 2007.

Box 8.4 The Staples Center, Los Angeles

Since 1999, its tenants have been the Los Angeles Lakers and the Los Angeles Clippers, which are NBA basketball teams, and the Los Angeles Kings of the National Hockey League. The Staples Center also hosts the Los Angeles Sparks of the WNBA [Women's National Basketball Association] and the Los Angeles D-Fenders of the NBA's D League. From 2000 to 2008 it was the home of the Los Angeles Avengers of the Arena Football League. It is the only arena to host five professional franchises. In spite of all this, the facility's sporting spectacles account for only half of its 250 annual events. It has 18,997 seats for Lakers basketball matches, 19,060 for Clippers games, 18,118 for ice hockey, 16,096 for American indoor football, 12,947 for WNBA matches and 20,000 for concerts and boxing. The facility offers every convenience imaginable to maximize income, with 2500 business seats, 32 party suites and 160 luxury suites, including 20 event suites.

Source: www.staplescenter.com/index.html?0 (last accessed 17 March 2010).

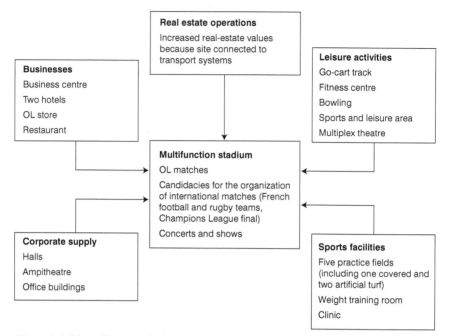

Figure 8.8 Diversification of Olympique Lyonnais's income, based on its future stadium

Source: www.lnr.fr (last accessed 18 March 2010).

The French club Olympique Lyonnais, with its new stadium, is hoping to see a similar diversification of income in the coming years (Figure 8.8).

Acquisition of a modern, spacious, multi-functional stadium is now a matter of survival for professional sports teams.

Notes

1 Marketing mix describes the whole set of decisions concerning the policies of production, pricing, distribution and advertising of the products of a firm or a brand.
2 In this chapter we will mainly be talking about stadiums, because this is the item on which academic and managerial thought has progressed the furthest. But our observations apply equally well to other 'arenas' (indoor spaces for basketball, volleyball and handball in Europe, and basketball and ice hockey in North America). Moreover, this separation is increasingly obsolete, since many of the major North American stadiums are now covered, and thus straddle the borderline between stadium and arena. In the NFL, 9 of the 32 teams already play in covered stadiums, which enable the 'control' of climatic hazards (cold, heat and bad weather) and increase the number of non-sporting events. In Europe, the Amsterdam Arena also has a retractable roof and is cited as one of the most successful examples of multi-functionality.
3 This section on experiential marketing arises from a conference and a discussion with Lionel Maltese, a senior lecturer at the Université Paul Cézanne d'Aix-Marseille (France) and a consultant on sports marketing. For additional information, see Caru *et al.* 2008.
4 Source: Jean-François Bourg, www.lexpansion.com/economie/le-rugby-show-biz-de-max-guazzini-tourneboule-l-ovalie_25447.html?pg=2, last accessed 17 March 2010.
5 Source: www.histoirenordiques.ca/souvenir20.html (last accessed 17 March 2010).

6 Source: www.lnr.fr (last accessed 17 March 2010).
7 Source: www.basketlfb.fr (last accessed 17 March 2010).
8 This problem is particularly acute in England and Germany, where major cities are close together, almost contiguous.
9 Source: Markess International, *Optimisation de la gestion des interactions client avec Internet et le mobile, 2009–2011*, www.markess.fr/demandedocument.php?refdoc=642 (last accessed 16 March 2010).
10 Source: Teletech International, *Le multicanal en centre d'appels*, www.teletech.fr (last accessed 16 March 2010).
11 Running Club for New Balance, Adidas Running Partners, Nike+, to mention the main community sites.
12 Source: www.lfp.fr (last accessed 17 March 2010).
13 The services provided and the objectives are the same as in the CRM policy practiced by the San Diego Padres, mentioned in Box 8.2.
14 This is why television broadcasters film the event in an 'accommodating' manner, focusing on the lower levels of the stands, which are usually better filled, so that the broadcast will be as favourable as possible to the event's organizer. The broadcaster and the seller of the rights have interests in common. Similarly, when the Stade de France thinks that a match will not sell out, only the lower ring of seats is put on sale, so as to avoid humiliating pictures of a scattered crowd.
15 Source: Helleu, 2010.
16 Frédéric Thiriez: *Les stades, un chantier bien entamé* (26 November 2007) www.lfp.fr/actualiteLFP/lireArticle.asp?idArticle=9248 (last accessed 20 January 2010).
17 In France, the amount of the contract signed between the MMA insurance company and the city of Le Mans to name its new stadium the 'MMA Arena' is one million euros per year, and extends for ten years. It will go into effect in 2011, when the new facility is inaugurated.
18 In January 2009 Bonham, a company based in Denver (USA) for more than 25 years, terminated its North American activities and moved to London. This website is therefore no longer active.
19 Opposition may arise when a legendary old site is re-baptized (Anfield Road in Liverpool, Old Trafford in Manchester, Camp Nou in Barcelona, the Marseilles Velodrome), but this does not apply in the case of a new facility.

References

Apostolopoulou, A., Clark, J. and Gladden, J.M. (2006), 'From H-Town to M-Town: the importance of Super-Bowl entertainment', *Sport Marketing Quarterly*, 15, 223–231.

Badot, O. and Cova, B. (1992), *Le Néo Marketing*, ESF Éditeur, Paris, France.

Baray, J. (2003), 'Optimisation de la localisation commerciale: une application du traitement du signal et du modèle p-médian', *Recherche et applications en Marketing*, 18(3), 31–44.

Besson, E. (2008), *Accroître la compétitivité des clubs de football professionnel français*, Paris, La documentation française, www.ladocumentationfrancaise.fr/ (last accessed 17 March 2010).

Bourg, J.-F. and Gouguet, J.-J. (2004), *Analyse économique du sport*, PUF, Paris.

Caru, A., Cova, B. and Maltese, L. (2008), 'Un approccio duale al marketing esperienziale: divertimento e approfondimento nell'immersione', *Mercati & Competitività*, 4, 17–40.

Cliquet, G. (1992), *Management stratégique des points de vente*. Sirey, Paris.

Costantini, D. and Besnier, F. (2010), *Arenas 2015: Rapport de la commission Grandes Salles*, www.ladocumentationfrancaise.fr/rapports-publics/104000122/ (last accessed 17 March 2010).

Desbordes, M. (2006), 'The economics of cycling', in Andreff, W., Szymanski, S. and Borland, J. (eds.), *The Edward Elgar Companion to the Economics of Sports*, 645–662.

Desbordes, M. (2008), 'Le marketing du sport en question', *Revue française de marketing*, 219 (4/5), 5–9.

Desbordes, M. and Falgoux, J. (2007), *Les événements sportifs*, Les Éditions d'Organisation, Paris, 3rd edition, preface by Michel Platini, 260 p.

Durand, C., Ravenel, L. and Bayle, E. (2005), 'The strategic and political consequences of using a demographic criteria for the organization of European leagues', *European Journal of Sport Sciences*, 4, 167–180.

Eiglier, P. and Langeard, E. (1987), *La servuction. Le marketing des services*, McGraw- Hill, Paris, France.

Halba, B. (1997), *Économie du sport*, Economica, Paris, France.

Helleu, B. (2007), *Régulation des ligues sportives professionnelles, une approche géographique. Le cas du football européen (1975–2005)*, doctoral thesis in sports sciences, Université de Rouen, France, 368 p.

Helleu, B. (2010), *Cours de marketing sur le management des stades*, mastère de management du sport, Université de Caen Basse-Normandie, France (unpublished).

Holbrook, M.B. and Hirschman, E. (1982), 'The experiential aspects of consumption', *Journal of Consumer Research*, 9 (2), 132–140.

Holt, D.B. (1995), 'How consumers consume: a typology of consumption practices', *Journal of Consumer Research*, 22 (1), 1–16.

Ineum Consulting (2008), *Football professionnel, finances et perspectives*, joint study with Euromed, Paris, France.

Kahle, L. R., Kambara, K. M. and Rose, G. M. (1996), 'A functional model of fan attendance motivations for college football', *Sport Marketing Quarterly*, 5 (4), 51–60.

Keller, K.L. (2003), *Strategic Brand Management: Building, Measuring, and Managing Brand Equity*, 2nd edition, Englewood Cliffs, NJ, USA, Prentice Hall.

Lestrelin, L. (2006), *L'autre public des matchs de football, sociologie du supporterisme à distance: le cas de l'Olympique de Marseille*, doctoral thesis in sociology, Université de Rouen, France, 996 p.

Ligue de football professionnel (2010), *Rapport sur les stades*, Paris, France.

Maltese, L. (2010), Conference on sport marketing, Euromed business school, Marseille, France, June 7th 2010.

Mullin, B.J., Hardy, S. and Sutton, W.A. (2007), *Sport Marketing, Human Kinetics*, Champaign, IL, USA, 3rd edition, 552 p.

Pine, B. J. and Gilmore, J.H. (1999), *The Experience Economy*, Harvard Business School Press, Boston, MA, 254 p.

Pooley, J. (1978), The sport fan: a social psychology of misbehaviour, *CAPHER Sociology of Sport Monograph Series*, Calgary, Canada.

Ravenel, L. (2009), *L'analyse des espaces sportifs: l'apport du géomarketing*, accreditation to direct research, Université de Franche-Comté, France, October, 248 p.

Séguin, P. and Valentin, J.L. (2008), *Grands stades – Rapport de la Commission Euro 2016*, Paris, France, La documentation française, www.ladocumentationfrancaise.fr/ (last accessed 17 March 2010).

Tribou, G. (2007), *Sponsoring sportif*, 3rd edition, Economica, Paris, France.

Van Uden, J. (2004), *Organisation and Complexity: Using Complexity Science to Theorise Organisational Aliveness*, Universal Publishers, Boca Raton, FL, USA.

Wann, D. L. and Branscombe, N. R. (1993), 'Sports fans: measuring degree of identification with the team', *International Journal of Sport Psychology*, 24, 1–17.

9   General conclusions

Some things to remember

André Richelieu and Michel Desbordes

We have reached the end of our journey. It is now time to evaluate and to reflect upon our experience; to take a step back and solidify what we've learned.

This book was structured in two parts: the first part dealt with brand management and the internationalization of sports organizations, particularly sports teams, in the context of globalization; the second part looked at sporting events and the marketing experience. In both parts, we referred to theoretical foundations to articulate our thoughts and to suggest managerial avenues, offering international examples, which allowed us to highlight the similarities and differences between North America and Europe.

More than a synthesis, we would like to prepare the ground for a jumping off point, an opening onto new horizons. On the one hand, because of the challenges that sports managers face today, and those they will face in the future, they will demand different solutions from those used 10, 20 or 30 years ago. On the other hand, insofar as we believe that sport is more than a field for applying marketing theories, we pose the question: What can sports marketing contribute to the understanding of marketing and brand management? In this respect, the first part of the book on strategic brand construction, the internationalization of sports brands as well as the internationalization strategies of these brands, gives rise to some interesting points (chapters by André Richelieu).

First, reputation gives a certain advantage to the team in its *quest* for internationalization. Whether through championships or tradition, star players, local or foreign, and even the management of the team on and off the field, a sports club has to pay particular attention to its image. Brand is a promise that each organization must deliver on to its consumers each time they are in contact with the brand. But what is it really all about today? How many times have you been seduced by the level of service offered by your mobile phone provider, your cable company, your bank or even your airline? These ideas about reputation and promise are that much more important in the world of sports, insofar as what the team sells are emotions, above all else. This is equally true for cities that see the opportunities in large global sporting events to make over their image in order to better position themselves on the sports scene, as well as on the cultural, economic and tourist scenes: the case of Beijing is a good example in this regard (chapter by Guojun Zeng *et al.*)

One must pay attention, however. Alter your reputation, break your promise and you could very well ruin the emotional connection that took so long to build with your fans. After repeated betrayals, fans will spend their money elsewhere, and perhaps never return. This is even truer for renowned teams. With prestige comes privilege, but also obligations, without which the team's social standing, locally and internationally, is threatened.

Second, venturing into international markets may no longer be optional. While globalization appears to be an 'inevitable tornado' (Valaskakis, 1990), organizations are required to not only look abroad, but also to consider ways to successfully penetrate international markets. Here, the NHL could take some inspiration from the NBA, which currently has seven regional offices in Europe: the NHL, none. And, at the risk of offending some general managers in the NHL, one must recognize that proposing games involving exotic teams from the southern part of the USA, deprived of any big names, to hockey fans of Sweden, Finland, the Czech Republic or Latvia, is not a big seller for the NHL brand. It would be like the Premier League of England trying to establish itself in North America by offering soccer fans the show put on by the Bolton Wanderers and Stoke City! (without taking anything away from these two teams).

In so doing, we return to the importance of context, in particular the calibre of the teams, the sport in question and the league's management system. These would have an impact on the internal and external catalysts that a team would be able to use in its international approach. Teams that are successful are able to transcend their market and their sport to become global symbols. From a brand management and finance perspective, this opens new possibilities to teams to solidify the connection with their fans via different points of contact: games at the stadium, the cyber platform of the internet (official website, online fan communities, social groups), the mascot, tours and exhibition matches, not to mention the licensed merchandise (chapters by André Richelieu). According to PriceWaterhouseCoopers (PriceWaterhouseCoopers, 2004, 2007), the sale of licensed products is to exceed US$20 billion in 2011, and this includes all sports and all teams in North America. This figure represents the marketing and financial opportunities that sports clubs are able to capitalize on when they enjoy a strong emotional connection with their supporters.

Third, and to create a link with the preceding point, the speed and the sequence of internationalization have become key issues for sports organizations. Insofar as sport is affected by globalization, some teams will have to, and will have the means to, be aggressive in international markets, in order to profit most from being the first on the scene. As the Vice President of Marketing for FC Barcelona affirmed, 'There will probably only be room for five or six global football team brands' (2004). These teams should be able to use a mass marketing strategy, involving significant resources and elevated risk. Other clubs, by virtue of their limited resources and their level of performance, as well as because of the nature of their sport, and the league's management system, could follow a niche interregional strategy with emphasis placed on the 'grass roots': that is to say, break from the foundation to join a younger clientele who will develop, over time, a strong relationship with the brand ('womb to tomb' marketing concept). Hence, the interest in focusing on smaller teams like SpVgg Vreden (chapter by Christoph Breuer *et al.*; see also Richelieu *et al.*, 2011).

Fourth, sports offer promising opportunities for co-branding, especially on the international level. International marketing experts underline the importance of adapting what you offer to the foreign market in order to ease consumer acceptance and to attain a desired level of 'seduction'. Hence, the concept of 'glocalization', across which brands adjust their offer to a local context to better connect with different consumers, all while preserving the brand's coherence (Cateora and Graham, 2006; Hollensen, 2007). As we have seen, some teams emerge onto the international market via a subsidiary team (the Conquistador strategy). Co-branding, however, can also be initiated through the activities of production and promotion in conjunction with local companies. This is the approach FC Barcelona used to penetrate China, Japan and Singapore (Richelieu *et al.*, 2008).

In a period of great economic change, professional sports teams have realized that brand is an asset, and the power brand management has to go beyond the local market (Bauer *et al.*, 2005). What we call globalization, simultaneously offers opportunities and threats to sports teams. Teams can no longer hide behind what once was, in the past, a purely local activity.

The book's second section allowed us to continue in the same vein, concentrating on the notion of the experience lived by the fan, from the perspective of the 'consumer/actor' (chapter by Boris Helleu). The consumer/actor, simultaneously an actor and a spectator in the arena of 'sportainment', is more demanding than before when it comes to the experience s/he has. The consumer/actor wants, in a growing number of cases, to be a stakeholder in the script. In fact, the more the consumer/actor is involved, the more s/he will assume possession of the product and the brand, and the more s/he will potentially remain loyal to it. Weekly games, however, no longer suffice. Today's consumer/actor needs to stay connected practically 24 hours a day, or at least be given the opportunity, notably via applications on mobile phones, social networks on the internet where s/he can connect with fans, players, trainers, managers and journalists in an interconnected network of networks.

The sporting event is an experiential product given the emotions generated by the event and how it is put together (chapters by Boris Helleu and Wladimir Andreff). The match can be seen as a culmination and a catalyst for a social communion where a series of actors take their seats, having devoted themselves to the team's status and brand to a level of quasi-divinity, as shown in the examples of FC Barcelona and the Juventus Football Club in Europe, as well as the Montreal Canadiens and the Chicago Cubs in North America. In this vein, we emphasized that the stadium had become a major boost to the development of a sports team's event and experience marketing. The stadium, or the arena, becomes a sanctuary, sometimes with its 'ghosts' that can radically change the tide in favour of the local team. Today, however, the profitability of a stadium also goes through a diversification and a durability of revenue thanks to the multi-functionality of the sports complex (sports games, concerts, movie theatres, restaurants, even shopping malls) (chapter by Michel Desbordes).

So, what does the future hold for sports marketing? In an attempt to find some clues, we looked at the following themes: 1) the arrival of emerging countries and their impact on sports marketing; 2) culture: global convergence via sports and sports marketing; 3) sports marketing and new media; and 4) money and sport.

To the first point, the arrival of emerging countries is at once a challenge and an opportunity for sports organizations in developing countries. It is not only a challenge insofar as emerging countries are proving to be tough competitors (their teams and athletes), but also via the organization of international calibre sporting events. Today we have South Africa with the FIFA World Cup, Malaysia and Singapore with F1 and, in the very near future, Russia and Brazil with the Olympic Games and the FIFA World Cup, not to mention Ukraine with the UEFA 2012 Euro Championship, etc. It is also an opportunity, given the economic development of these often young and populous countries, with a growing middle class and increasing wealth, as well as more lenient tobacco and alcohol regulations with regard to potential sponsorship deals.

Second, sport is a vehicle of social cohesion by virtue of the feeling of belonging and pride that it generates in a community, whether that is physical or by allegiance. Sports break through barriers and, to this end, they become a powerful cultural common denominator between people: sports get the conversation going, as we often say! The World Cup of soccer is, in this respect, an eloquent example, when the whole world becomes a spectator, even actor, during the eventful moments among 32 participating nations. As a case in point, despite an absence dating back to 1986, Canada is the theatre of heightened emotion come World Cup time: in the Jean-Talon district of Montreal, the Italian *tifosi* vibrate to the rhythm of the *Squadra Azzurra*, fans from Algeria shout 'Viva Algeria' at the top of their lungs, the Portuguese fans hold their breath for Cristiano Ronaldo's free kick, Greek supporters hold out for a repeat of 2004 to let their joy explode, etc. As much as sport unites people, it can also divide them due to the tribal dimension of sport, the 'us against them' aspect; it seems even truer in a context of globalization where the preservation of national identity is sometimes presented as an act of survival. The risk of things getting out of control is there, and this is a danger that sports must be wary of, so that they do not transform into a weapon of populist demagogy.

Third, sports should profit from the expansion of new media. As a matter of fact, they already do. New media is legendary in that it allows teams, leagues, players, federations, etc. to stay connected with their fans on a continual basis, from a distance. This is the case with the 'satellite supporters' we discussed in the book, but also with platforms such as Facebook and Twitter, to name just a few. The phenomenon will likely grow, allowing the most reputed and dynamic organizations to expand their reach and their sphere of influence on a global scale. But let's take care to not make new media and technology an end in itself, at the risk of creating distance with the fans, instead of reducing it.

Fourth, sport has become a business where money talks, as exemplified by the merger of sport and entertainment, or 'sportainment' (chapters by André

Richelieu). If fans react in an emotional, even passionate, manner, the management, more often than not, are motivated by the bottom line. This sometimes leads to bizarre decisions in the eyes of the fans who view it as a betrayal to trade the star goalie, the prolific scorer or the best pitcher in the league for recruits whose future remain, at best, hypothetical. Sport is, above all, about emotion, and star players have the ability to solidify these feelings by playing the role of emotional anchors, helping to reinforce the feeling of belonging to the club. Reconciling the emotional and 'rational' aspects remains a challenge for many teams, who sometimes seem too ready to sacrifice the privileged relationship they maintain with their fans for the benefits of a promising future that rarely ever comes. This can only weaken the club's brand.

It is the same for professional players and their own brands. Many people ask themselves, what motivation can one still have when one earns so much money, especially when it is a matter of wearing the national jersey? The now infamous strike, orchestrated by the players of the French football team during the World Cup in South Africa, was much discussed, perhaps more than the competition itself. Is this strike the reflection, pushed to the extreme, of the evolution of professionalism that has turned players into egotistical 'entrepreneurs', where pride in playing goes along with the size of one's bonus? The question lacks finesse, admittedly, but it is something we must think about, by virtue of the consequences that it poses to the brand image of teams, federations and even countries, as underlined by then French Minister of Sport, Madame Bachelot: 'The image of France has been tarnished' (*L'Express* 2010).

To finish this fourth axis of reflection, we shall ask ourselves what will be the impact of betting on the integrity of the sport, the leagues and international competitions, especially with the sums at stake? According to an article in Singapore's *Sunday Times*, the betting profits for each football game can reach 1.5 million euros (Toh, 2011). It remains to be seen if, and in what way, we can truly manage the influence of betting on sports in order to avoid repeat spin-offs, even more so in a global society connected to the Internet.

What will sport and sports marketing be like in 10 or 20 years? We have attempted, in this book, to offer areas of reflection and management tools to managers who operate in an industry that has changed enormously in recent years and that will continue to do so. And this, driven by the tornado called globalization, with its many challengers coming from emerging countries, and with the constraints linked to the business of sport and the cultures that remain, like the sport, tribal in their expression of allegiance, such as the Montreal Canadiens, the Marseille Olympique or even the Bafana Bafana of the new South Africa.

References

Bauer, H. H., N. E. Sauer and P. Schmitt (2005). 'Customer-based brand equity in the team sport industry'. *European Journal of Marketing*, 39 (5/6): 496–513.

Cateora, P. R. and J. L. Graham (2006). *International Marketing*, Canadian edition, Homewood, IL: Irwin.

L'Express (2010). 'Bachelot: "Vous avez terni l'image de la France"', June 21.

Hollenson, S. (2007). *Global marketing: A decision-oriented approach*, 4th edition, London, UK: Prentice Hall.

PriceWaterhouseCoopers (2004). 'Global outlook for the sports market'. *Global entertainment and media outlook report: 2004–2008*. New York.

PriceWaterhouseCoopers (2007). 'Global outlook for the sports market'. *Global entertainment and media outlook: 2007–2011*. New York.

Richelieu, A., S. Lopez and M. Desbordes (2008). 'The internationalization of a sports team brand: The case of European soccer teams'. *International Journal of Sports Marketing and Sponsorship*, 9 (4): 29–44.

Richelieu, A., T. Pawlowski and C. Breuer (2011). 'Football brand management: Minor League vs. Champions League'. *Journal of Sponsorship*, 4 (2): 178–189.

Toh, Kezia (2011). 'Match-fixer caught in net', *Sunday Times* (Singapore), 24 July 2011, p. 10.

Valaskakis, K. (1990). *Canada in the Nineties: Meltdown or renaissance*. Ottawa: World Media.

Vice President of Marketing for FC Barcelona (2004). Personal interview. Barcelona, Spain, May 2004.

Index